TWO YOGA SAMHITAS

English Translation Accompanied by Sanskrit Text in Roman Transliteration

Swami Vishnuswaroop

Divine Yoga Institute
Kathmandu, Nepal

DEDICATION

Tasmai Shri Gurave Namah!

This book is dedicated to my Guru Swami Satyananda Saraswati, Founder of Bihar School of Yoga, Munger, India.

-Swami Vishnuswaroop

CONTENTS

Title Page
Dedication
Gheranda Samhita 1
Introduction 2
Chapter Topics 4
Chapter One 6
Chapter Two 21
Chapter Three 33
Chapter Four 57
Chapter Five 59
Chapter Six 83
Chapter Seven 89
Goraksha Samhita 96
Introduction 97
Chapter Topics 99
Pūrva Śatakam 101
Uttara Śatakam 123
A Key to Transliteration 148
Also by this author 149
About the author 150
About the Publisher 152

GHERANDA SAMHITA

घेरण्ड संहिता

Book One

English Translation Accompanied by Sanskrit Text in Roman Transliteration

Translated into English by
Swami Vishnuswaroop

Published by
Divine Yoga Institute
Kathmandu, Nepal

INTRODUCTION

Gheraṇḍa Samhitā is a classical yogic text. Its author is Sage *Gheraṇḍa*. The form of yoga he taught in *Gheraṇḍa Samhitā* is called *Ghaṭastha Yoga*. Initially, it deals with the body, *prāna* and the mind through various yogic practices step by step and finally, leads to *Ātmajñāna* (knowledge of the Self).

It is said that *Gheraṇḍa Samhitā* was composed in the Seventeenth Century. But not so much is known about Sage *Gheraṇḍa* regarding his place of birth. His system of yoga is called '*Saptāṅga Yoga*' i.e. the yoga of seven limbs or parts. We know '*Aṣṭāṅga Yoga*' (i.e. the eight limbs of yoga) by Sage *Patañjali* and '*Ṣaḍāṅga Yoga*' (i.e. the six limbs of yoga) by Guru *Gorakhanātha*. All these systems of yoga with their specific limbs/parts are equally respected and followed in the yogic tradition.

The first aspect of yogic practice described in *Gheraṇḍa Samhitā* is *ṣaṭkarma*, the six yogic cleansing practices. Their practice is important to get rid of diseases from the body and purify it properly. The second aspect of yogic practice discussed is the āsana. The importance of āsana practice is that they help create firmness and stability in the body. The third aspect of practice described is the *mudrā* which is used to control the flow of *prāṇa* and retain and circulate it within the body. The fourth aspect of practice he talked is *pratyāhāra*. According to Sage *Gheraṇḍa*, when body is purified through *ṣaṭkarma*, it is made firm and stable by āsana and *prāṇa* is controlled and retained by *mudrā*, then one can naturally do the practice of *pratyāhāra*. The fifth aspect of practice he taught is *prānāyāma*. In most of the *prānāyāma* practices he included *mantras* with them. Practice of *prānāyāma* with specific *mantras* creates direct impact on energy field within the body and mind through the vibrations of the *mantras* which eventually contribute for the expansion of awareness.

The sixth aspect of discourse in *Gheraṇḍa Samhitā* is *dhyāna*. The state of *dhyāna* arises naturally when the body is pure, firm and stable, *prāṇa* is controlled and the mind is withdrawn within itself. It describes three types of *dhyāna* for developing awareness and one-pointedness of the mind. The seventh and final aspect described in *Gheraṇḍa Samhitā* is *samādhi*. Its achievement is the final goal of yoga.

It is very interesting to know that in the second verse of first chapter of *Gheraṇḍa Samhitā Caṇḍakapāli* expresses his desire to learn *Ghaṭastha Yoga* which is the cause of *tattvajñāna* (knowledge of the truth). What is this *Ghaṭastha Yoga*? It simply means body based yoga (i.e. *ghaṭa* - body, *stha* – based, *yoga* – yoga).

The two common meanings of the word '*ghaṭa*' is 'a body', 'a large vessel or water pot'. It also means the mind, the heart and the soul. A *ghaṭa* (large vessel or water pot) is composed of five elements, so is the body. In this body as *ghaṭa* abide *prāna* (the vital energy), mind (with its four components) and five senses, heart (feeling, emotion, attachment) and an independent *Ātmā* (the Self which is regarded as the source and support of all beings).

Therefore, according to Sage *Gheraṇḍa Ghaṭastha Yoga* begins with the body, creates balance and harmony on the *prānic*, mental and emotional levels for higher level of awakening and finally, leads to *samādhi*, the Self-realization which is the ultimate goal of human life.

Publisher

CHAPTER TOPICS

Chapter One

Discourse On Śaṭkarma

Salutations to Ādīśvara - Body Based Yoga - The Seven Means of Purification - The Six Cleansing Practices - The Internal Cleansing - Vātasāra Dhauti - Vārisāra Dhauti – Agnisāra -Bahiṣkṛta Dhauti – Prakṣālana - Dantadhauti - Jihvā Dhauti - Karṇa Dhauti - Kapālarndhra Dhauti - Hṛddhauti – Vamanadhauti - Vāsadhauti – Mūlaśodhana – Vasti - Jala vasti - Sthala Vasti – Neti – Laulikī - Trāṭaka – Kapālabhāti – Vātakrama - Vyutkrama – Śītkrama

Chapter Two

Discourse On Āsana

Kinds of Āsana: 1. Siddhāsana, 2. Padmāsana, 3. Bhadrāsana, 4. Muktāsana, 5. Vajrāsana, 6. Svastikāsana, 7. Simhāsana, 8. Gomukhāsana, 9. Vīrāsana, 10. Dhanurāsana, 11. Mṛtāsana, 12. Guptāsana, 13. Mātsyāsana, 14. Matsyendrāsana, 15. Gorakṣāsana, 16. Paścimottānāsana, 17. Utkaṭāsana, 18. Saṅkaṭāsana, 19. Mayūrāsana, 20. Kukkuṭāsana, 21. Kūrmāsana, 22. Uttāna Kūrmakāsana, 23. Uttāna Maṇḍukāsana, 24. Vṛkṣāsana, 25. Maṇḍukāsana, 26. Garuḍāsana, 27. Vṛṣāsana, 28. Salabhāsana, 29. Makarāsana, 30. Uṣṭrāsana, 31. Bhujaṅgāsana, 32. Yogāsana

Chapter Three

Discourse On Mudrā

Twenty-Five Mudrās: 1. Mahā Mudrā, 2. Nabho Mudra, 3. Uḍḍīyāna Bandha, 4. Jālandhara Bandha, 5. Mūla Bandha, 6. Mahā Bandha, 7. Mahā Bedha Mudrā, 8. Khecarī Mudrā, 9. Viparīta Karani Mudrā, 10. Yoni Mudrā, 11. Vajroṇi Mudrā, 12. Śakti Cālinī Mudra, 13. Tāḍāgī Mudrā, 14. Māṇḍukī Mudrā, 15. Śāmbhavī Mudrā - Pañcadhāraṇās (The Five Concentrations): 16. Pārthivī Dhāraṇā, 17. Āmbhasī Dhāraṇā, 18. Āgneyī Dhāraṇā,

19. Vāyavīya Dhāraṇā, 20. Ākāśī Dhāraṇā, 21. Aśvinī Mudrā, 22. Pāśinī Mudrā, 23. Kākī Mudrā, 24. Mātaṅginī Mudrā 25. Bhujaṅginī Mudrā

Chapter Four

Discourse On Pratyāhāra

Pratyāhāra Destroys All Enemies - Pratyāhāra Controls the Mind - Pratyāhāra: Controlling the Sense Stimuli - Pratyāhāra: Mind Under the Control of the Self

Chapter Five

Discourse On Prānāyāma

Place of Practice - Time of Practice - Moderation in Diet - Forbidden Foods - Purification of Nāḍī - Types of Kumbhaka - Sahita Prāṇāyāma - Sagarbha Prāṇāyāma - Nigarbha Prāṇāyāma - Sūryabheda Prāṇāyāma - Prāṇa Vāyus - Locations of Prāṇa Vāyus - Ujjāyī Prāṇāyāma - Śītalī Prāṇāyāma - Bhastrikā Prāṇāyāma - Bhrāmarī Prāṇāyāma - Mūrcchā Prāṇāyāma - Kevalī Prāṇāyāma

Chapter Six

Discourse On Dhyāna

Three Types of Dhyāna: Sthūla Dhyāna - Another Method - Jyoti Dhyāna - Sūkṣma Dhyāna

Chapter Seven

Discourse On Samādhi

Samādhi: The Supreme Yoga - Samādhi: Union With Paramātmā - Types of Samādhi - Dhyānayoga Samādhi - Nādayoga Samādhi - Rasanānanda Samādhi - Layasiddhi Samādhi - Bhaktiyoga Samādhi - Manomūrcchā Samādhi - Greatness of Samādhi Yoga

CHAPTER ONE

Discourse On Śaṭkarma

Salutations to Ādīśvara

आदीश्वराय प्रणमामि तस्मै येनोपदिष्टा हठयोग विद्या ।
विभ्राजते प्रोन्नतराजयोगमं आरोढुमिच्छोरधिरोहिणीव ॥

ādīśvarāya praṇamāmi tasmai
yenopadiṣṭā haṭhayoga vidyā /
virājate pronnatarājayogaṃ
ārodhumicchādhirohiṇīva //

Salutation to *Śrī Ādinātha* (the primordial Lord *Śiva*) who imparted the knowledge of *Haṭha Yoga* that shines forth as a stairway for those who desire to climb highly advanced *Rāja Yoga*.

एकदा चण्डकापालिर्गत्वा घेरण्डकुट्टिरम् ।
प्रणम्य विनयाद्भक्त्या घेरण्डं परिपृच्छति ॥ १॥

ekadā caṇḍakāpālirgatvā gheraṇḍakuṭṭiram /
praṇamya vinayādbhaktayā gheraṇḍaṃ paripṛcchati //1//

One day *Caṇḍakapāli* went to the cottage of Sage *Gheraṇḍa*, saluted him with due respect and devotion and asked him. -1.

Body Based Yoga

चण्डकापालिरुवाच ।
घटस्थयोगं योगेश तत्त्वज्ञानस्य कारणम् ।
इदानीं श्रोतुमिच्छामि योगेश्वर वद प्रभो ॥ २॥

caṇḍakapāliruvāca /
ghaṭasthayogaṃ yogeśa tattvajñānasya kāraṇam /
idānīṃ śrotumicchāmi yogeśvara vada prabho //2//

Caṇḍakapāli said: - O Lord of Yoga! I wish to learn *ghaṭas-thayoga* (body based yoga) which is the cause of *tattvajñāna* (knowledge of the truth). O Lord of Yogīs! O Lord! Please tell me about it. -2.

घेरण्ड उवाच ।

साधु साधु महाबाहो यन्मां त्वं परिपृच्छसि ।

कथयामि च ते वत्स सावधानोऽवधारय ॥ ३॥

sādhu sādhu mahābāho yanmāṃ tvaṃ paripṛcchasi /

kathayāmi ca te vatsa sāvadhāno'vadhāraya //3//

Gheraṇḍa said: - O Mighty One! Well, you asked me. O child, I shall tell you. Listen to it very carefully. -3.

नास्ति मायासमं पापं नास्ति योगात्परं बलम् ।

नास्ति ज्ञानात्परो बन्धुर्नाहङ्कारात्परो रिपुः ॥ ४॥

nāsti māyāsamaṃ pāpaṃ nāsti yogātparaṃ balam /

nāsti jñānātparo bandhurnāhaṅkārārātparo ripuḥ //4//

There is no noose equal to *māyā* (illusion). There is no power equal to Yoga. There is no greater friend than *jñānā* (knowledge). There is no greater enemy than *ahaṅkāra* (ego). -4.

अभ्यासात्कादिवर्णानां यथा शास्त्राणि बोधयेत् ।

तथा योगं समासाद्य तत्त्वज्ञानं च लभ्यते ॥ ५॥

abhyāsātkādivarṇanām yathā śāstrāṇi bodhayet /

tathā yogaṃ samāsādya tattvajñānaṃ ca labhyate //5//

Just like by learning alphabets through practice all the *śāstrās* (branches of learning) are known, so by practicing yoga properly *tattvajñāna* (knowledge of the truth) is gained. -5.

सुकृतैर्दुष्कृतैः कार्यैर्जायते प्राणिना घटः ।

घटादुत्पद्यते कर्म घटीयन्त्रं यथा भ्रमेत् ॥ ६॥

sukṛtairduṣkṛtaiḥ kāryairjāyate prāṇinām ghaṭaḥ /

ghaṭādutpadyate karma ghaṭīyantraṃ yathā bhramet //6//

The physical bodies of all creatures are produced as the result of their good or bad actions. The karma (action) is originated from the body and its cycle continues just like the circle of a *ghaṭīyantra* (water-wheel). -6.

ऊर्ध्वाधोभ्रमतेयद्वद् घटीयन्त्रं गवांवशात् ।
तद्वत्कर्मवशाज्जीवो भ्रमते जन्ममृत्युभिः ॥ ७॥
urdhvārdhobhramateyadvat ghaṭīyantraṃ gavāṃvaśāt/
tadvatkarmavaśājjīvo bhramate janmamṛtyubhiḥ //7//

Just like the water-wheel goes up and down as it is moved by the bullocks, so the *jīva* (the embodied Self) goes through the cycle of birth and death due to its (past) karma. -7.

आमकुम्भ इवाम्भस्थो जीर्यमाणः सदा घटः ।
योगानलेन सन्दह्य घटशुद्धिं समाचरेत् ॥ ८॥
āmakumbha ivāmbhastho jīryamāṇaḥ sadā ghaṭaḥ /
yogānalena sandahyā ghaṭaśuddhiṃ samācaret //8//

Like a raw clay pot filled with water is destroyed (as it melts quickly), so the body is always deteriorated soon. One should purify the body baking it well by the fire of yoga. -8.

The Seven Means of Purification

शोधनं दृढता चैव स्थैर्यं धैर्यं च लाघवम् ।
प्रत्यक्षं च निर्लिप्तं च घटस्थसप्तसाधनम् ॥ ९॥
śodhanaṃ dṛḍhatā caiva
sthairyaṃ dhairyaṃ ca lāghavam /
pratyakṣaṃ ca nirliptaṃ ca
ghaṭasthasaptasādhanam //9//

The seven means of cleaning the physical body are: - purification, firmness, stability, endurance, lightness, direct knowledge and total detachment (from the world). -9.

षट्कर्मणा शोधनं च आसनेन भवेद्दृढम् ।
मुद्रया स्थिरता चैव प्रत्याहारेण धीरता ॥ १०॥
प्राणायामाल्लाघवं च ध्यानात्प्रत्यक्षमात्मनः ।
समाधिना निर्लिप्तं च मुक्तिरेव न संशयः ॥ ११॥
ṣaṭkarmaṇā śodhanaṃ ca āsanena bhaveddṛḍham /
mudrayā sthiratā caiva pratyāhāreṇa dhīratā //10//
prāṇāyāmāllāghavaṃ ca dhyānātpratyakṣamātmanaḥ /
samādhinā nirliptaṃ ca muktireva na samśayaḥ //11//

The purification is achieved through the practice of *ṣaṭkarma* (the six yogic cleansing practices); firmness through āsanas; stability through *mudrās*; endurance through *pratyāhāra*; lightness (of the body) through *prāṇāyāma*; direct knowledge through *dhyāna*; and total detachment (from the world) through *samādhi* which is certainly *mukti* (liberation) without any doubt. -10-11.

The Six Cleansing Practices

धौतिर्बस्तिस्तथा नेतिर्नौलिकी त्राटकं तथा ।
कपालभातिश्चैतानि षट्कर्माणि समाचरेत् ॥ १२॥

dhautirvastistathā netiḥ laulikī trāṭakaṃ tathā /
kapālabhātiścetāni ṣaṭkarmāṇi samācaret //12//

The *ṣaṭkarmas* to be practiced are *dhauti, vasti, neti, laulika, trāṭaka and kapālabhāti*. -12.

अन्तर्धौतिर्दन्तधौतिर्हृद्धौतिर्मूलशोधनम् ।
धौतिं चतुर्विधां कृत्वा घटं कुर्वन्ति निर्मलम् ॥ १३॥

antardhautirdantadhautirhṛddhutirmūlaśodhanam /
dhautiṃ caturvidāṃ kṛtvā ghaṭaṃ kurvanti nirmalam //13//

Antardhauti (internal cleansing), *dantadhauti* (cleaning of teeth), *hṛddhuti* (cleaning of the heart i.e. the gullet, the lungs and the stomach) and *mūlaśodhana* (cleaning of the rectum) are the four kinds *dhautis* which purify the physical body. -13.

The Internal Cleansing

वातसारं वारिसारं वह्निसारं बहिष्कृतम् ।
घटस्य निर्मलार्थाय ह्यन्तर्धौतिश्चतुर्विधा ॥ १४॥

vātasāraṃ vārisāraṃ vanhisāraṃ bahiṣkṛtam //
ghaṭasya nirmalārthāya antardhutiścaturvidhā //14//

There are four types of *antardhauti* for the purification of the physical body. They are: - *vātasāra* (purification by air), *vārisāra* (purification by water), *vanhisāra* (purification by fire) and *bahiṣkṛta* (expulsion through rectum). -14.

Vātasāra Dhauti

काकचञ्चुवदास्येन पिबेद्वायुं शनैः शनैः ।
चालयेदुदरं पश्चाद्वर्त्मना रेचयेच्छनैः ॥ १५॥

kākacañcuvadāsyena pibedvāyuṃ śanaiḥ śanaiḥ /
cālayeduduraṃ pascadvartmanā recayecchanaiḥ //15//

Inhale the air slowly through the mouth like a beak of a crow, fill the stomach and move the abdomen, and then slowly expel the air moving out through the downward passage. -15.

वातसारं परं गोप्यं देहनिर्मलकारणम् ।
सर्वरोगक्षयकरं देहानलविवर्धकम् ॥ १६॥

vātasāraṃ paraṃ gopyaṃ deha nirmalakārakam /
sarva rogakṣayakaraṃ dehānalavivardhakam //16//

Vātasāra is a highly secret practice. It is the purifier of the physical body. It destroys all diseases and increases digestive fire. -16.

Vārisāra Dhauti

आकण्ठं पूरयेद्वारि वक्त्रेण च पिबेच्छनैः ।
चालयेदुदरेणैव चोदराद्रेचयेदधः ॥ १७॥

ākaṇṭhaṃ pūrayedvāri vaktreṇa ca pibetcchanaiḥ /
cālayeddudareṇaiva codarādrecayedadhaḥ //17//

Drink the water through the mouth filling up to the throat, drink it slowly; and move it through the abdomen and then expel it forcibly through the rectum. -17.

वारिसारं परं गोप्यं देहनिर्मलकारकम् ।
साधयेद्यः प्रयत्नेन देवदेहं प्रपद्यते ॥ १८॥

vārisāraṃ paraṃ gopyaṃ dehanirmalakārakam /
sādhayettatprayatnena devadehaṃ prapadyate //18//

Vārisāra is a highly secret practice. It is the purifier the body. One who carefully practices it, his body is transformed into a divine body. -18.

वारिसारं परां धौतिं साधयेद्यः प्रयत्नतः ।
मलदेहं शोधयित्वा देवदेहं प्रपद्यते ॥ १९॥

vārisāraṃ parāṃ dhautiṃ sādhayedyaḥ prayatnataḥ /
maladehaṃ sodhayitvā devadehaṃ prapadyate //19//

Vārisāra is the best *dhauti*. One who practices it carefully purifies the impurities of his body and transforms it into the *deva-deha* (divine body). -19.

Agnisāra

नाभिग्रन्थिं मेरुपृष्ठे शतवारं च कारयेत् ।
उदरामयजं त्यक्त्वा जाठराग्निं विवर्धयेत् ॥ २०॥

nābhigranthiṃ merupṛṣṭhe śatavāraṃ ca kārayet /
agnisārameṣā dhautiryogināṃ yogasiddhidā //20//

Pull in the navel knot (center) towards the spinal column and then push out one hundred times. This is *agnisāradhauti* which gives perfection in yoga. -20.

अग्निसारमियं धौतिर्योगिनां योगसिद्धिदा ।
एषा धौतिः परा गोप्या देवानामपि दुर्लभा ।
केवलं धौतिमात्रेण देवदेहो भवेद्ध्रुवम् ॥ २१॥

udarāmayajaṃ tyaktvā jaṭharāgniṃ vivardhayet /
eṣā dhautiḥ parā gopyā devānāmapi durlabhā /
kevalaṃ dhautimātreṇa devadeho bhaveddhruvam //21//

By its practice all diseases of the stomach are cured and digestive fire is increased. This *dhauti* should be kept highly secret, and it is difficult to attain even by gods. One certainly gets a divine body through the practice of this *dhauti* alone. -21.

Bahiṣkṛta Dhauti

काकीमुद्रां साधयित्वा पूरयेदुदरं मरुत् ।
धारयेदर्धयामं तु चालयेदधोवर्त्मना ।
एषा धौतिः परा गोप्या न प्रकाश्या कदाचन ॥ २२॥

kākīmudrāṃ sādhayitvā pūrayedudaraṃ marut /
dhārayedardhayāmaṃ tu cālayedadhovartmanā /
eṣā dhautiḥ parā gopyā na prakāśyā kadācana //22//

Fill the stomach with air through the practice of *kākīmudrā*, hold it there for one and a half hours, and then force it to move downwards. This *dhauti* should be kept highly secret and not to be disclosed to anyone. -22.

Prakṣālana

नाभिदघ्ने जले स्थित्वा शक्तिनाडीं विसर्जयेत् ।
कराभ्यां क्षालयेन्नाडीं यावन्मलविसर्जनम् ।
तावत्प्रक्षाल्य नाडीं च उदरे वेशयेत्पुनः ॥ २३॥

nābhimagnajale sthitvā śaktināḍīṃ visarjayet /

karābhyāṃ kṣālayennāḍīṃ yāvanmalavisarjanam /

tāvatprakṣālya nāḍīṃ ca udare viśayetpunaḥ //23//

Stand in navel-deep water, gently draw out *śaktināḍī* (the intestine) and carefully wash it with the hands until it is clean and then draw it back again into the abdomen. -23.

इदं प्रक्षालनं गोप्यं देवानामपि दुर्लभम् ।

केवलं धौतिमात्रेण देवदेहो भवेद्ध्रुवम् ॥ २४॥

idaṃ prakṣālanaṃ gopyaṃ devānāmapi durlabham /

kevalaṃ dhautimātreṇa devadeho bhavet dhruvam //24//

This *prakṣālana* (washing practice) should be kept secret. It is difficult to attain even by gods. Through this practice alone one certainly obtains a divine body. -24.

यामार्धधारणाशक्तिं यावन्न साधयेन्नरः ।

बहिष्कृतं महद्धौतिस्तावच्चैव न जायते ॥ २५॥

yamārdha dhāraṇāśaktiṃ yāvanna dhārayennaraḥ /

bahiṣkṛtaṃ mahaddhautistāvaccaiva na jāyate //25//

As long as one does not have the power of retaining the breath for one and half hours, so long he should not attempt to do *bahiṣkṛta dhauti*, the great purification practice. -25.

Dantadhauti

दन्तमूलं जिह्वामूलं रन्ध्रं च कर्णयुग्मयोः ।

कपालरन्ध्रं पञ्चैते दन्तधौतिं विधीयते ॥ २६॥

dantamūlaṃ jihvāmūlaṃ randhraṃ karṇayugmayoḥ /

kapālarandhraṃ pañcaite dantadhautirvidhīyate //26//

Purification of the root of the teeth, the root of the tongue, the two holes of the ears (counted as two cleaning practices) and the frontal sinuses are known as five kinds *dantadhauti*. -26.

खादिरेण रसेनाथ मृत्तिकया च शुद्धया ।

मार्जयेद्दन्तमूलं च यावत्किल्बिषमाहरेत् ॥ २७॥

khādireṇa rasenātha śuddhamṛttikayā tathā /

mārjayeddantamūlaṃ ca yāvaṭkilviṣamāharet//27//

Rub the root of the teeth with catechu powder/juice or with pure earth until the impurities are removed. -27.

दन्तमूलं परा धौतिर्योगिनां योगसाधने ।
नित्यं कुर्यात्प्रभाते च दन्तरक्षाय योगवित् ।
दन्तमूलं धावनादिकार्येषु योगिनां मतम् ॥ २८॥

dantamūlaṃ parādhutiryogināṃ yoga sādhane /
nityaṃ kuryātprabhāte ca dantarakṣāṃ ca yogavit /
dantamūlaṃ dhāvanādikāryeṣu yogināṃ matam //28//

The cleaning the root of teeth is a great *dhauti* for yogīs in their yogic *sādhanā* (practice). It should be done regularly in the morning for the protection of the teeth. The knowers of yoga regard that this *dhauti* is one of the important acts of yogīs like their other practices. -28.

Jihvā Dhauti

अथातः संप्रवक्ष्यामि जिह्वाशोधनकारणम् ।
जरामरणरोगादीन्नाशयेद्दीर्घलम्बिका ॥ २९॥

athātaḥ sampravakṣyāmi jihvāśodhana kāraṇam /
jarāmaraṇarogādīnnāśayeddīrghalambikā //29//

Now I shall explain you about the reason of cleaning the tongue. This practice of *dīrghalambikā* (elongation of the tongue) destroys old age, death and disease, etc. -29.

तर्जनीमध्यमाऽनामा अङ्गुलित्रययोगतः ।
वेशयेद्गलमध्ये तु मार्जयेल्लम्बिकामूलम् ।
शनैः शनैर्मार्जयित्वा कफदोषं निवारयेत् ॥ ३०॥

tarjanīmadhyamānāmā aṅgulitrayayogataḥ /
veśayedgalamadhye tu mārjayellambikāmūlam /
śanaiḥ śanaiḥ mārjayitvā kaphadoṣaṃ nivārayet //30//

Insert the index, middle and ring fingers jointly into the throat, rub and clean well the root of the tongue and remove the imbalance of *kapha* (phlegm) rubbing and cleaning it slowly and regularly. -30.

मार्जयेन्नवनीतेन दोहयेच्च पुनः पुनः ।
तदग्रं लोहयन्त्रेण कर्षयित्वा शनैः शनैः ॥ ३१॥

mārjayennavanītena dohayecca punaḥ punaḥ /
tadagraṃ lohayantreṇa karṣayitvā śanaiḥ śanaiḥ //31//

Having the tongue cleaned, rub it with butter and milk it again and again. Then holding the tip of the tongue with an iron tongs, pull it out slowly and slowly. -31.

नित्यं कुर्यात्प्रयत्नेन रवेरुदयकेऽस्तके ।
एवं कृते च नित्यं सा लम्बिका दीर्घतां व्रजेत् ॥ ३२॥

nityaṃ kuryātprayatnena raverudayake'stake /
evaṃ kṛte ca nityaṃ sā lambikā dīrghatāṃ vrajet //32//

It should be done carefully everyday at the time of rising and setting of the sun. In this way, through regular practice the tongue becomes longer. -32.

Karṇa Dhauti

तर्जन्यङ्गुल्य काग्रेण मार्जयेत्कर्णरन्ध्रयोः ।
नित्यमभ्यासयोगेन नादान्तरं प्रकाशयेत् ॥ ३३॥

tarjanyanāmikā yogānmārjayet karṇarandhrayoḥ /
nityamabhyāsa yogena nādāntaraṃ prakāśayet //33//

The holes of the ears should be cleaned with the index and/or ring fingers. The inner mystical sounds become evident through the regular practice of this yogic method. -33.

Kapālaradhra Dhauti

वृद्धाङ्गुष्ठेन दक्षेण मर्दयेद्भालरन्ध्रकम् ।
एवमभ्यासयोगेन कफदोषं निवारयेत् ॥ ३४॥

vṛddhāṅguṣṭhena dakṣeṇa mārjayedbhālarandhrakam /
evamabhyāsayogena kaphadoṣaṃ nivārayet //34//

The top opening of the head should be patted with the thumb of the right hand. The imbalance of *kapha* is removed through the practice of this yogic method. -34.

नाडी निर्मलतां याति दिव्यदृष्टिः प्रजायते ।
निद्रान्ते भोजनान्ते च दिवान्ते च दिने दिने ॥ ३५॥

nāḍī nirmalatām yāti divyadṛṣṭiḥ prajāyate /
nidrānte bhojanānte ca divānte ca dine dine //35//

The *nāḍīs* (*prānic* channels) become pure (by this practice) and *divyadṛṣṭi* (clairvoyance) is achieved. It should be practiced daily at the end of sleep, at the end of meals, and at the end of the day.

-35.

Hṛddhauti

हृद्धौतिं त्रिविधां कुर्याद्दण्डवमनवाससा ॥ ३६॥

hṛddhautiṃ trividhāṃ kuryāddaṇḍavamanavāsasā //36//

There are three kinds *hṛddhauti* (cleaning of the heart): - *daṇḍadhauti* (cleaning by using stalk), *vamanadhauti* (cleaning by vomiting) and *vāsadhauti* (cleaning by using cloth). -36.

रम्भादण्डं हरिद्दण्डं वेत्रदण्डं तथैव च ।

हृन्मध्ये चालयित्वा तु पुनः प्रत्याहरेच्छनैः ॥ ३७॥

rambhādaṇḍaṃ hariddaṇḍaṃ vetradaṇḍaṃ tathaiva ca /

hṛnmadhye cālayitvā tu punaḥ pratyāharecchanaiḥ //37//

Use a stalk of the soft part of a banana plant or a stalk of the turmeric or a stalk of cane and insert it into the gullet and move it there (several times) and then take it out slowly. -37.

कफपित्तं तथा क्लेदं रेचयेदूर्ध्ववर्त्मना ।

दण्डधौतिविधानेन हृद्रोगं नाशयेद्ध्रुवम् ॥ ३८॥

kaphaṃ pittaṃ tathā kledaṃ recayedūrdhvavartmanā /

daṇḍadhautividhānena hṛdrogaṃ nāśayet dhruvam //38//

The phlegm, bile and other watery impurities should be expelled out through the opening of the mouth. The heart disease is certainly destroyed by the proper practice of this *daṇḍadhauti*. -38.

Vamanadhauti

भोजनान्ते पिबेद्वारि चाऽऽकण्ठपूरितं सुधीः ।

ऊर्ध्वां दृष्टिं क्षणं कृत्वा तज्जलं वमयेत्पुनः ।

नित्यमभ्यासयोगेन कफपित्तं निवारयेत् ॥ ३९॥

bhojanānte pibetvāri cākaṇṭhaṃ pūritaṃ sudhiḥ /

urdhvā dṛṣṭiṃ kṣaṇaṃ kṛtvā tatjalaṃ vamayetpunaḥ /

nityamabhyāsayogena kaphapittaṃ nivārayet //39//

The wise practitioner at the end of his meal should drink water filling up to the throat and looking upwards for a short time should vomit up the water. The *kapha* (phlegm) and *pitta* (bile) are cured through this regular yogic practice. -39.

Vāsadhauti

चतुरङ्गुल विस्तारं सूक्ष्मवस्त्रं शनैर्ग्रसेत् ।
पुनः प्रत्याहरेदेतत्प्रोच्यते धौतिकर्मकम् ॥ ४०॥

caturaṅgula vistāraṃ sukṣmavastraṃ śanairgraset /
punaḥ pratyāharedetatprocyate dhautikarmakam //40//

Slowly swallow a thin cloth having the width of four fingers and slowly take it out. This is called *vāsa/vastradhauti*. -40.

गुल्मज्वरप्लीहाकुष्ठकफपित्तं विनश्यति ।
आरोग्यं बलपुष्टिश्च भवेत्तस्य दिने दिने ॥ ४१॥

gulmajvaramlaplīhakuṣṭhakaphapittaṃ vinasyati /
ārogyaṃ balapuṣṭiśca bhavettasya dine dine //41//

The practice of this *dhauti* cures enlarged glands and spleen, fever, leprosy and *kapha* and *pitta* related disorders. Good health, strength and nourishment are gradually acquired through this practice. -41.

Mūlaśodhana

अपानक्रूरता तावद्यावन्मूलं न शोधयेत् ।
तस्मात्सर्वप्रयत्नेन मूलशोधनमाचरेत् ॥ ४२॥

apānakrūratā tāvadyāvanmūlaṃ na śodhayet /
tasmātsarvaprayatnena mūlaśodhanamācaret //42//

The *apānakrūratā* (the cruelty of *apāna vāyu*) cannot be eliminated unless the rectum is not purified. Therefore, purification of the rectum should be done with all effort. -42.

पीतमूलस्य दण्डेन मध्यमाङ्गुलिनाऽपि वा ।
यत्नेन क्षालयेद्गुह्यं वारिणा च पुनः पुनः ॥ ४३॥

pītamūlasya daṇḍena madhyamāṅgulinā'pi vā /
yatnena kṣālayetguhyaṃ vāriṇā ca punaḥ punaḥ //43//

The rectum should be carefully cleaned by means of a turmeric stalk or the middle finger with water again and again. -43.

वारयेत्कोष्ठकाठिन्यमामाजीर्णं निवारयेत् ।
कारणं कान्तिपुष्ट्योश्च वह्निमण्डलदीपनम् ॥ ४४॥

vārayetkoṣṭhakāṭhinyamāmājīrṇa nivārayet /
kāraṇaṃ kāntipuṣṭyocca dīpanaṃ vanhimaṇḍalam //44//

The practice of *mūlaśodhana*destroys constipation, indigestion and digestive disorders. It increases the beauty and vitality of the body and activates the digestive fire. -44.

Vasti

जलबस्तिः शुष्कबस्तिर्बस्तिः स्याद्द्विविधा स्मृता ।
जलबस्तिं जले कुर्याच्छुष्कबस्तिं सदा क्षितौ ॥ ४५॥

jala vastiḥ śuṣkavastirvasti ca dvividhau smṛtā /
jala vastiṃ jale kuryācchuṣkavastiṃ sadā kṣitau //45//

The *vasti* is considered of two kinds: - *jala vasti* and *śuṣka vasti*. *Jala vasti* is practiced in water and *śuṣka vasti* is always practiced on land. -45.

Jala vasti

नाभिमग्नजले पायुं न्यस्तवानुत्कटासनम् ।
आकुञ्चनं प्रसारं च जलबस्तिं समाचरेत् ॥ ४६॥

nābhimagnajale pāyuṃ nyastavānutkaṭāsanam /
ākuñcanaṃ prasāraṃ ca jala vastiṃ samācaret //46//

Go into water up to the navel deep and perform *utkaṭāsana*. Then contract and expand the anus muscles for the practice of *jala vasti*. -46.

प्रमेहं च उदावर्तं क्रूरवायुं निवारयेत् ।
भवेत्स्वच्छन्ददेहश्च कामदेवसमो भवेत् ॥ ४७॥

prameham ca udāvartaṃ kruravāyuṃ nivārayet /
bhavetsvacchandadehaśca kāmadeva samo bhavet //47//

This practice cures *prameha* (diabetes), *udāvarta* (digestive disorders) and *kruravāyu* (severe disorders of the *vāyu*). The body becomes free from all restraints and one attains the beauty equal to *kāmadeva* (the god of love). -47.

Sthala Vasti

बस्तिं पश्चिमोत्तानेन चालयित्वा शनैरधः ।
अश्विनीमुद्रया पायुमाकुञ्चयेत्प्रसारयेत् ॥ ४८॥

paścimottānato vastiṃ calayitva śanaiḥ śanaiḥ /
aśvinīmudrayā pāyumākuñcayetprasārayet //48//

After assuming the *paścimottānāsana*, move the intestines

slowly in the lower region and then contract and expand the anus muscles through the practice of *aśvinīmudrā*. -48.

एवमभ्यासयोगेन कोष्ठदोषो न विद्यते ।
विवर्धयेज्जाठराग्निमामवातं विनाशयेत् ॥ ४९॥

evamabhyāsayogena koṣṭhadoṣo na vidyate /
vivarddhayejjaṭharāgnimāmavātaṃ vināśayet //49//

Thus, constipation does not exist through this yogic practice. The digestive fire is increased and flatulence is destroyed. -49.

Neti

वितस्तिमानं सूक्ष्मसूत्रं नासानाले प्रवेशयेत् ।
मुखान्निर्गमयेत्पश्चात्प्रोच्यते नेतिकर्मकम् ॥ ५०॥

vitastimānaṃ sūkṣmasūtraṃ nāsānale praveśayet /
mukhānnirgamayetpaścāt procyate netikarmakam //50//

Insert into the nostril a thin thread about ten-inch long and then it should be taken out through the mouth. This is called *neti karma*. -50.

साधनान्नेतिकार्यस्य खेचरीसिद्धिमाप्नुयात् ।
कफदोषा विनश्यन्ति दिव्यदृष्टिः प्रजायते ॥ ५१॥

sādhanānnetikāryasya khecarisiddhimāpnuyāt /
kaphadoṣā vinasyanti divyadṛṣṭiḥ prajāyate //51//

khecari siddhi is obtainedthrough the practice of *neti*. It destroys *kapha doṣas* (disorders of the *kapha*) and *divyadṛṣṭi* (clairvoyance) is attained. -51.

Laulikī

अमन्दवेगेन तुन्दं भ्रामयेदुभपार्श्वयोः ।
सर्वरोगान्निहन्तीह देहानलविवर्धनम् ॥ ५२॥

amandavegena tundaṃ bhrāmayedubhapārśvayoḥ /
sarvarogānnihantīha dehānalavivarddhanam //52//

Rotate the abdominal muscles very quickly from one side to another. The practice of *Laulikī* destroys all diseases and increases *deha anala* (the bodily fire i.e. digestive fire). -52.

Trāṭaka

निमेषोन्मेषकं त्यक्त्वा सूक्ष्मलक्ष्यं निरीक्षयेत् ।

यावदश्रूणि पतन्ति त्राटकं प्रोच्यते बुधैः ॥ ५३॥

nimeṣonmeṣaṃ tyaktvā sūkṣmalakṣyaṃ nirīkṣayet /

patanti yāvadaśrūṇi trāṭakaṃ procyate budhaiḥ //53//

Having stopped the blinking of eyes, gaze at a small object until tears shed down. This is called *trāṭaka* by the wise. -53.

एवमभ्यासयोगेन शाम्भवी जायते ध्रुवम् ।

नेत्ररोगा विनश्यन्ति दिव्यदृष्टिः प्रजायते ॥ ५४॥

evamabhyāsayogena śāmbhavī jāyate dhruvam /

netrarogā vinasyanti divyadṛṣṭiḥ prajāyate //54//

The state of *śāmbhavī mudrā*is attained through this yogic practice. This practice destroys all diseases of the eyes and bestows *divyadṛṣṭi* (clairvoyance). -54.

Kapālabhāti

वातक्रमव्युत्क्रमेण शीत्क्रमेण विशेषतः ।

भालभातिं त्रिधा कुर्यात्कफदोषं निवारयेत् ॥ ५५॥

vātakrameṇa vyutkrameṇa śītkrameṇa viśeṣaluḥ /

bhālabhātiṃ tridhā kuryātkaphadoṣaṃ nivārayet //55//

There are three kinds of *kapālabhāti* especially: - *vātakrama, vyut- krama* and *śītkrama*. They destroy all disorders arising from *kapha* (phlegm). -55.

Vātakrama

इडया पूरयेद्वायुं रेचयेत्पिङ्गलां पुनः ।

पिङ्गलया पूरयित्वा पुनश्चन्द्रेण रेचयेत् ॥ ५६॥

iḍayā pūrayedvāyuṃ recayetpiṅgalayā punaḥ /

piṅgalayā pūrayitvā punaścandreṇa recayet //56//

Inhale the air through the left nostril and exhale through the right nostril and again inhale it through the right nostril and exhale it through the left nostril. -56.

पूरकं रेचकं कृत्वा वेगेन न तु धारयेत् ।

एवमभ्यासयोगेन कफदोषं निवारयेत् ॥ ५७॥

purakaṃ rechakaṃ kṛtvā vegena na tu dhārayet /

evamabhyāsayogena kapha doṣaṃ nivārayet //57//

The inhalation and exhalation should be done without any

force. The disorder of the *kapha* (phlegm) is destroyed through this yogic practice. -57.

Vyutkrama

नासाभ्यां जलमाकृष्य पुनर्वक्त्रेण रेचयेत् ।
पायं पायं व्युत्क्रमेण श्लेष्मदोषं निवारयेत् ॥ ५८॥

nāsābhyāṃ jalamākṛsya punarvaktreṇa recayet /
pāyaṃ pāyaṃ vyutkrameṇa śleṣmādoṣaṃ nivārayet //58//

Draw water through both nostrils and expel it through the mouth, again draw water through the mouth and expel it through the nostrils. In this way, drawing water and expelling it repeatedly destroys the disorder of the *kapha* (phlegm). -58.

Śītkrama

शीत्कृत्य पीत्वा वक्त्रेण नासानलैर्विरेचयेत् ।
एवमभ्यासयोगेन कामदेवसमो भवेत् ॥ ५९॥

śītkṛtya pītvā vaktreṇa nāsānālairvirecayet /
evamabhyāsayogena kāmadeva samo bhavet //59//

Drink water through the mouth with a hissing sound and expel it through the nostrils. One becomes equal to *kāmadeva* (the God of love) through this yogic practice. -59.

न जायते वार्द्धकं च ज्वरो नैव प्रजायते ।
भवेत्स्वच्छन्ददेहश्च कफदोषं निवारयेत् ॥ ६०॥

na jāyate vārddhakaṃ ca jvaro naiva prajāyate /
bhavetsvacchanda dehaśca kapaha doṣaṃ nivārayet //60//

One who practices it does not become old and his body does not become frail. The body becomes free (from diseases), healthy and *kapha doṣa* (disorder of phlegm) is removed. -60.

इति श्रीघेरण्डसंहितायां घेरण्डचण्डसंवादे
षट्कर्मशोधनं नाम प्रथमोपदेशः॥

iti śrīgheraṇḍasamhitāyāṃ gheraṇḍacaṇḍasaṃvāde
ṣaṭkarmasādhanaṃ nāma prathamopadeśaḥ //

Thus ends the First Chapter of *Gheraṇḍa Samhitā* entitled *Ṣaṭkarma* practice.

CHAPTER TWO

Discourse On Āsana

घेरण्ड उवाच ।
आसनानि समस्तानि यावन्तो जीवजन्तवः ।
चतुरशीतिलक्षाणि शिवेन कथितानि च ॥ १॥

gheraṇḍa uvāca /
āsanāni samastāni yāvanto jīvajantavaḥ /
caturaśīti lakṣāṇi śivena kathitāni ca //1//

Sage *Gheraṇḍa* said: - There are as many āsanas as there are living beings in the universe. Lord *Śiva* has described eighty-four hundred thousand āsanas. -1.

तेषां मध्ये विशिष्टानि षोडशोनं शतं कृतम् ।
तेषां मध्ये मर्त्यलोके द्वात्रिंशदासनं शुभम् ॥ २॥

teṣāṃ madhye viśiṣṭani ṣoḍaśonaṃ śataṃ kṛtam/
teṣāṃ madhye martyaloke dvātriṃśadāsanaṃ śubham //2//

Of these, eighty-four are the excellent; and of these eighty-four, thirty-two are auspicious in this *martyaloka* (world of mortals). -2.

Kinds of Āsana

सिद्धं पद्मं तथा भद्रं मुक्तं वज्रं च स्वस्तिकम् ।
सिंहं च गोमुखं वीरं धनुरासनमेव च ॥ ३॥
मृतं गुप्तं तथा मात्स्यं मत्स्येन्द्रासनमेव च ।
गोरक्षं पश्चिमोत्तानमुत्कटं सङ्कटं तथा ॥ ४॥
मयूरं कुक्कुटं कूर्मं तथा चोत्तानकूर्मकम् ।
उत्तानमण्डूकं वृक्षं मण्डूकं गरुडं वृषम् ॥ ५॥
शलभं मकरं चोष्ट्रं भुजङ्गं च योगासनम् ।

द्वात्रिंशदासनानि तु मर्त्यलोके हि सिद्धिदम् ॥ ६॥

siddhaṃ padmaṃ tathā bhadraṃ muktaṃ vajraṃ ca svastikam /
simhaṃ ca gomukhaṃ vīraṃ dhanurāsanameva ca //3//
mṛtaṃ guptaṃ tathā mātsyaṃ matsyendrāsanameva ca /
gorakṣaṃ paścimottānamuṭaṭaṃ saṅkaṭaṃ tathā //4//
mayūraṃ kukkuṭaṃ kūrmaṃ tathā cottānakūrmakam /
uttānamaṇḍukaṃ vṛkṣaṃ maṇḍukaṃ garuḍaṃ vṛṣam //5//
salabhaṃ makaraṃ coṣṭraṃ bhujaṅgaṃ yogamāsanam /
dvātrimśadāsanāni tu martyaloke hi siddhidam //6//

The thirty-two āsanas which certainly bestow*siddhi* (perfection) in this mortal world are: - 1. *siddhāsana*, 2. *padmāsana*, 3. *bhadrāsana*, 4. *muktāsana*, 5. *vajrāsana*, 6. *svastikāsana*, 7. *simhāsana*, 8. *gomukhāsana*, 9. *vīrāsana*, 10. *dhanurāsana*, 11. *mṛtāsana*, 12. *guptāsana*, 13. *mātsyāsana*, 14. *matsyendrāsana*, 15. *gorakṣāsana*, 16. *paścimottānāsana*, 17. *utkaṭāsana*, 18. *saṅkaṭāsana*, 19. *mayūrāsana*, 20. *kukkuṭāsana*, 21. *kūrmāsana*, 22. *uttāna kūrmakāsana*, 23. *uttāna maṇḍukāsana*, 24. *vṛkṣāsana*, 25. *maṇḍukāsana*, 26. *garuḍāsana*, 27. *vṛṣāsana*, 28. *salabhāsana*, 29. *makarāsana*, 30. *uṣṭrāsana*, 31. *bhujaṅgāsana* and 32. *yogāsana*. -3-6.

1. Siddhāsana

योनिस्थानकमङ्घ्रिमूलघटितं सम्पीड्य गुल्फेतरं
मेढ्रोपर्यथ संनिधाय चिबुकं कृत्वा हृदि स्थापितम् ।
स्थाणुः संयमितेन्द्रियोऽचलदृशा पश्यन्भ्रुवोरन्तरे
एवं मोक्षविधायते फलकरं सिद्धासनं प्रोच्यते ॥ ७॥

yonisthānakamaṅghrimūlaghaṭitaṃ sampiḍya gulphetaram
meḍhroparyatha sannidhāya cibukaṃ kṛtvā hṛdi sthāpitam /
sthāṇuḥ samyamitendriyo'caladṛśā paśyanbhruvorantaram
hyetanmokṣakapāṭabhedanakaraṃ siddhāsanaṃ procyate //7//

A yogi who has restrained his senses should place one heel at the perineum, theother heel above the penis pressing the pubis and the chin on the chest. Remaining steady and upright, he should fix his gaze constantly between the two eyebrows. This is called *siddhāsana* which breaks open the door to liberation. -7.

2. Padmāsana

वामोरूपरि दक्षिणं हि चरणं संस्थाप्य वामं तथा
दक्षोरूपरि पश्चिमेन विधिना कृत्वा कराभ्यां दृढम् ।
अङ्गुष्ठौ हृदये निधाय चिबुकं नासाग्रमालोकयेत्
एतद्व्याधिविकारनाशनकरं पद्मासनं प्रोच्यते ॥ ८॥

vāmorupari dakṣiṇaṃ hi caraṇaṃ samsthāpya vāmaṃ tathā
dakṣorūpari paścimena vidhinā dhṛtvā karābhyāṃ dṛdham /
aṅguṣṭhau hṛdaye nidhāya cibukaṃ nāsāgramālokayet
etadvyādhivikāranāśanakaraṃ padmāsanaṃ procyate //8//

Place the right foot on the left thigh and the left foot on the right thigh. Then, place the arms behind the back crosswise, firmly grab the big toes and rest the chin on the chest and fix the gaze on the tip of the nose. This is called *padmāsana* which destroys all kinds of diseases. -8.

3. Bhadrāsana

गुल्फौ च वृषणस्याधो व्युत्क्रमेण समाहितः ।
पादाङ्गुष्ठौ कराभ्यां च धृत्वा च पृष्ठदेशतः ॥ ९॥
जालन्धरं समासाद्य नासाग्रमवलोकयेत् ।
भद्रासनं भवेदेतत्सर्वव्याधिविनाशकम् ॥ १०॥

gulphau ca vṛṣaṇasyādhovyutkramena samāhitaḥ /
pādanguṣṭhau karābhyāṃ ca dhṛtvā vai pṛṣṭhadeśataḥ //9//
jālandharaṃ samāsādya nāsāgramavalokayet /
bhadrāsanaṃ bhavedetatsarvavyādhivināśakam //10//

Turn both heels upward and keep them under the scrotum and grasp the big toes behind the back. After performing the *jālandhara Bandha*, gaze on the tip of the nose. This is *bhadrāsana*, the destroyer of all diseases. -9-10.

4. Muktāsana

पायुमूले वामगुल्फं दक्षगुल्फं तथोपरि ।
समकायशिरोग्रीवं मुक्तासनं तु सिद्धिदम् ॥ ११॥

pāyumūle vāmagulphaṃ dakṣagulphaṃ tathopari /
samakāyaśirogrīvaṃ muktāsanaṃ tu siddhidam //11//

One should place the left heel at the base of the anus and the right heel above it. The body, head and neck should be kept straight. This is called *muktāsana* which gives perfection. -11.

5. Vajrāsana

जङ्घाभ्यां वज्रवत्कृत्वा गुदपार्श्वे पदावुभौ ।
वज्रासनं भवेदेतद्योगिनां सिद्धिदायकम् ॥ १२॥

jaṅghābhyāṃ vajravatkṛtvā gudāpārśve padāvubhau /
vajrāsanaṃ bhavedetadyogināṃ siddhidāyakam //12//

Making the thighs solid like thunderbolt, the legs are placed by the side of the anus. This is v*ajrāsana* which gives perfection to yogis. -12.

6. Svastikāsana

जानूर्वोरन्तरे कृत्वा योगी पादतले उभे ।
ऋजुकायः समासीनः स्वस्तिकं तत्प्रचक्षते ॥ १३॥

jānūrvorantare kṛtvā yogī pādatale ubhe /
ṛjukāyasamāsīnaḥ svastikaṃ tatpracakṣate //13//

Placing the soles of both feet between the calves and thighs, sit with the body straight and remain stable. That is called *svastikāsana*. -13.

7. Simhāsana

गुल्फौ च वृषणस्याधो व्युत्क्रमेणोर्ध्वतां गतौ ।
चितिमूलौ भूमिसंस्थौ करौ च जानुनोपरि ॥ १४।
व्यक्तवक्त्रो जलन्धरं च नासाग्रमवलोकयेत् ।
सिंहासनं भवेदेतत्सर्वव्याधिविनाशकम् ॥ १५॥

gulphau ca vṛṣaṇasyādho vyutkrameṇordhvatāṃ gatau /
citiyugmaṃ bhūmisamsthaṃ karau ca jānunopari //14//
vyāttavaktro jalandhreṇa nāsāgramavalokayet /
simhāsanaṃ bhavedetatsarvavyādhivināśakam //15//

Place both the heels under the scrotum with the feet crosswise turning upward. Place the knees on the ground and hands on them with open mouth. Then, practice *jālandhara bandha* and fix the gaze on the tip of the nose. This is called *simhāsana*, the destroyer of all diseases. -14-15.

8. Gomukhāsana

पादौ च भूमौ संस्थाप्य पृष्ठपार्श्वे निवेशयेत् ।
स्थिरकायं समासाद्य गोमुखं गोमुखाऽऽकृतिः ॥ १६॥

pādau ca bhūmau saṃsthāpya pṛṣṭhapārśve niveśayet /
sthiraṃ kāyaṃ samāsādhya gomukhaṃ gomukhākṛtiḥ //16//

Place both feet on the ground with the heels crosswise on each side of the buttocks. Sit calmly keeping the body stable with the mouth raised. This is *gomukhāsana* forming the shape of the mouth of a cow. -16.

9. Vīrāsana

एकं पादमथैकस्मिन्विन्यसेदूरुसंस्थितम् ।
इतरस्मिंस्तथा पश्चाद्वीरासनमितीरितम् ॥ १७॥

ekaṃ pādamathaikasminvinyasedūrusaṃsthitam /
itarasminstathā paścādvīrāsanamitīritam //17//

Place the right foot near the thigh of left foot. Then bend the left knee and turn the foot backwards. This is called *vīrāsana.* -17.

10. Dhanurāsana

प्रसार्य पादौ भुवि दण्डरूपौ
करौ च पृष्ठे धृतपादयुग्मम् ।
कृत्वा धनुस्तुल्यपरिवर्तिताङ्गं
निगद्य योगी धनुरासनं तत् ॥ १८॥

prasārya pādau bhuvi daṇḍarūpau
karau ca pṛṣṭhe dhṛtapādayugmam /
kṛtvā dhanurvatparivartitāṅgaṃ
nigadhyate vai dhanurāsanaṃ tat //18//

Lie down facing on the ground and extend both legs like a stick. Then grab both ankles with hands and stretch the body making it like a bow. This is called *dhanurāsana.* -18.

11. Mṛtāsana

उत्तानं शववद्भूमौ शयानं तु शवासनम् ।
शवासनं श्रमहरं चित्तविश्रान्तिकारणम् ॥ १९॥

uttānaṃ śavavat bhūmau śayanaṃ tu śavāsanam /

savāsanaṃ śramaharaṃ cittaviśrāntikārakam //19//

Lying down on the ground like a dead person is *śavāsana*. *Śavāsana* removes fatigue and relaxes the mind. -19.

12. Guptāsana

जानूर्वोरन्तरे पादौ कृत्वा पादौ च गोपयेत् ।

पादोपरि च संस्थाप्य गुदं गुप्तासनं विदुः ॥ २०॥

jānūrvorantare pādau kṛtvā pādau ca gopayet /

pādopari ca samsthāpya gudaṃ guptāsanaṃ viduḥ //20//

Keep both feet in the middle of the knees and thighs, and place the anus area between the feet. This is called *guptāsana*. -20.

13. Matyāsana

मुक्तपद्मासनं कृत्वा उत्तानशयनं चरेत् ।

कूर्पराभ्यां शिरो वेष्ट्यं रोगघ्नं मत्स्यासनम् ॥ २१॥

muktapadmāsanaṃ kṛtvā uttānaśayanaṃ caret /

kūrparābhyāṃ śiro veṣṭyaṃ rogaghnaṃ mātsyamāsanam //21//

After performing *muktapadmāsana*, lie flat on the ground resting the head between the two elbowsof the hands. This is called *mātsyāsana*, the destroyer of diseases. -21.

14. Matsyendrāsana

उदरं पश्चिमाभासं कृत्वा तिष्ठत्ययत्नतः ।

नम्रितं वामपादं हि दक्षजानूपरि न्यसेत् ॥ २२॥

तत्र याम्यं कूर्परं च याम्यकरेऽपि च।

भ्रुवोर्मध्ये गतां दृष्टिः पीठं मात्स्येन्द्रमुच्यते ॥ २३॥

udaraṃ paścimābhāsaṃ kṛtvā tiṣṭhatyayatnataḥ /

namritaṃ vāmapādaṃ hi dakṣajānūpari nyaset //22//

tatra yāmyaṃ kūrparaṃ ca yāmyakare'pi ca /

bhruvormadhye gatāṃ dṛṣṭiḥ pīṭhaṃ mātsyendram-ucyate //23//

After pulling the abdomen backward, remain upright with due effort. Bend the left leg and place the heel/foot on the right thigh. Place the right elbow on the leg, the chin on the right hand and fix the gaze between the eyebrow center. This is called *matsyendrāsana*. -22-23.

15. Gorakṣāsana

जानूर्वोरन्तरे पादौ उत्तानौ व्यक्तसंस्थितौ ।
गुल्फौ चाच्छाद्य हस्ताभ्यामुत्तानाभ्यां प्रयत्नतः ॥ २४॥
कण्ठसङ्कोचनं कृत्वा नासाग्रमवलोकयेत् ।
गोरक्षासनमित्याहुर्योगिनां सिद्धिकारणम् ॥ २५॥

jānūrvorantare pādau uttānau vyaktasamsthitau /
gulphau cācchādya hastābyāmuttānābhyāṃ prayatnataḥ //24//
kaṇṭhasaṅkocanaṃ kṛtvā nāsāgramavalokayet /
gorakṣāsanamityāhuryogināṃ siddhikārakam //25//

Keep the both feet turned upward concealed in the middle of the knees and the thighs, and then cover the heels carefully with both the hands turned upward. After contracting the throat, fix the gaze at the tip of the nose. This is called *gorakṣāsana* which gives perfection to yogis. -24-25.

16. Paścimottānāsana

प्रसार्य पादौ भुवि दण्डरूपौ
विन्यस्तभालं चितियुग्ममध्ये ।
यत्नेन पादौ च धृतौ कराभ्यां
तत्पश्चिमोत्तानमिहासनं स्यात् ॥ २६॥

prasārya pādau bhuvi daṇḍarūpau
vinyastabhālaṃ citiyugmamadhye /
yatnena pādau ca dhṛtau karābhyāṃ
tatpaścimottānamihāsanaṃ syāt //26//

Stretch both legs out on the ground like a stick and place the forehead between the knees and then grasp the big toes carefully with the hands. This is *paścimottānāsana*. -26.

17. Utkaṭāsana

अङ्गुष्ठाभ्यामवष्टभ्य धरां गुल्फौ च खे गतौ ।
तत्रोपरि गुदं न्यस्य विज्ञेयं तुत्कटासनम् ॥ २७॥

aṅguṣṭhabhyāmavaṣṭabhya dharāṃ gulphau ca khe gatau /
tatropari gudaṃ nyasya vijñeyaṃ tūtkaṭāsanam // 27//

Keep the big toes on the ground with the heels raised up in the air and place the area of the anus on the heels. This is known as *utkaṭāsana*. -27.

18. Saṅkaṭāsana

वामपादचितेर्मूलं विन्यस्य धरणीतले ।
पाददण्डेन याम्येन वेष्टयेद्वामपादकम् ।
जानुयुग्मे करयुग्ममेतत्सङ्कटमासनम् ॥ २८॥

vāmapādacitermūlaṃ vinyasya dharaṇītale /
pāda daṇḍenayāmyena veṣṭayedvāmapādakam /
jānuyugme karayugmetatsaṅkaṭāsanam //28//

Keeping the left shin and foot on the ground, wrap the right leg around the left leg and then place both the hands on the knees. This is called *saṅkaṭāsana*. -28.

19. Mayūrāsana

पाण्योस्तलामाभ्यामवलम्ब्य भूमिं
तत्कूर्परस्थापितनाभिपार्श्वम् ।
उच्चासनो दण्डवदुत्थितः खे
मायूरमेतत्प्रवदन्ति पीठम् ।।२९।।

pāṇyostalābhyāmavalambya bhūmiṃ
taṭūrparasthāpitanābhipārśvam /
uccāsano daṇḍavadutthitaḥ khe
māyūrametatpravadanti pīṭham //29//

Placing the palms of both hands firmly on the floor, keep both elbows on each side of the navel region. Then raise both legs and the body like a stick in the air. This is called *mayūrāsana*. -29.

20. Kukkuṭāsana

पद्मासनं समासाद्य जानूर्वोरन्तरे करौ ।
कूर्पराभ्यां समासीनो उच्चस्थः कुक्कुटासनम् ॥ ३१॥

padmāsanaṃ samāsādhya jānūrvorantare karau /
kūrparābhyāṃ samāsīno uccasthaḥ kukkuṭāsanam //31//

Sitting in *padmāsana*, insert the hands between the thighs and calves. Place the palms firmly on the floor and raise the body with the support of the elbows. This is called *kukkuṭāsana*. -31.

21. Kūrmāsana

गुल्फौ च वृषणस्याधो व्युत्क्रमेण समाहितौ ।
ऋजुकायशिरोग्रीवं कूर्मासनमितीरितम् ॥ ३२॥

gulphau ca vṛṣaṇasyādho vyutkrameṇa samāhitau /
ṛjukāyaśirogrīvaṃ kūrmāsanamitīritam //32//

Place both heels under the scrotum/testes opposite to one another and keep the body, head and neck straight. This is called *kūrmāsana*. -32.

22. Uttāna Kūrmāsana

कुक्कुटासनबन्धस्थं कराभ्यां धृतकन्धरम् ।
पीठं कूर्मवदुत्तानमेतदुत्तानकूर्मकम् ॥ ३३॥

kukkuṭāsanabandhasthaṃ karābhyāṃ dhṛtakandharam /
pīṭhaṃ kūrmavaduttānametaduttānakurmakam //33//

Perform *kukkuṭāsana*, then hold the shoulders with the hands and straighten the body like a tortoise. This is *uttānakūrmāsana*. -33.

23. Maṇḍukāsana

पादतलौ पृष्ठदेशे अङ्गुष्ठे द्वौ च संस्पृशेत् ।
जानुयुग्मं पुरस्कृत्य साधयेन्मण्डूकासनम् ॥ ३४॥

pṛṣṭhadeśe pādatalāvaṅguṣṭhau dvau ca samspṛśet /
jānuyugmaṃ puraṣkṛtya sādhyenmaṇḍūkāsanam //34//

Bring both feet behind the back and join the big toes keeping the knees apart in front. Thus, *maṇḍūkāsana* is practiced. -34.

24. Uttāna Maṇḍūkāsana

मण्डूकासनमध्यस्थं कूर्पराभ्यां धृतं शिरः ।
एतद्भेकवदुत्तानमेतदुत्तानमण्डूकम् ॥ ३५॥

maṇḍūkāsanamadhyasthaṃ kūrparābhyāṃ dṛtaṃ śiraḥ /
etadbhekavaduttānametaduttānamaṇḍukam //35//

Performing *maṇḍūkāsana*, the head is held on the elbows lifting up the torso like a frog. This is *uttānamaṇḍukāsana*. -35.

25. Vṛkṣāsana

वामोरुमूलदेशे च याम्यं पादं निधाय तु ।
तिष्ठेत्तु वृक्षवद्भूमौ वृक्षासनमिदं विदुः ॥ ३६॥

vāmorumūladeśe ca yamyaṃ pādaṃ nidhāya vai /

tiṣṭhettu vṛkṣavatbhūmau vṛkṣāsanamidaṃ viduḥ//36//

Placing the right foot at the root of the left thigh, stand straight on the ground like a tree. This is called *vṛkṣāsana*. -36.

26. Garuḍāsana

जङ्घोरुभ्यां धरां पीड्य स्थिरकायो द्विजानुना ।
जानूपरि करद्वन्द्वं गरुडासनमुच्यते ॥ ३७॥

jaṅghorubhyāṃ dharāṃ pīḍya sthirakāyo dvijānunā /
jānūpari karadvandvaṃ garuḍāsanamucyate //37//

Pressing the ground firmly with both the thighs and knees, keep the body stable and place both hands on the knees. This is called *garuḍāsana*. -37.

27. Vṛṣāsana

याम्यगुल्फे पायुमूले वामभागे पदेतरम् ।
विपरीतं स्पृशेद्भूमिं वृषासनमिदं भवेत् ॥ ३८॥

yāmyagulphe pādamūle vāmabhāge padetaram /
viparītaṃ spṛśedbhūmim vṛṣāsanamidaṃ bhavet //38//

Placing the anus on the right heel, bring the left heel on the left side of the anus and keep the left foot on the ground facing backwards. This is called the *vṛṣāsana*. -38.

28. Śalabhāsana

अध्यास्य शेते करयुग्मवक्ष
आलम्ब्य भूमिं करयोस्तलाभ्याम् ।
पादौ च शून्ये च वितस्ति चोर्ध्वं
वदन्ति पीठं शलभं मुनीन्द्राः ॥ ३९॥

adhyāsya śete karayugmavakṣa
ālambya bhumiṃ karayostalābhyām /
pādau ca śūnye ca vitasti cordhyaṃ
vadanti pīṭhaṃ śalabhaṃ munīndrāḥ //39//

Lie down facing on the ground. Keep both arms by the sides of the chest placing the palms firmly on the ground and raise both legs in the air. This is called *śalabhāsana* by the great sages. -39.

29. Makarāsana

अध्यास्य शेते हृदयं निधाय

भूमौ च पादौ च प्रसार्यमाणौ ।
शिरश्च धृत्वा करदण्डयुग्मे
देहाग्निकारं मकरासनं तत् ॥ ४०॥

adyāsya śete hṛdayaṃ nidhāya
bhūmau ca pādau prasāryamāṇau /
śiraśca dhṛtvā karadaṇḍayugme
dehāgnikāraṃ makarāsanaṃ tat //40//

Lie down facing on the ground with the chest touching the floor. Spread out the legs and hold the head on the arms. This is *makarāsana* which activates the bodily fire. -40.

30. Uṣṭrāsana

अध्यास्य शेते पदयुग्मव्यस्तं
पृष्ठे निधायापि धृतं कराभ्याम् ।
आकुञ्च्य सम्यग्ध्युदरास्यगाढं
उष्ट्रं च पीठं यतयो वदन्ति ॥ ४१॥

adhyāsya śete padayugmavyastaṃ
pṛṣṭhe nidhāyāpi dhṛtaṃ karābhyām/
ākuñcya samyagdhyudarāsyagāḍhaṃ
uṣṭraṃ ca pīṭhaṃ yatayo vadanti //41//

Lie down facing on the ground. Bending both legs, cross them behind the back. Holding the feet with the hands, contract the mouth and the abdomen forcefully. This is called *uṣṭrāsana* by the ascetics. -41.

31. Bhujaṅgāsana

अङ्गुष्ठनाभिपर्यन्तमधोभूमौ विनिन्यसेत् ।
धरां करतलाभ्यां धृत्वोर्ध्वंशीर्षं फणीव हि ॥ ४२॥
देहाग्निर्वर्धते नित्यं सर्वरोगविनाशनम् ।
जागर्ति भुजङ्गीदेवी भूजङ्गासनसाधनात् ॥ ४३॥

aṅguṣṭhanābhiparyantamadhobhūmau ca vinyaset /
dharāṃ karatalabhyāṃ dhṛtvordhvaśīrṣaṃ phaṇīva hi //42//
dehāgnivarddhate nityaṃ sarvarogavināśanam /
jāgarti bhujaṅgīdevī bhujaṅgāsanasādhanāt //43//

Place the body facing down from the toes to the navel on the floor. Placing the palms of the hands firmly on the floor, raise the head like a snake. This is *bhujaṅgāsana* which increases the fire of the body and destroys all diseases. *Bhujaṅgīdevī* (i.e. the divine serpent power) is awakened by the practice of this asana. -42-43.

32. Yogāsana

उत्तानौ चरणौ कृत्वा संस्थाप्योपरि जानुनोः ।
आसनोपरि संस्थाप्य चोत्तानं करयुग्मकम् ॥ ४४॥
पूरकैर्वायुमाकृष्य नासाग्रमवलोकयेत् ।
योगासनं भवेदेतद्योगिनां योगसाधने ॥ ४५॥

uttānau caraṇau kṛtvā samsthāpyopari jānunoḥ /
āsanopari samsthāpya cottānaṃ karayugmakam //44//
pūrakairvāyumākṛṣya nāsāgramavalokayet /
yogāsanaṃ bhavedetadyogināṃ yogasādhane //45//

Turning the feet upwards, place them on the opposite knees. Keep both hands on the knees with the palm turned upwards. Inhale, hold the air inside and fix the gaze at the tip of the nose. This is *yogāsana* which should be practiced by the yogis. -44-45.

इति श्रीघेरण्डसंहितायां महर्षिघेरण्डनृपचण्डकापालिसंवादे
घटस्थयोगे द्वात्रिंशासनवर्णनं नाम द्वितीयोपदेशः ॥

iti śrīgheraṇḍasamhitāyāṃ gheraṇḍacaṇḍasaṃvāde
āsanaprayogo nāma dvitīyopadeśaḥ /

Thus ends the Second Chapter of *Gheraṇḍa Samhitā*
entitled Āsana Practice.

CHAPTER THREE

Discourse On Mudrā

Types of Mudrās

घेरण्ड उवाच ।
महामुद्रा नभोमुद्रा उड्डीयानं जलन्धरम् ।
मूलबन्धं महाबन्धं महावेधश्च खेचरी ॥ १॥
विपरीतकरी योनिर्वज्रोली शक्तिचालनी ।
ताडागी माण्डुकीमुद्रा शाम्भवी पञ्चधारणा ॥ २॥
अश्विनी पाशिनी काकी मातङ्गी च भुजङ्गिनी ।
पञ्चविंशतिमुद्राश्च सिद्धिदा इह योगिनाम् ॥ ३॥

gheraṇḍa uvāca /
mahāmudrā nabhomudrā uḍḍīyānaṃ jalandharam /
mūlabandho mahābandho mahāvedhaśca khecarī //1//
viparītakarī yonirvajroṇi śakticalanī /
tāḍāgī māṇḍukī mudrā śāmbhavī pañcadhāraṇā //2//
aśvinī pāśinī kākī mātaṅgī ca bhujaṅginī /
pañcavimśatimudrāśca siddhidā iha yogināṃ //3//

Sage *Gheraṇḍa* said: - *Mahā mudrā, nabho mudrā, uḍḍīyāna bandha, jālandhara bandha, mūla bandha, mahā bandha, mahā bedha mudrā, khecarī mudrā, viparīta karani mudrā, yoni mudrā, vajroṇi mudrā, śakti cālinī mudrā, tāḍāgī mudrā, māṇḍukī mudrā, śāmbhavī mudrā, pañcadhāraṇās* (the five concentrations), *aśvinī mudrā, pāśinī mudrā, kākī mudrā, mātaṅginīmudrā* and *bhujaṅginī mudrā* are the twenty-five *mudrās* which give *siddhi* (perfection) to yogis. -1-3.

मुद्राणां पटलं देवि कथितं तव संनिधौ ।

येन विज्ञातमात्रेण सर्वसिद्धिः प्रजायते ॥ ४॥
गोपनीयं प्रयत्नेन न देयं यस्य कस्यचित् ।
प्रीतिदं योगिनां चैव दुर्लभं मरुतामपि ॥ ५॥

mudrāṇām paṭalaṃ devi kathitaṃ tava sannidhau /
yena vijñātamātreṇa sarva siddhiḥ prajāyate //4//
gopanīya prayatnena na deyaṃ yasyakasyacit /
prītidaṃ yoginaṃ caiva durlabhaṃarutāmapi //5//

Mahesvara talking to *Devi* about *mudrās* said: - O *Devi*! I have told you about the chapter dealing with the *mudrās*. Through their knowledge alone leads to all perfection/mastery in yoga. This knowledge of the *mudrās* should be kept secret with due effort. It should not be imparted to everyone. Their knowledge gives bliss to yogis which is not easily available even to the Gods. -4-5.

1. Mahāmudrā

पायुमूलं वामगुल्फे संपीड्य दृढयत्नतः ।
याम्यपादं प्रसार्याथ करोपात्तपदाङ्गुलः ॥ ६॥
कण्ठसङ्कोचनं कृत्वा भ्रुवोर्मध्यं निरीक्षयेत् ।
महामुद्राभिधा मुद्रा कथ्यते चैव सूरभिः ॥ ७॥
क्षयकासं गुदावर्तप्लीहाजीर्णज्वरं तथा ।
नाशयेत्सर्वरोगांश्च महामुद्रा च साधनात् ॥ ८॥

pāyumūlaṃ vāmagulphe sampīḍya dṛḍhayatnataḥ /
yāmyapādaṃ prasāryātha karopāttapadāṅgulaḥ //6//
kaṇṭhaṃ saṅkocanaṃ kṛtvā bhruvormadhyaṃ nirīkṣayet /
mahāmudrābhidhā mudrā kathyate caiva sūrabhiḥ //7//
kṣayakāsaṃ gudāvartaplīhājīrṇajvaraṃ tathā /
nāsayetsarvarogāmśca mahāmudrā ca sādhanāt //8//

Pressing the anus area with the left heel carefully, stretch the right leg in front and take hold of the toes with both hands. After contracting the throat, focus the gaze in the middle of the eyebrow center. This is called *mahā mudrā* by the wise. The practice of *mahā mudrā* cures tuberculosis, disorders of phlegm, constipation, enlarged spleen and fever. Through the practice/mastery of *mahā mudrā* all diseases are cured. -6-8.

2. Nabho Mudrā

यत्र यत्र स्थितो योगी सर्वकार्येषु सर्वदा ।
ऊर्ध्वजिह्वः स्थिरो भूत्वा धारयेत्पवनं सदा ।
नभोमुद्रा भवेदेषा योगिनां रोगनाशिनी ॥ ९॥

yatra yatra sthito yogī sarvakāryeṣu sarvadā /
urdhvajihvaḥ sthiro bhūtvā dhārayetpavanaṃ sadā /
nabhomudrā bhavedeṣā yogināṃ roganāśinī //9//

Wherever a yogi is and whatever activity he is engaged in, he should steadily turn the tongue upwards and always retain the breath. This is *nabho mudrā* which destroys all the diseases of the yogi. -9.

3. Uḍḍiyāna Bandha

उदरे पश्चिमं तानं नाभेरूर्ध्वं तु कारयेत् ।
उड्डीनं कुरुते यस्मादविश्रान्तं महाखगः ।
उड्डीयानं त्वसौ बन्धो मृत्युमातङ्गकेसरी ॥ १०॥
समग्राद्बन्धनाद्ध्येतदुड्डीयानं विशिष्यते ।
उड्डीयाने समभ्यस्ते मुक्तिः स्वाभाविकी भवेत् ॥ ११॥

udare paścimaṃ tānaṃ nābhirūrdhvaṃ tu kārayet /
uḍḍīnaṃ kurute yasmādaviśrāntaṃ mahākhagaḥ /
uḍḍīyānaṃ tvasau bandho mṛtumūlaṅgakesarī //10//
samagrād bandhanāddhyetaduḍḍīyānaṃ viśiṣyate /
uḍḍīyāne samabhyste muktiḥ svābhāvikī bhavet //11//

Contract the abdomen equally above the navel towards the back. Consequently, the great dynamic bird (*prāna*) flies upward. This is called *uḍḍīyāna bandha*. It is a victorious lion over the elephant of death. Of all the *bandhas, Uḍḍīyāna bandha* is the chief one. Liberation is accomplished naturally through its proper practice. -10-11.

4. Jālandhara Bandha

कण्ठसङ्कोचनं कृत्वा चिबुकं हृदये न्यसेत् ।
जालन्धरे कृते बन्धे षोडशाधारबन्धनम् ।
जालन्धरमहामुद्रा मृत्योश्च क्षयकारिणी ॥ १२॥

सिद्धो जालन्धरो बन्धो योगिनां सिद्धिदायकः ।
षण्मासमभ्यसेद्यो हि स सिद्धो नाऽत्र संशयः ॥ १३॥

kaṇṭhasaṅkocanaṃ kṛtvā cibukaṃ hṛdaye nyaset /
jālandharekṛte bandhe ṣoḍaśādhārabandhanam //12//
jālandharamahāmudrā mṛtyośca kṣayakāriṇī /
siddho jālandharo bandho yogināṃ siddhidāyakaḥ /
ṣaṇmāsamabhyasedyo hi sa siddho nātra samśayaḥ //13//

While contracting the throat, place the chin on the chest. This is the practice of *jālandhara bandha*. The sixteen *ādhāras* (bases or supports) are controlled by this practice. This great *mudrā* named *jālandhara bandha* destroys death. Mastery over *jālandhara bandha* bestows *siddhis* to yogis. A yogi certainly becomes a *siddha* (perfected one) by just practicing it for six months. There is no doubt about it. -12-13.

5. Mūlabandha

पार्ष्णिना वामपादस्य योनिमाकुञ्चयेत्ततः ।
नाभिग्रन्थिं मेरुदण्डे सुधीः संपीड्य यत्नतः ॥ १४॥
मेढ्रं दक्षिणगुल्फेन दृढबन्धं समाचरेत् ।
नाभेरूर्ध्वमधश्चापि तानं कुर्यात्प्रयत्नतः ।
जराविनाशिनी मुद्रा मूलबन्धो निगद्यते ॥ १५॥
संसारसागरं तर्तुमभिलषति यः पुमान् ।
सुगुप्तो विरलो भूत्वा मुद्रामेतां समभ्यसेत् ॥ १६॥
अभ्यासाद्बन्धनस्यास्य मरुत्सिद्धिर्भवेद्ध्रुवम् ।
साधयेद्यत्नतस्तर्हि मौनी तु विजिताऽलसः ॥ १७॥

pārṣṇinā vāmapādasya yonimākuñcayettataḥ /
nābhigranthiṃ merudaṇḍe sudhiḥ sampīḍya yatnataḥ //14//
meḍhram dakṣiṇagulphena dṛḍhabandhaṃ samācaret /
jarāvināśinī mudrā mūlabandho nigadhyate //15//
samsārasāgaraṃ tartumabhilaṣati yaḥ pumān /
sugupto viralo bhūtvā mudrāmetāṃ samabhyaset //16//
abhyāsādbandhanasyāsya marutsiddhirbhaveddhruvam /
sādhayedyatnatastarhi mauni tu vijitālasaḥ //17//

Pressing the genital area between the anus and testes with

the left heel, contract the anus. Press the navel knot close to the spinal column with due effort and firmly press the genital organ with the right heel. This is called *mūla bandha* which destroys old age. The wise yogis who wish to cross the ocean of the world should practice this *mudrā* in a secret and solitary place. *Maruta siddhi* (perfection of *prāna* or *vāyu*) is certainly attained through this practice. Therefore, one should practice it with due effort in silence without laziness. -14-17.

6. Mahābandha

वामपादस्य गुल्फेन पायुमूलं निरोधयेत् ।
दक्षपादेन तद्गुल्फं संपीड्य यत्नतः सुधीः ॥ १८॥
शनैः शनैश्चालयेत्पार्ष्णिं योनिमाकुञ्चयेच्छनैः ।
जालन्धरे धरेत्प्राणं महाबन्धो निगद्यते ॥ १९॥
महाबन्धः परो बन्धो जरामरण नाशनः ।
प्रसादादस्य बन्धस्य साधयेत्सर्ववाञ्छितम् ॥ २०॥

vāmapādasya gulphena pāyumūlaṃ nirodhayet /
dakṣapādena tadgulphaṃ sampīḍya yatnataḥ sudhīḥ //18//
śanakaiścālayetpārṣṇi yonimākuñcayecchanaiḥ /
jālandhare dharetprāṇaṃ mahābandho nigadyate //19//
mahābandhaḥ paro bandho jarāmaraṇa nāśanaḥ /
prasādādasya bandhasya sādhayetsarvavāñchitam //20//

Closing the anus with the left heel, press the left heel with the right foot with due effort. Slowly contract and expand the perineum and retain the breath by applying *jālandhara bandha.* This is called *mahā bandha.* It is the supreme *bandha* (of all the *bandhas*) and is the destroyer of old age and death. All desires objects are accomplished through the grace of this *bandha.* -18-20.

7. Mahāvedha Mudrā

रूपयौवनलावण्यं नारीणां पुरुषं विना ।
मूलबन्धमहाबन्धौ महावेधं विना तथा ॥ २१॥
महाबन्धं समासाद्य कुम्भकं परेत्पुड्डीन।
महावेधः समाख्यातो योगिनां सिद्धिदायकः ॥ २२॥
महाबन्धमूलबन्धौ महावेधसमन्वितौ ।
प्रत्यहं कुरुते यस्तु स योगी योगवित्तमः ॥ २३॥

न मृत्युतो भयं तस्य न जरा तस्य विद्यते ।
गोपनीयः प्रयत्नेन वेधोऽयं योगिपुङ्गवैः ॥ २४॥

rūpayauvanalāvaṇyaṃ nārīṇām puruṣam vinā /
mūlabandhamahābandhau mahāvedhaṃ vinā tathā //21//
mahābandhaṃ samāsādya kumbhakaṃ careduḍḍīna /
mahāvedaḥ samākhyāto yogināṃ siddhidāyakaḥ //22//
mahābandhamūlabandhau mahāvedasamanvitau /
pratyahaṃ kurute yastu say yogī yogavittamaḥ //23//
na mṛtyuto bhayaṃ tasya na jarā tasya vidyate /
gopanīyaḥ prayatnena vedho'yaṃ yogipuṅgavaiḥ //24//

As the beauty, youth and charisma of a woman are worthless without a man, similarly are the *mūla bandha* and *mahā bandha* without *mahā veda*. First perform *mahā bandha* and then while doing *uḍḍīyāna bandha* retain the breath by *kumbhaka*. This is called *mahā veda*, the giver of *siddhis* to all yogis. The yogi who practice *mahā bandha* and *mūla bandha* daily along with *mahā veda*, becomes the best of all yogis. There is no fear of old age and death for him. The wise yogi should carefully keep this *vedha* secret. -21-24.

8. Khecarī Mudrā

जिह्वाधो नाडीं सञ्छित्य रसनां चालयेत्सदा ।
दोहयेन्नवनीतेन लौहयन्त्रेण कर्षयेत् ॥ २५॥
एवं नित्यं समभ्यासाल्लम्बिका दीर्घतां व्रजेत् ।
यावद्गच्छेद्भ्रुवोर्मध्ये तदा सिध्यति खेचरी ॥ २६॥
रसनां तालुमूले तु शनैः शनैः प्रवेशयेत् ।
कपालकुहरे जिह्वा प्रविष्टा विपरीतगा ।
भ्रुवोर्मध्ये गता दृष्टिर्मुद्रा भवति खेचरी ॥ २७॥

jihvādho nāḍīṃ sañchitya rasanāṃ cālayetsadā /
dohayennavanītena lauhayantreṇa karṣayet //25//
evaṃ nityaṃ samabhyāsāllambika dīrghatāṃ vrajet /
yāvadgacchedbhruvormadhye tadā sidhyati khecari //26//
rasanāṃ tālumūle tu śanaiḥ śanaiḥ praveśayet /
kapālakuhare jihvā praviṣṭā viparītagā /

bhruvormadhye gatā dṛṣtirmudrā bhavati khecari //27//

Cutting the tendon (frenulum) at the base of the tongue, move the tongue constantly. Rub it with fresh butter and milk it out slowly with a pair of iron forceps. In this way, the tongue is elongated through proper regular practice. When the tongue reaches the eyebrow center, then *khecari mudrā* is accomplished. Thus, insert the tongue into the base of the palate slowly and gently. Turning the tongue upwards and backwards, take and enter the tongue into the holes of the nasal passage. Keep the gaze fixed at the eyebrow center. This becomes *khecari mudrā*. -25-27.

न च मूर्च्छा क्षुधा तृष्णा नैवालस्यं प्रजायते ।
न च रोगो जरा मृत्युर्देवदेहः स जायते ॥ २८॥
नाग्निना दह्यते गात्रं न शोषयति मारुतः ।
न देहं क्लेदयन्त्यापो दशेन्न भुजङ्गमः ॥ २९॥
लावण्यं च भवेद्गात्रे समाधिर्जायते ध्रुवम् ।
कपालवक्त्रसंयोगे रसना रसमाप्नुयात् ॥ ३०॥

na ca mūcchā kṣudhā tṛṣṇā naivālasyaṃ prajāyate /
na ca rogo jarā mṛtyurdevadehaḥ sa jāyate //28//
nāgninā dahyate gātraṃ na śoṣayati mārutaḥ /
na dehaṃ cledayantyāpo daśenna bhujaṅgamaḥ //29//
lāvaṇyaṃ ca bhavedgātre samādhirjāyate dhruvaṃ /
kapālavaktrasamyoge rasanā rasamāpnuyāt //30//

Through the practice of *khecari mudrā* neither there is faint nor hunger, nor thirst, nor laziness. Neither there is disease, nor old age, nor death. The body becomes divine. The physical body is neither burnt by fire, nor dried up by air, nor it is made wet by water, nor it is affected by the poison of snake bite. The body becomes beautiful. *Samādhi* is certainly accomplished. Various juices are obtained through the union of the tongue between the forehead and mouth. -28-30.

नानारससमुद्भूतमानन्दं च दिने दिने ।
आदौ च लवणं क्षारं च ततस्तिक्तकषायकम् ॥ ३१॥
नवनीतं घृतं क्षीरं दधितक्रमधूनि च ।

द्राक्षारसं च पीयूषं जायते रसनोदकम् ॥ ३२॥

nānārasasamudbhūtamānandaṃ ca dine dine /
ādau ca lavaṇaṃ kṣāraṃ ca tatastiktakaṣāyakam //31//
nanītaṃ gṛtaṃ kṣīraṃ dadhitakramadhūni ca /
drākṣārasaṃ ca pīyūsaṃ jāyate rasanodakam //32//

Various types of juices are produced every day and a blissful state is experienced. At first salty and alkaline, then bitter and astringent tastes are felt and then taste of butter, ghee, milk, yogurt, buttermilk, honey, grape juice are felt and finally, the taste of nectar arises. -31-32.

9. Viparīrakaraṇī Mudarā

नाभिमूले वसेत्सूर्यस्तालुमूले च चन्द्रमाः ।
अमृतं ग्रसते सूर्यस्ततो मृत्युवशो नरः ॥ ३३॥
ऊर्ध्वं च योजयेत्सूर्यं चन्द्रं चाप्यध आनयेत् ।
विपरीतकरी मुद्रा सर्वतन्त्रेषु गोपिता ॥ ३४॥
भूमौ शिरश्च संस्थाप्य करयुग्मं समाहितः ।
ऊर्ध्वपादः स्थिरो भूत्वा विपरीतकरी मता ॥ ३५॥
मुद्रां च साधयेन्नित्यं जरा मृत्युं च नाशयेत् ।
स सिद्धः सर्वलोकेषु प्रलयेऽपि न सीदति ॥ ३६॥

nābhimūle vasetsūryastālumūle ca candramāḥ /
amṛtaṃ grasate sūryastato mṛtyuvaśo naraḥ //33//
urdhvaṃ ca yojayetsūryaṃ candraṃ cāpyadha ānayet /
viparītakaraṇī mudrā sarvatantreṣu gopitā //34//
bhūmau śiraśca samsthāpya karayugmaṃ samāhitaḥ /
urdhvapādaḥ sthiro bhūtvā viparītakarī matā // 35//
mudrā ca sādhayennityaṃ jarā mṛtu ca nāśayet /
sa siddhaḥ sarvalokeṣu pralaye'pi na sīdati //36//

The sun (i.e. the solar plexus) is situated at the root of the navel and the moon is situated at the root of the palate. A man is subject to death because the sun devours the nectar. Hence, the sun should be brought upward and the moon downward. This is *viparītakaraṇī mudrā* which is kept secret in all the *tantras*. Placing the head on the ground, support with both hands spreading out. Raise both legs and remain stable. This is *viparītakaraṇī mudrā*. By daily practice of this *mudrā* one destroys old age and death. He becomes an adept in all the worlds and does not suffer even at the time of dissolution. -33-36.

10. Yoni Mudrā

सिद्धासनं समासाद्य कर्णचक्षुर्नसामुखम् ।
अङ्गुष्ठतर्जनी मध्यानामादिभिश्च धारयेत् ॥ ३७॥
काकीभिः प्राणं सङ्कृष्य अपाने योजयेत्ततः ।
षट्चक्राणि क्रमाद्ध्यात्वा हुं हंसमनुना सुधीः ॥ ३८॥
चैतन्यमानयेद्देवीं निद्रिता या भुजङ्गिनी ।
जीवेन सहितां शक्तिं समुत्थाप्य पराम्बुजे ॥ ३९॥
शक्तिमयः स्वयं भूत्वा परं शिवेन सङ्गमम् ।
नानासुखं विहारं च चिन्तयेत्परमं सुखम् ॥ ४०।
शिवशक्तिसमायोगादेकान्तं भुवि भावयेत् ।
आनन्दमानसो स्वयं भूत्वा अहं ब्रह्मेति सम्भवेत् ॥ ४१॥
योनिमुद्रा परा गोप्या देवानामपि दुर्लभा ।
सकृत्तु लाभसंसिद्धिः समाधिस्थः स एव हि ॥ ४२॥

siddhāsanaṃ samāsādya karṇacakṣurnasāmukham/
aṅguṣṭha madhyanāmādibhśca dhārayet // 37//
kākībhiḥ prāṇasamkṛṣya apāne yojayettataḥ /
ṣaṭcakrāṇi kramātdhyātvā hum haṃsamanunā sudhiḥ //38//
caitanyamānayeddevīṃ nidritā yā bhujaṅginī /
jīvena sahitāṃ śaktiṃ samutthāpya parāmbuje //39//
śaktimayaḥ svayaṃ bhutvā paraṃ śivena saṅgamam /
nānasukhaṃ vihāraṃ ca cintayetparamam sukham //40//
śivaśaktisamāyogādekāntaṃ bhuvibhāvayet /
ānandamānaso svayaṃ bhūtvā ahaṃ brahmeti sambhavet //41//
yonimudrā parā gopyā devānāmapi durlabhā /
sakṛttu lābhasaṃsiddhiḥ samādhisthaḥ sa eva hi //42//

Sitting in *siddhāsana*, close the ears with both thumbs, the eyes with the index fingers, both nostrils with the middle fingers and mouth with the ring fingers and the little fingers. Pull the *prāṇa* through *kākīmudrā* and join it with the *apāna*. Meditating on the six *cakras* according to their order, awaken the sleeping *kuṇḍalinī śakti* through the practice of the *mantras* '*hūm*' and '*haṃsa*'. Raise the *Śakti* along with the individual soul and bring it to *sahasrāra* (the thousand petalled lotus). Being one full of *Śakti* and united with supreme *Śiva* feel that "I am roaming with *Śiva* with all the happiness and I am augmented by *Śakti* and enjoying a blissful state". Contemplate absolutely on the union of *Śiva* and *Śakti* in this world. Being oneself blissful through their union, realize oneself that "I am also *Brahman*". This *yoni mudrā* is highly secret. It is rare even for the Gods. He who accomplishes perfection in it through regular practice, naturally attains the state of *samādhi*. -37-42.

ब्रह्महा भ्रूणहा चैव सुरापी गुरुतल्पगः ।
एतैः पापैर्न लिप्यते योनिमुद्रानिबन्धनात् ॥ ४३॥
यानि पापानि घोराणि उपपापानि यानि च ।
तानि सर्वाणि नश्यन्ति योनिमुद्रानिबन्धनात् ।
तस्मादभ्यासनं कुर्याद्यादि मुक्तिं समिच्छति ॥ ४४॥

brahmahā bhrūṇahā caiva surāpi gurutalpagaḥ /
etaiḥ pāpairna lipyate yonimudrā nibandhanāt //43//
yāni pāpāni ghoraṇi upapāpāni yāni ca /
tāni sarvāṇi nasyanti yonimudrā nibandhanāt /
tasmādabhyāsanaṃ kuryādyādi muktiṃ samicchati //44//

By the practice this *mudrā* one gets rid of sins like killing a *brāhmaṇa* or a fetus, drinking alcohol or violating the bed of the teacher. All types of great sins and small sins are eradicated by the practice of *yoni mudrā*. Therefore, one should practice it if he sincerely wishes for liberation. -43-44.

11. Vajroṇi Mudrā

धरामवष्टभ्य करयोस्तलाभ्याम्
उर्ध्वे क्षिपेत्पादयुगं शिरः खे ।
शक्तिप्रबोधाय चिरजीवनाय
वज्रोणिमुद्रा मुनयो वदन्ति ॥ ४५॥
अयं योगे योग श्रेष्ठो योगिनां मुक्तिकारणम् ।

अयं हितप्रदो योगो योगिनां सिद्धिदायकः ॥ ४६॥
एतद्योगप्रसादेन बिन्दुसिद्धिर्भवेद्ध्रुवम् ।
सिद्धे बिन्दौ महायत्ने किं न सिध्यति भूतले ॥ ४७॥
भोगेन महता युक्तो यदि मुद्रां समाचरेत् ।
तथापि सकला सिद्धिर्भवति तस्य निश्चितम् ॥ ४८॥

dharāmavaṣṭabhya karayostalābhyāṃ
urdve kṣipetpādayugaṃ śiraḥ khe /
śaktiprabodhāya cirajīvanāya
vajroṇimudrā munayoḥ vadanti //45//
ayaṃ yoge yoga śreṣṭho yogināṃ muktikāraṇam /
ayaṃ hitaprado yogo yogināṃ siddhidāyakaḥ //46//
etadyogaprasādena bindusiddhirbhaveddhruvam /
siddhe vindu mahāyatne kiṃ na sidhyati bhūtale //47//
bhogena mahatā yukto yadi mudrāṃ samācaret /
tathāpi sakalā siddhirbhavati tasya niścitam //48//

Placing both palms firmly on the ground, raise both legs and the head in the air. The *munis* (seers) have called it *vajroṇi mudrā* which awakens the *Śakti* and provides long life. Due to the grace of this yogic *mudrā*, *bindu siddhi* (perfection in the retention of seminal fluid) is certainly accomplished. When *bindu siddhi* is attained with the highest effort, what cannot be achieved in this world? Even though engaged in great enjoyments, one can certainly attain all the *siddhis* through the perfection of this *mudrā.* -45-48.

12. Śakticālinī Mudrā

मूलाधारे आत्मशक्तिः कुण्डली पर देवता ।
शयिता भुजगाकारा सार्ध त्रिवलयान्विता ॥ ४९॥
यावत्सा निद्रिता देहे तावज्जीवः पशुर्यथा ।
ज्ञानं न जायते तावत्कोटियोगं समभ्यसेत् ॥ ५०॥

mūlādhāre ātmaśaktiḥ kuṇḍalī para devatā /
śayitā bhujagākārā sārdha trivalayānvitā //49//
yāvatsā nidritā dehe tāvajjīvaḥ paśuryathā /
jñānaṃ na jāyate tāvat koṭiyogaṃ samabhyaset //50//

The supreme goddess *kuṇḍalinī*, the power of the Self, sleeps in *mūlādhāra* in the form of a serpent coiled in three and a half rounds. As long as she is asleep, *jīva* (a living being) remains in ignorance like an animal. Until then the knowledge does not arise even though one may practice ten million types of yoga. -49-50.

उद्घाटयेत्कवाटं च यथा कुञ्चिकया हठात् ।
कुण्डलिन्याः प्रबोधेन ब्रह्मद्वारं प्रभेदयेत् ॥ ५१॥
नाभिं संवेष्ट्य वस्त्रेण न च नग्नो बहिः स्थितः ।
गोपनीयगृहे स्थित्वा शक्तिचालनमभ्यसेत् ॥ ५२॥

udghāṭayeṭavāṭaṃ ca yathā kuñcikayā haṭhāt /
kuṇḍalinyāḥ prabodhena brahmadvāraṃ prabhedayet //51//
nābhiṃ samveṣṭya vastreṇa na ca nagno bahiḥ sthitaḥ /
gopanīyagṛhe sthitvā śakticālanamabhyset //52//

Just like a door is opened after opening the lock with a key, in the same way *brahmadvāra* (the door to *Brahma*) is opened forcibly when *kuṇḍalinī* is awakened. *Śakticālana* should be practiced in a solitary shelter/home covering the navel with a piece of cloth wrapped around (the waist/loins). It should not be practiced being naked in an open area (staying outside). -51-52.

वितस्तिप्रमितं दीर्घं विस्तारे चतुरङ्गुलम् ।
मृदुलं धवलं सूक्ष्मं वेष्टनाम्बरलक्षणम् ।
एवमम्बरयुक्तं च कटिसूत्रेण योजयेत् ॥ ५३॥
भस्मना गात्रं संलिप्य सिद्धासनं समाचरेत् ।
नासाभ्यां प्राणमाकृष्य अपाने योजयेद्बलात् ॥ ५४॥
तावदाकुञ्चयेद्गुह्यं शनैरश्विनिमुद्रया ।
यावद्गच्छेत्सुषुम्णायां वायुः प्रकाशयेद्धठात् ॥ ५५॥
तदा वायुप्रबन्धेन कुम्भिका च भुजङ्गिनी ।
बद्धश्वासस्ततो भूत्वा ऊर्ध्वमार्गं प्रपद्यते॥ ५६॥

vitastipramitaṃ dīrghaṃ vistāre caturaṅgulam /
mṛdulaṃ dhavalaṃ sūkṣmaṃ veṣṭanāmbaralakṣaṇam /
evamambarayuktaṃ ca katisūtreṇa yojayet //53//
bhasmanā gātraṃ samlipya siddhāsanaṃ samācaret /

nāsābhyāṃ prāṇamākṛṣya apāne yojayetbalāt //54//
tāvadākuñcayedguhyaṃ śanairaśvinimudrayā /
yāvadgacchetsuṣumṇāyāṃ vāyuḥ prakāśayeddhaṭhāt //55//
tadā vāyuprabandhena kumbhikā ca bhujaṅginī /
baddhaśvāsastato bhūtvā ūrdvāmārgaṃ prapadhyate //56//

The wrapping cloth should be soft, white and fine measuring about 10 centimeters wide and 23 centimeters long. Fasten this cloth around the navel with a *katisūtra* (a cotton thread/rope which is worn around the loins). Smearing the ashes on the whole body, sit in *siddhāsana*. Drawing the *prāṇa* inside, join it by force with the *apāna*. Contract the anus slowly by practicing *aśvini mudrā* until the *prāṇa* passes through the *suṣumṇā* and manifests forcibly there. Thus, with the *prāṇa* held by *kumbhaka,* the *kuṇḍalinī* in the form of serpent being suffocated awakens and then follows the upward passage. – 53-56.

विना शक्तिचालनेन योनिमुद्रा न सिध्यति ।
आदौ चालनमभ्यस्य योनिमुद्रां समभ्यसेत् ॥ ५७॥
इति ते कथितं चण्डकापाले शक्तिचालनम् ।
गोपनीयं प्रयत्नेन दिने दिने समभ्यसेत् ॥ ५८॥

vinā śakticālena yonimudrā na sidhyati /
ādau cālanamabhasya yonimudrāṃ samabhyaset //57//
iti te kathitaṃ caṇḍakāpale śakticālanam /
gopanīya prayatnena dine dine samabhyaset //58//

Without the practice of *śakticālana mudrā*, *yoni mudrā* cannot be accomplished. First one should practice *śakticālana* properly and then duly practice *yoni mudrā*. O *Caṇḍakapāli!* Thus, I have told you about *śakticālana mudrā*. Keeping it secret with care, practice it daily. -57-58.

मुद्रेयं परमा गोप्या जरामरणनाशिनी ।
तस्मादभ्यसनं कार्यं योगिभिः सिद्धिकाङ्क्षिभिः ॥ ५९॥
नित्यं योऽभ्यसते योगी सिद्धिस्तस्य करे स्थिता ।
तस्य विग्रहसिद्धिः स्याद्रोगाणां सङ्क्षयो भवेत् ॥ ६०॥

mudreyam paramā gopyā jaramaraṇanaśinī /

tasmādabhyasanaṃ kāryaṃ yogibhiḥ siddhikāṅkṣibhiḥ //59//
nityaṃ yo'bhyasate yogī siddhistasya kare sthitā /
tasya vigrahasiddhiḥ syādrogāṇāṃ saṅkṣayo bhavet //60//

This *mudrā* is highly secret. It destroys old age and death. Therefore, the yogis and those who are desirous of *siddhis* (perfections) should do its practice. The yogi who practices it daily, the *siddhis* dwell in his hand. He attains *vigraha siddhi* (perfection of the body) and all his diseases are eliminated entirely. -59-60.

13. Taḍāgi Mudrā

उदरं पश्चिमोत्तानं कृत्वा च तडागाकृति ।
ताडागी सा परामुद्रा जरा मृत्यु विनाशिनी ॥ ६१॥

udaraṃ paścimottānaṃ kṛtvā ca taḍāgākṛtiḥ /
tāḍāgi sā parāmudrā jarā mṛtyu vināśinī //61//

Sitting in *paścimottānāsana*, enlarge the abdomen fully like a shape of a pond. This is *tāḍāgi,* a great *mudrā* which destroys old age and death. -61.

14. Māṇḍukī Mudrā

मुखं समुद्रितं कृत्वा जिह्वामूलं प्रचालयेत् ।
शनैर्ग्रसेदमृतं तां माण्डुकीं मुद्रिकां विदुः ॥ ६२॥
वलितं पलितं नैव जायते नित्ययौवनम् ।
न केशे जायते पाको यः कुर्यान्नित्यमाण्डुकीम् ॥ ६३॥

mukhaṃ saṃudritaṃ kṛtvā jihvāmūlaṃ pracālayet /
śanairgrasedamṛtaṃ tāṃ māṇḍukīṃ mudrikāṃ viduḥ //62//
valitaṃ palitaṃ naiva jāyate nityayauvanam /
na keśe jāyate pāko yaḥ kuryānnityamāṇḍukīm //63//

Keeping the mouth closed, rotate the tongue inside the palate and taste the nectar slowly by the tongue. This is called *māṇḍukīmudrā*. By the practice of this *mudrā* regularly wrinkles and grey hairs never appear in the body. Long-lasting youth is attained. -62-63.

15. Śāmbhavī Mudrā

नेत्राञ्जनं समालोक्य आत्मारामं निरीक्षयेत् ।

सा भवेच्छाम्भवी मुद्रा सर्वतन्त्रेषु गोपिता ॥ ६४॥
अथ शाम्भवीमुद्रायाः फलकथनम् ।
वेदशास्त्रपुराणानि सामान्यगणिका इव ।
इयं तु शाम्भवीमुद्रा गुप्ता कुलवधूरिव ॥ ६५॥
स एव आदिनाथश्च स च नारायणः स्वयम् ।
स च ब्रह्मा सृष्टिकारी यो मुद्रां वेत्ति शाम्भवीम् ॥ ६६॥

netrāñjanaṃ samālokya ātmārāmaṃ nirīkṣayet /
sā bhavetcchāmbhavī mudrā sarvatantreṣu gopitā //64//
vedaśāstrapurāṇāni sāmānyagaṇikā iva /
iyaṃ tu śāmbhavīmudrā guptā kulavadhūriva //65//
sa eva ādināthaśca sa ca nārāyaṇaḥ svayam /
sa ca brahmā sṛṣṭikarī yo mudrāṃ vetti śāmbhavīm //66//

Fix the gaze steadily between the eyebrows, observe the Self within. This is *śāmbhavī mudrā* which is kept secret in all the *tantras*. The *Vedas, Śāstras* and *Purāṇas* are like ordinary women, but *śāmbhavī mudrā* is like a lady of a noble family. One who knows *śāmbhavī mudrā* is himself *Ādinātha*, *Nārāyaṇa* and *Brahmā*, the creator of the world. -64-66.

सत्यं सत्यं पुनः सत्यं सत्यमुक्तं महेश्वरः ।
शाम्भवीं यो विजानीयात्स च ब्रह्म न चान्यथा ॥ ६७॥

satyaṃ satyaṃ punaḥ satyaṃ satyamuktaṃ maheśvaraḥ /
śāmbhavīm yo vijānīyātsa ca brahma na cānyathā //67//

Maheśvara says: - "It is true, it is true and it is verily true again that he who knows *śāmbhavī mudrā* is certainly *Brahma*. There is no doubt about it." -67.

Pañcadhāraṇā

कथिता शाम्भवी मुद्रा श्रृणुष्व पञ्चधारणाम् ।
धारणानि समासाद्य किं न सिध्यति भूतले ॥ ६८॥
अनेन नरदेहेन स्वर्गेषु गमनागमम् ।
मनोगतिर्भवेत्तस्य खेचरत्वं न चान्यथा ॥ ६९॥

kathitā śāmbhavimudrā śruṇuṣva pañcadhāraṇām /
dhāraṇāni samāsādya kiṃ na sidhyati bhūtale //68//
anena naradehena svargeṣu gamanāgamam /

manogatirbhavettasya khecaratvaṃ na cānyathā //69//

Śāmbhavī mudrā has been explained above. Now listen to *pañca dhāraṇā* (the five concentrations which are *pārthivī, āmbhasī, āgneyī, vāyavīya* and *ākāśī*). After having mastery over them, what cannot be accomplished in this universe? With this human body one can travel to heaven and come back to earth. By these *dhāraṇās* one acquires *manogati* (the power to go anywhere at one's will with the speed of mind) and *khecaratva* (the ability to travel in space). -68-69.

16. Pārthivī Dhāraṇā

यत्तत्वं हरितालदेशरचितं भौमं लकाराऽन्वितं
वेदास्त्रं कमलासनेन सहितं कृत्वा हृदिस्थायिनम् ।
प्राणस्तत्र विलीय पञ्चघटिकाश्चित्तान्वितां धारयेत्
एषा स्तम्भकरी सदा क्षितिजयं कुर्यादधोधारणा ॥ ७०॥
पार्थिवीधारणामुद्रां यः करोति तु नित्यशः ।
मृत्युञ्जयः स्वयं सोऽपि स सिद्धो विचरेद्भुवि ॥ ७१॥

yattvaṃ haritāladeśaracitaṃ bhaumaṃ lakārānvitaṃ
vedāstraṃ kamalāsanenasahitaṃ kṛtvā hṛdisthāpitam /
prāṇastatra vilīya pañcaghaṭikāścittānvitāṃ dhārayet
eṣā stambhakarī sadā kṣitijayaṃ kuryādadhodhāraṇā //70//
pārthivīdhāraṇāmudrāṃ yaḥ karoti tu nityaśaḥ /
mṛtuñjayaḥ svayaṃ so'pi sa siddho vicaredbhuvi //71//

The earth element has yellow color, the *bīja mantra* relating to it is '*lam*', it has a square shape and its god in lotus pose is *Brahmā*. Establish this *tattva* in the heart, dissolve the *prāṇa* thereby *kumbhaka* and focus the mind on it for five *ghaṭikās* (two hours). This is called *adhodhāraṇā*. By perfecting this practice one always acquires steadiness and conquers the earth. One who practises *prithvidhāraṇā* daily conquers death himself. He becomes a *siddha* (perfected one) and roams on this earth. -70-71.

17. Āmbhasī Dhāraṇā

शङ्खेन्दुप्रतिमं च कुन्दधवलं तत्त्वं किलालं शुभं
तत्पीयूषवकारबीजसहितं युक्तं सदा विष्णुना ।

प्राणं तत्र विलीय पञ्चघटिकाश्चित्तान्वितां धारयेत्
एषा दुःसहतापपापहरिणी स्यादाम्भसी धारणा ॥ ७२॥

śaṅkhendupratimaṃ ca kundadhavalaṃ
tattvaṃ kilālaṃ śubham /
tatpīyūṣavakārbījasahitaṃ yuktaṃ sadā viṣṇunā /
prāṇaṃ tatra vilīya pañcaghatikāścitānvitāṃ dhārayet /
eṣā duḥsahatāpapāpahariṇī syādāmbhasī dharaṇā //72//

The water element has white color which is like the color of a jasmine flower or a conch or the moon. It has a circular shape and the *bīja mantra* of this ambrosial element is '*vam*'. It is always associated with Lord *Viṣṇu*. Focus on this element in the heart and dissolve the *prāṇa* there through *kumbhaka* practice for five *ghaṭikās* (two hours). This is *āmbhasī dhāraṇā* which destroys pains, sufferings and sins all together. -72.

आम्भसीं परमां मुद्रां यो जानाति स योगवित् ।
जले च गंभीरे घोरे मरणं तस्य नो भवेत् ॥ ७३॥
इयं तु परमा मुद्रा गोपनीया प्रयत्नतः ।
प्रकाशात्सिद्धिहानिः स्यात्सत्यं वच्मि च तत्त्वतः ॥ ७४॥

āmbhāsīṃ paramāṃ mudrāṃ yo jānāti sa yogavit /
jale ca ghore gambhīre maraṇaṃ tasya no bhavet //73//
iyaṃ tu paramā mudrā gopanīyā prayatnataḥ /
prakāśātsiddhihāniḥ syātsatyaṃ vacmi ca tattvataḥ //74//

Āmbhasī is a supreme *mudrā*. One who knows it is the knower of yoga. A person never dies even in very deep water through the practice of this *mudrā*. Keep this supreme *mudrā* carefully secret. The *siddhi* is destroyed by disclosing it. Surely, I have told you the truth. -73-74.

18. Āgneyī Dhāraṇā

यन्नाभिस्थितमिन्द्रगोपसदृशं बीजं त्रिकोणान्वितं
तत्त्वं वह्निमयं प्रदीप्तमरुणं रुद्रेण यत्सिद्धिदम् ।
प्राणं तत्र विलीय पञ्चघटिकाश्चित्तान्वितं धारयेत्
एषा कालगभीरभीतिहरणी वैश्वानरी धारणा ॥ ७५॥

yannābhisthitamindragopasadṛśaṃ bījaṃ trikoṇānvitaṃ,

tattvaṃ vahnimayaṃ pradīptamaruṇaṃ rudreṇa yatsiddhidam /
prāṇaṃ tatra vilīya pañcaghatikāścittānvitaṃ dhārayet,
eṣā kālagabhīrabhītihariṇī vaisvānarī dhāraṇā //75//

The fire element is located at the navel region. Its color is red like the cochineal insect. It has a triangular shape. Its *bīja mantra* is '*ram*' and it deity is *Rudra*. This element is full of flaming fire and has the radiance of the sun. It is the giver of *siddhi* (perfection). Contemplating on this element, dissolve the *prāṇa* there for five *ghaṭikās* (two hours). This is *vaisvānarī dhāraṇā* which destroys the fear of horrible death. -75.

प्रदीप्ते ज्वलिते वह्नौ यदि पतति साधकः ।
एतन्मुद्राप्रसादेन स जीवति न मृत्युभाक् ॥ ७६॥

pradīpte jvalite vahnau patito yadi sādhakaḥ /
etanmudrā prasādena sa jīvati na mṛtyubhāk //76//

If a *sādhaka* falls into a flaming fire, he remains alive and does not face the jaws of death by the grace of this *mudrā*. -76.

19. Vāyavīya Dhāraṇā

यद्भिन्नाञ्जनपुञ्जसंनिभमिदं धूम्राऽवभासं परं,
तत्त्वं सत्त्वमयं यकारसहितं यत्रेश्वरो देवता ।
प्राणं तत्र विलीय पञ्चघटिकाश्चित्तान्वितं धारयेदत्
एषा खे गमनं करोति यामिनां स्याद्वायवी धारणा ॥ ७७॥

yadbhinnāñjanapuñjasannibhamidaṃ
dhūmrāvabhāsaṃ paraṃ,
tattvaṃ sattvamayam yakārasahitaṃ yatreśvaro devatā /
prāṇaṃ tatra vilīya pañcaghatikāścittānvitaṃ dhārayet,
eṣā khe gamanaṃ karoti yāmināṃ syādvāyavī dhāraṇā //77//

The color of the air element is black like collyrium or smoke. Its *bīja mantra* is '*yam*'. This *tattva* is full of *sāttvika* qualities and its *devatā* (god/deity) is *Iśvara*. Focus on this element in the heart and dissolve the *prāṇa* there by *kumbhaka* practice with concentrated mind for five *ghaṭikās* (two hours). This is *vāyavī dhāraṇā*. The practitioner travels in space by the practice of this *mudrā*.

-77.

इयं तु परमा मुद्रा जरामृत्युविनाशिनी ।
वायुनाम्रियते नापि खे च गतिप्रदायिनी ॥ ७८॥
शठाय भक्तिहीनाय न देयं यस्यकस्यचित् ।
दत्ते च सिद्धिहानिः स्यात्सत्यं वच्मि च चण्ड ते ॥ ७९॥

iyaṃ tu paramā mudrā jarāmṛtyuvināśinī /
vāyunāmriyate nāpi khe ca gatipradāyinī //78//
śaṭhāya bhaktihīnāya na deyaṃ yasyakasyacit /
datte ca siddhihāniḥ syātsatyaṃ vacmi ca caṇḍe te //79//

This is a foremost *mudrā* which destroys decay and death. One cannot be killed because of air and gains the power to fly in space. This *dhāraṇā* should never be taught to those who are wicked and devoid of devotion. If it is given, *siddhi* is verily destroyed. O *Caṇḍakapāli!* Surely, I have told you the truth. -78-79.

20. Ākāśī Dhāraṇā

यत्सिन्धौ वरशुद्धवारिसदृशं व्योमाख्यमुद्भासते
तत्त्वं देवसदाशिवेन सहितं बीजं हकारान्वितम् ।
प्राणं तत्र विलीय पञ्चघटिकाश्चित्तान्वितं धारयेद्
एषा मोक्षकवाटभेदनकरी कुर्यान्नभोधारणा ॥ ८०॥

yatsindhau varaśuddhavārisadṛśaṃ vyomākhyamudbhāsate,
tattvaṃ devasadāśivena sahitaṃ bījaṃ hakārānvitam /
prāṇaṃ tatra vilīya pañcaghatikāścittānvitaṃ dhārayet,
eṣā mokṣakapāṭabhedanakarī kuryānnabhodhāraṇā //80//

The eather element has the colour of pure ocean water. Its *bīja mantra* is '*haṃ*' and its deity is *Sadāśiva*. Dissolve the *prāṇa* by *kumbhaka* practice with concentrated mind there for five *ghaṭikās* (two hours). This is *nabho dhāraṇā mudrā* which opens the gate to liberation. It should be practiced. -80.

आकाशीधारणां मुद्रां यो वेत्ति स च योगवित् ।
न मृत्युर्जायते तस्य प्रलये नावसीदति ॥ ८१॥

ākāśīdhāraṇāṃ mudrāṃ yo vetti sa yogavit /
na mṛtyurjāyate tasya pralaye nāvasīdati //81//

One who knows *ākāśı dhāraṇā mudrā* is the knower of yoga.

He does not die even at the time of dissolution. – 81.

21. Aśvinī Mudrā

आकुञ्चयेद्गुदद्वारं प्रकाशयेत् पुनः पुनः ।
सा भवेदश्विनी मुद्रा शक्तिप्रबोधकारिणी ॥ ८२॥
अश्विनी परमा मुद्रा गुह्यरोगविनाशिनी ।
बलपुष्टिकरी चैव अकालमरणं हरेत् ॥ ८३॥

ākuñcayed gudadvāraṃ prakāśayet punaḥ punaḥ /
sā bhavedaśvinīmudrā śaktiprabodhakāriṇī //82//
aśvinī paramā mudrā guhyarogavināśinī /
balapuṣṭikarī caiva akālamaraṇaṃ haret //83//

Contract and expand the anus area repeatedly. It is called *aśvinī mudrā.* It awakens the *kuṇḍalinī śakti*. This is a foremost *mudrā* which destroys all hidden diseases (i.e. anus, rectum and reproductive organs). It provides physical strength and nourishment, and prevents untimely death. -82-83.

22. Pāśinī Mudrā

कण्ठपृष्टे क्षिपेत्पादौ पाशवद् दृढबन्धनम् ।
सा एव पाशिनी मुद्रा शक्तिप्रबोधकारिणी ॥ ८४॥
पाशिनी महती मुद्रा बलपुष्टिविधायिनी ।
साधनीया प्रयत्नेन साधकैः सिद्धिकाङ्क्षिभिः ॥ ८५॥

kaṇṭhapṛṣṭhe kṣipetpādau pāśavad dṛḍhabandhanam /
sā eva pāśinī mudrā śaktiprabodhakāriṇī //84//
paśinī mahatī mudrā balapuṣṭividhāyinī /
sādhaniyā prayatnena sādhakaiḥ siddhikāṅkṣibhiḥ //85//

Cast both legs behind the neck and tie up them firmly like a noose. This is called *pāśinī mudrā*. It awakens the *kuṇḍalinī śakti*. *Pāśinī* is a great *mudrā* which gives strength and nourishment. A *sādhaka* desirous of *siddhi* should practice it with due effort. -84-85.

23. Kākī Mudrā

काकचञ्चुवदास्येन पिबेद्वायुं शनैः शनैः ।
काकी मुद्रा भवेदेषा सर्वरोगविनाशिनी ॥ ८६॥
काकीमुद्रा परा मुद्रा सर्वतन्त्रेषु गोपिता ।

अस्याः प्रसादमात्रेण काकवन्नीरुजो भवेत् ॥ ८७॥

kākacañcuvadāsyena pibedvāyuṃ śanaiḥ śanaiḥ /
kākī mudrā bhvedeṣā sarvarogavināśinī //86//
kākīmudrā parā mudrā sarvatantreṣu gopitā /
asyāḥ prasādamātreṇa kākavannīrujo bhavet //87//

Inhale slowly through the mouth making its shape like a beak of a crow. This is *kākī mudrā*, the destroyer of all diseases. This is an important *mudrā* kept secret in all the *tantras*. By the grace of this *mudrā*, one becomes free from diseases like a crow. -86-87.

24. Mātaṅginī Mudrā

कण्ठमग्नेजले स्थित्वा नासाभ्यां जलमाहरेत् ।
मुखान्निर्गमयेत्पश्चात् पुनर्वक्त्रेण चाहरेत् ॥ ८८॥
नासाभ्यां रेचयेत्पश्चात् कुर्यादेवं पुनः पुनः ।
मातङ्गिनी परा मुद्रा जरामृत्यु विनाशिनी ॥ ८९॥

kaṇṭhamagnejale sthitvā nāsābhyāṃ jalamāharet /
mukhānnirgamayetpaścāt punarvaktreṇa cāharet //88//
nāsābhyāṃ recayetpaścāt kuryādevaṃ punaḥ punaḥ /
mātaṅginī parā mudrā jarāmṛtyu vināśinī //89//

Stand in water up to the neck level deep. Inhale drawing the water up through the nostrils and expel it out through the mouth. Then draw the water through the mouth and expel it through the nostrils. This practice should be repeated. This is a great *mātaṅginī mudrā* which destroys old age and death. -88-89.

विरले निर्जने देशे स्थित्वा चैकाग्रमानसः ।
कुर्यान्मातङ्गिनीं मुद्रां मातङ्ग इव जायते ॥ ९०॥
यत्र यत्र स्थितो योगी सुखमत्यन्तमश्नुते ।
तस्मात्सर्वप्रयत्नेन साधयेत् मुद्रिकां पराम् ॥ ९१॥

virale nirjane deśe sthitvā caikāgramānasaḥ /
kuryānmātaṅginī mudrāṃ mātaṅga iva jāyate //90//
yatra yatra sthito yogī sukhamatyantamaśnute /
tasmātsarvaprayatnena sādhayet mudrikāṃ parām //91//

A yogi should practice it remaining alone in an isolated place with a concentrated mind. By this *mudrā* he becomes strong like an elephant. Wherever he stays, he remains in a great happiness. Therefore, this great *mudrā* should be perfected with the highest effort. -90-91.

25. Bhujaṅginī Mudrā

वक्त्रं किञ्चित्सुप्रसार्य चाऽनिलं गलया पिबेत् ।
सा भवेद्भुजङ्गी मुद्रा जरामृत्युविनाशिनी ॥ ९२॥
यावच्च उदरे रोगमजीर्णादि विशेषतः ।
तत्सर्वं नाशयेदाशु यत्र मुद्रा भुजङ्गिनी ॥ ९३॥

vaktraṃ kiñcitsuprasārya cānilaṃ galayā pibet /
sā bhavedbhujaṅgī mudrā jarāmṛtyuvināśinī //92//
yāvacca udare rogamajīrṇādi viśeṣataḥ /
tatsarvaṃ nāśayedāśu yatra mudrā bhujaṅginī //93//

Opening the mouth a little wide, draw air through the throat. This becomes *bhujaṅginī mudrā*, the destroyer of old age and death. All digestive disorders, especially indigestion, etc. are destroyed at once by the mastery over this *mudrā*. -92-93.

अथ मुद्राणां फलकथनम् ।
इदं तु मुद्रापटलं कथितं चण्डकापाले ।
वल्लभं सर्वसिद्धानां जरामरणनाशनम् ॥ ९४॥
शठाय भक्तिहीनाय न देयं यस्य कस्यचित् ।
गोपनीयं प्रयत्नेन दुर्लभं मरुतामपि ॥ ९५॥
ऋजवे शान्तचित्ताय गुरुभक्तिपराय च ।
कुलीनाय प्रदातव्यं भोगमुक्ति प्रदायकम् ॥ ९६॥

idaṃ tu mudrāpaṭalaṃ kathitaṃ caṇḍakāpāle /
vallabhaṃ sarvasiddhānāṃ jarāmaraṇanāsanam //94//
śaṭhāya bhaktihīnāya na deyaṃ yasya kasyacit /
gopaniyaṃ prayatnena durlabhaṃ marutāmapi //95//
ṛjave śāntacittāya gurubhakti parāya ca /
kulīnāya pradātavyaṃ bhogamukti pradāyakam //96//

Now the benefits of the *mudrās* are described.

O *Caṇḍakapāli!* Here I have told you the chapter on *mudrās*. They are dear to all *siddhas.* They destroy old age and death. Do not teach them to people who are wicked and devoid of devotion.

Keep them secret carefully as they are rare even to gods. These *mudrās* should be taught to those who are mentally peaceful, devoted to their gurus and who belong to a noble family. These *mudrās* provide both worldly enjoyments and liberation. -94-96.

मुद्राणां पटलं ह्येतत्सर्वव्याधिविनाशनम् ।
नित्यमभ्यासशीलस्य जठराग्निविवर्धनम् ॥ ९७॥
न तस्य जायते मृत्युर्नास्य जरादिकं तथा ।
नाग्निजलभयं तस्य वायोरपि कुतो भयम् ॥ ९८॥
कासः श्वासः प्लीहा कुष्ठं श्लेष्मरोगाश्च विंशतिः ।
मुद्राणां साधनाच्चैव विनश्यन्ति न संशयः ॥ ९९॥

mudrāṇāṃ paṭalaṃ hyetatsarvavyādhi vināśanam /
nityamabhyāsa śīlasya jaṭharāgnivivardhanam //97//
na tasya jāyate mṛtyurnāsya jarādikaṃ tathā /
nāgnijalabhayaṃ tasya vāyorapi kuto bhayam //98//
kāsaḥ śvāsaḥ plihā kuṣṭhaṃ śleṣmarogāśca viṃśatiḥ //
mudrāṇāṃ sadhanāccaiva vinasyanti na saṃśayaḥ //99//

All diseases are destroyed by these *mudrās* explained in this chapter. The digestive fire of a *sādhaka* is activated through their regular practice. He is not touched by death and old age. He has no fear of fire, water and air. Twenty types of diseases like cough, asthma, spleen disorders, leprosy and phlegm, etc., are destroyed through the practice of these *mudrās*. There is no doubt about it. -97-99.

बहुना किमिहोक्तेन सारं वच्मि च चण्ड ते ।
नास्ति मुद्रासमं किञ्चित्सिद्धिदं क्षितिमण्डले ॥ १००॥

bahunā kimihoktena sāram vacmi ca caṇḍa te /
nāsti mudrāsamaṃ kiñcitsiddhidam kṣitimaṇḍale //100//

O *Caṇḍakapāli!* What shall I tell you more? I have explained you in summary. There is nothing equal to these *mudrās* for granting *siddhis* in this world. -100.

इति श्रीघेरण्डसंहितायां घेरण्डचण्डसंवादे
मुद्राप्रयोगो नाम तृतीयोपदेशः ॥

iti śrīgheraṇḍasaṃhitāyāṃ gheraṇḍacaṇḍasaṃvāde

mudrāprayogo nāma tṛtīyopadeśaḥ /
Thus ends the Third Chapter of *Gheraṇḍa Samhitā* entitled *Mudrā* Practice.

CHAPTER FOUR

Discourse On Pratyāhāra

घेरण्ड उवाच ।
अथातः संप्रवक्ष्यामि प्रत्याहारमनुत्तमम् ।
यस्य विज्ञानमात्रेण कामादिरिपुनाशनम् ॥ १॥

gheraṇḍa uvāca /
athātaḥ sampravakṣyāmi pratyāhārakamuttamam /
yasya vijñānamātreṇa kāmādiripunāśanam //1//

Sage *Gheraṇḍa* said: - Now I shall describe you the highest practice of *pratyāhāra*. By knowing this alone, all the enemies like *kāmā* (craving, lust), etc. are destroyed. -1.

यतो यतो निश्चरति मनश्चञ्चलमस्थिरम् ।
ततस्ततो नियम्यैतदात्मन्येव वशं नयेत् ॥ २॥

yato yato niścarati manaścancalamasthiram /
tatastato niyamyaitadātmanyeva vaśaṃ nayet //2//

Whenever the mind wanders and become unstable, subduing it, bring it back under control of *Ātma* (the Self). -2.

पुरस्कारं तिरस्कारं सुश्राव्यं वा भयानकम् ।
मनस्तस्मान्नियम्यैतदात्मन्येव वशं नयेत् ॥ ३॥

puraskāraṃ tiraskāraṃ suśrāvyaṃ vā bhayānakam /
manastamānniyamyaitadātmanyeva vaśam nayet //3//

Respect or condemnation, hearing of good words or very bad words, subdue the mind in all these (contradictions) and bring it back under control of *Ātma* (the Self). -3.

सुगन्धे वाऽपि दुर्गन्धे मनो घ्राणेषु जायते ।
तस्मात्प्रत्याहरेदेतदात्मन्येव वशं नयेत् ॥ ४॥

sugandhe vā'pi durgandhe mano ghrāṇeṣu jāyate /

tasmātpratyāharedetadātmanyava vaśaṃ nayet //4//

Whether there is a good or bad smell, the mind goes to it. Therefore, withdraw the mind from it (smell) and keep it under the control of the Self. -4.

मधुराम्लकतिक्तादिरसं गतं यदा मनः ।

तस्मात्प्रत्याहरेदेतदात्मन्येव वशं नयेत् ॥ ५॥

madhurāmlakatiktādirasaṃ gataṃ yadā manaḥ /

tasmātpratyāharedetadātmanyava vaśaṃ nayet //5//

Whenever the mind becomes attracted to sweet, sour, bitter and other (kinds) of tastes, withdraw it from them and bring it under the control of the Self. -5.

इति श्रीघेरण्डसंहितायां घेरण्डचण्डसंवादे

प्रत्याहारप्रयोगो नाम चतुर्थोपदेशः ॥

iti śrīgheraṇḍasamhitāyāṃ gheraṇḍacaṇḍasamvāde

pratyāhārāprayogo nāma caturthopadeśaḥ /

Thus ends the Fourth Chapter of *Gheraṇḍa Samhitā* entitled *Pratyāhāra* Practice.

CHAPTER FIVE

Discourse On Prāṇāyāma

घेरण्ड उवाच ।
अथातः संप्रवक्ष्यामि प्राणायामस्य यद्विधिम् ।
यस्य साधनमात्रेण देवतुल्यो भवेन्नरः ॥ १॥

gheraṇḍa uvāca /
athātaḥ sampravakṣyāmi prāṇāyāmasya yadviddhim /
yasya sādhanamātreṇa devatulyo bhvennaraḥ //1//

Sage *Gheraṇḍa* said: - Now I shall explain you about the rules of *prāṇāyāma*. By its mere practice, a man becomes similar to a god. -1.

आदौ स्थानं तथा कालं मिताहारं तथापरम् ।
नाडीशुद्धिं ततः पश्चात्प्राणायामं च साधयेत् ॥ २॥

ādau sthānaṃ tathā kālaṃ mitahāraṃ tatha param /
nāḍīśuddhiṃ ca tataḥ paścātprāṇāyāmaṃ ca sādhayet //2//

First one should find a place and suitable time (for practice), eat in moderation and purify the *nāḍīs.* After that, he should practice *praṇayāma*. -2.

Place of Practice

दूरदेशे तथाऽरण्ये राजधान्यां जनान्तिके ।
योगारम्भं न कुर्वीत कृतश्चेत्सिद्धिहा भवेत् ॥ ३॥

dūradeśe tathā'raṇye rājadhānyāṃ janāntike /
yogārambhaṃ na kurvīta kṛtaścetsiddhiha bhavet //3//

One should not commence yogic practices in a far away land, in a forest, in a capital city or in the crowd. If one does so, he will not achieve *siddhi* (perfection). -3.

अविश्वासं दूरदेशे अरण्ये रक्षिवर्जितम् ।
लोकारण्ये प्रकाशश्च तस्मात् त्रीणि विवर्जयेत् ॥ ४॥

aviśvāsaṃ dūradeśe araṇye rakṣivarjitam /
lokāraṇye prakāśaśca tasmāt trīṇi vivarjayet //4//

One cannot believe people in a far away land. One is without protection in a forest. In the middle of dense population, one is open to public. Therefore, these three places should be avoided. -4.

सुदेशे धार्मिके राज्ये सुभिक्षे निरुपद्रवे ।
तत्रैकं कुटिरं कृत्वा प्राचीरैः परिवेष्टितम् ॥ ५॥

sudeśe dhārmike rājye subhikṣe nirupadrave /
kṛtvā tatraikaṃ kuṭīraṃ prācīraiḥ pariveṣṭitam //5//

In a good religious country where foods are sufficiently available in alms and is free from any disturbances, one should make a hut there and erect a wall around it. -5.

वापीकूपतडागं च प्राचीरमध्यवर्ति च ।
नात्युच्चं नातिनिम्नं च कुटिरं कीटवर्जितम् ॥ ६॥

vāpīkūpataḍāgaṃ ca prācīramadhyavarti ca /
nātyuccaṃ nātinimnaṃ ca kuṭīraṃ kīṭavarjitam //6//

There should be a well, a pond or a water source in the center of the boundary. The hut should be neither too high nor too low and be free from insects. -6.

सम्यग्गोमयलिप्तं च कुटिरं तत्र निर्मितम् ।
एवं स्थाने हि गुप्ते च प्राणायामं समभ्यसेत् ॥ ७॥

samyaggomayaliptaṃ ca kuṭīrantatra nirmitam /
evaṃ sthāneṣu gupteṣu prāṇāyāmaṃ samabhyaset //7//

The hut should be smeared well with cow-dung. In a hut built in this way located in a hidden place, one should practice *prāṇāyāma*. -7.

Time of Practice

हेमन्ते शिशिरे ग्रीष्मे वर्षायां च ऋतौ तथा ।
योगारम्भं न कुर्वीत कृते योगो हि रोगदः ॥ ८॥

hemante śiśire grīṣme varṣāyāṃ ca ṛtau tathā /

yogārambhaṃ na kurvīta kṛte yogo hi rogadaḥ //8//

One should not commence yogic practices during *hemanta* (winter), *śiśira* (cold), *grīṣma* (hot) and *varṣā* (rainy)seasons. If one does so in these seasons, the yoga indeed causes diseases for him. -8.

वसन्ते शरदि प्रोक्तं योगारम्भं समाचरेत् ।

तथा योगी भवेत्सिद्धो रोगान्मुक्तो भवेद्ध्रुवम् ॥ ९॥

vaśante śaradi proktaṃ yogārambhaṃ samācaret /

tatha yogī bhavet siddho rogānmukto bhaved dhruvam //9//

It is said that one should begin the practice of yoga in spring (*vaśanta*) and autumn (*śarada*) seasons. Thus, the yogi certainly becomes successful and free from diseases. -9.

चैत्रादिफाल्गुनान्ते च माघादिफाल्गुनान्तिके ।

द्वौ द्वौ मासावृतुभागावनुभावश्चतुश्चतुः ॥ १०॥

caitrādiphālgunānte ca māghādiphālgunāntike /

dvau dvau māsau ṛtubhāgau anubāvaścatuścatuḥ //10//

There are twelve months in a year from *caitrā* (March) to *phālguna* (February) and each season having two months duration follows in order starting from *māgha* to *phālguna*. But each season is also experienced for four months. -10.

द्वौ द्वौ मासावृतुभागावनुभावश्चतुश्चतुः ॥ १०॥

वसन्तश्चैत्र वैशाखौ ज्येष्ठाषाढौ च ग्रीष्मकौ ।

वर्षा श्रावणभाद्राभ्यां शरदाश्विनकार्तिकौ ।

मार्गपौषौ च हेमन्तः शिशिरो माघफाल्गुनौ ॥ ११॥

vasantaścaitra vaiśākhau jyeṣṭhāṣāḍhā ca grīṣmakau /

varṣā śrāvaṇabhādrābhyāṃ śaradāśvinakārtikau /

mārgapauṣau ca hemantaḥ śiśiro māghaphālgunau //11//

Caitra and *vaiśākha* (March and April) is *vasanta* (spring); *jyeṣṭha āṣāḍha* (May and June) is *grīṣma* (summer); *śrāvaṇa* and *bhādrā* (July and August) is *varṣā* (rainy season); *āśvina* and *kārtika* (September and October) is *śarada* (autumn); *mārgaśīrṣa and pauṣa* (November and December) is *hemanta* (winter); and *māgha* to *phālguna* (January and February) is *śiśira* (cold). -11.

अनुभावं प्रवक्ष्यामि ऋतूनां च यथोदितम् ।
माघादिमाधवान्तेषु वसन्तानुभवं विदुः ॥ १२॥
चैत्रादि चाषाढान्तं च निदाघानुभवं विदुः ।
आषाढादि चाश्विनान्तं प्रावृषानुभवं विदुः ॥ १३॥
भाद्रादि मार्गशीर्षान्तं शरदोऽनुभवं विदुः ।
कार्तिकादिमाघमासान्तं हेमन्तानुभवं विदुः ।
मार्गादि चतुरो मासान् शिशिरानुभवं विदुः ॥ १४॥

anubhāvaṃ pravakṣyāmi ṛtūnāṃ ca yothoditam /
māghādimādhavānteṣu vasantānubhavaṃ viduḥ //12//
caitrādi cāṣāḍhāntaṃ ca nidāghānubhavaṃ viduḥ /
āṣāḍhādi cāśvināntaṃ prāvṛṣānubhavaṃ viduḥ //13//
bhādrādi mārgaśīrṣantaṃ śarado'nubhavaṃ viduḥ /
kārtikādimāghamāsāntaṃ hemantānubhavaṃ viduḥ /
mārgādi caturo māsān śiśirānubhavaṃ vidūḥ //14//

Now I explain you about the seasons which are experienced as below. From *māgha* to *mādhava/vaiśākha* (January to April) spring is experienced; from *caitrā* to *āṣāḍha* (March to June) summer is experienced; from *āṣāḍha* to *āśvina* (June to September) monsoon is experienced; from *bhādra* to *mārgaśīrṣa* (August to November) autumn is experienced; from *kārtika* to *māgha* (October to January) winter is experienced; and from *mārgaśīrṣa* to *phālguna* (November to February) cold is experienced. -12-14.

वसन्ते वापि शरदि योगारम्भं समाचरेत् ।
तदा योगी भवेत्सिद्धो विनाऽऽयासेन कथ्यते ॥ १५॥

vasante vāpi śaradi yogārambhaṃ samācaret /
tadā yogo bhavetsiddho vinā''yāsena kathyate //15//

It is said that yogic practices should be commenced either in *vasanta* (spring) or *śarada* (autumn). Thus, one attains success in his yogic practices without trouble. -15.

Moderation in Diet

मिताहारं विना यस्तु योगारम्भं तु कारयेत् ।
नानारोगो भवेत्तस्य किञ्चिद्योगो न सिध्यति ॥ १६॥

mitāhāraṃ vinā yastu yogārambhaṃ tu kārayet /

nānārogo bhavettasya kiñcityogo na sidhyati //16//

One who does yogic practices without moderation in diet gets various diseases and certainly does not attain perfection/success in yoga. -16.

शाल्यन्नं यवपिष्टं वा गोधूमपिष्टकं तथा ।

मुद्गं माषचणकादि शुभ्रं च तुषवर्जितम् ॥ १७॥

śālyannaṃ yavapiṣṭaṃ vā godhūmapiṣṭakaṃ tathā /

mudgaṃ māṣacaṇakādi śubhraṃ ca tuṣavarjitam //17//

One who practices yoga should eat food made from rice, barley or wheat flour and pulses like *mudga* (green beans), *māṣa* (black gram), *caṇaka* (chick peas), etc. which are clean and without husks. 17.

पटोलं पनसं मानं कक्कोलं च शुकाशकम् ।

द्राढिकां कर्कटीं रम्भां डुम्बरीं कण्टकण्टकम् ॥ १८॥

आमरम्भां बालरम्भां रम्भादण्डं च मूलकम् ।

वार्ताकीं मूलकम् ऋद्धिं योगी भक्षणमाचरेत् ॥ १९॥

paṭolaṃ panasaṃ mānaṃ kakkolam ca śukāśakam /

drāḍhikāṃ karkaṭīṃ rambhāṃ ḍumbarīṃ kaṇṭakaṇṭakam //18//

āmarambhāṃ bālarambhāṃ rambhādaṇḍaṃ ca mūlakam /

vārtākīṃ mūlakaṃ ṛddhiṃ yogī bhakṣaṇamācaret //19//

A yogi can eat pointed gourd (trichosanthes dioica), jackfruit, root vegetables, berries, bitter gourd, cucumber, figs, plantain, plantain stem and roots, eggplants, radish and medicinal roots and fruits. -18-19.

बालशाकं कालशाकं तथा पटोलपत्रकम् ।

पञ्चशाकं प्रशंसीयाद्वास्तूकं हिलमोचिकाम् ॥ २०॥

bālaśākaṃ kālaśākaṃ tathā poṭalapatrakam /

pañcaśākaṃ praśamsīyādvāstūkaṃ himalocikām //20//

Five green vegetables *bālaśāka, kālaśāka, poṭalapatra, vāstūka* and *himalocika* are recommended for a yogi. -20.

शुद्धं सुमधुरं स्निग्धमुदरार्धविवर्जितम् ।

भुञ्जते सुरसं प्रीत्या मिताहारमिमं विदुः ॥ २१॥

śuddhaṃ sumadhuraṃ snigdhaṃ udarārdhavivarjitam /

bhujyate surasamprītyā mitāhāramimaṃ viduḥ //21//

Eating pure, sweet and cool foods (cooked with ghee or butter); drinking good juices with pleasure and keeping half of the stomach empty is called moderation in diet by the wise. -21.

अन्नेन पूरयेदर्धं तोयेन तु तृतीयकम् ।

उदरस्य तुरीयांशं संरक्षेद्वायुचारणे ॥ २२॥

annena pūrayedardhaṃ toyena tu tṛtīyakam /

udarasya turīyāmśaṃ samrakṣedvāyucāraṇe //22//

Half of the stomach should be filled with food; the third quarter (of it) with water and *turīyāmśa* (the last part or fourth quarter) should be reserved for *vāyucāraṇa* (the movement of air). -22.

Forbidden Foods

कट्वम्लं लवणं तिक्तं भृष्टं च दधि तक्रकम् ।

शाकोत्कटं तथा मद्यं तालं च पनसं तथा ॥ २३॥

kaṭvamlaṃ lavaṇaṃ tiktaṃ bhṛṣṭaṃ ca dadhi takrakam /

śākotkaṭaṃ tathā madyaṃ tālaṃ ca panasaṃ tathā //23//

While doing yogic practice for the first time, one should give up bitter, sour, salty, astringent and roasted food items, curd, buttermilk, heavy vegetables, wine, palm nuts and over-ripe jack fruits. -23.

कुलत्थं मसूरं पाण्डुं कूष्माण्डं शाकदण्डकम् ।

तुम्बीकोलकपित्थं च कण्टबिल्वं पलाशकम् ॥ २४॥

kulatthaṃ masuraṃ pāṇḍuṃ kūṣmāṇḍaṃ śākadaṇḍakam /

tumbīkolakapitthaṃ ca kaṇṭabilbaṃ palāśakam //24//

One should avoid horse gram, lentils, *pāṇḍu* (a kind of fruit), pumpkin, vegetable stems, gourds, *kaṇṭabilba* (feronia elephantum) and *palāśaka* (butea frondosa). -24.

कदम्बं जम्बीरं बिम्बं लकुचं लशुनं विषम् ।

कामरङ्गं पियालं च हिङ्गुशाल्मलिकेमुकम् ॥ २५॥

kadambaṃ jambīraṃ bimbaṃ lakucaṃ laśunaṃ viṣam /

kāmaraṅgaṃ piyālaṃ ca hiṅguśālmalīkemukam //25//

Also he should avoid fruit like berries, limes, garlic and onions, asafoetida, *śālmalī* and *kemuka*. -25.

योगारम्भे वर्जयेच्च पथस्त्रीवह्निसेवनम् ।
नवनीतं घृतं क्षीरं गुडं शर्करादि चैक्षवम् ॥ २६॥
पक्वरम्भां नारिकेलं दाडिम्बमशिवासवम् ।
द्राक्षां तु लवनीं धात्रीं रसमम्लविवर्जितम् ॥ २७॥

yogārambhe varjayecca pathastrivahnisevanam /
navanītaṃ ghṛtaṃ kṣīraṃ guḍaṃ śarkarādi caikṣavam //26//
pakvarambhāṃ nārikelaṃ dāḍimbamaśivāsavam /
drākṣāṃ tu lavalīṃ dhātriṃ rasamamlavivarjitam //27//

When one begins yogic practice for the first time, he should avoid travelling, the company of the women and serving the fire (for heating the body). He should also avoid fresh butter, clarified butter, milk, sugar-candy, jaggery, ripe banana, coconut, pomegranate, grapes, *lavalī* fruit, myrobalans and acidic juices. – 26-27.

एलाजातिलवङ्गं च पौरुषं जम्बु जाम्बलम् ।
हरीतकीं खर्जूरं च योगी भक्षणमाचरेत् ॥ २८॥
लघुपाकं प्रियं स्निग्धं तथा धातुप्रपोषणम् ।
मनोऽभिलषितं योग्यं योगी भोजनमाचरेत् ॥ २९॥

elājātilavaṅgaṃ ca pauruṣaṃ jambu jāmbalam /
harītakīṃ kharjūraṃ ca yogī bhakṣaṇamācaret //28//
laghupākaṃ priyaṃ snigdhaṃ tathā dhātupraposaṇam /
mano'bhilaṣitaṃ yogyaṃ yogī bhojanamācaret //29//

A yogi can eat cardamom, nutmeg, cloves, stimulants, *harītakī* and dates. He should eat easily digestible, agreeable and cool foods which nourish the humors of the body and appeal to his mind. -28-29.

काठिन्यं दुरितं पूतिमुष्णं पर्युषितं तथा ।
अतिशीतं चाति चोष्णं भक्ष्यं योगी विवर्जयेत् ॥ ३०॥

kāṭhinyaṃ duritaṃ pūtimuṣṇaṃ paryuṣitaṃ tathā /
atiśītaṃ cāticoṣṇaṃ bhakṣyaṃ yogī vivarjayet //30//

He should avoid the foods which are hard (difficult to digest), rotten, stale, heating, very cold and very hot. -30.

प्रातःस्नानोपवासादिकायक्लेशविधिं तथा ।
एकाहारं निराहारं यामान्ते च न कारयेत् ॥ ३१॥

prātaḥsnānopavāsādi kāyakleśavidhiṃ tathā /
ekāhāraṃ nirāhāraṃ yāmānte ca na kārayet //31//

He should not take early morning baths, do fasting or do any activity that causes pain for the body. He should avoid eating only once a day, not eating at all and eating at the end of every three hours (between meals). -31.

एवं विधिविधानेन प्राणायामं समाचरेत् ।
आरम्भे प्रथमे कुर्यात्क्षीराज्यं नित्यभोजनम् ।
मध्याह्ने चैव सायाह्ने भोजनद्वयमाचरेत् ॥ ३२॥

evaṃ vidhividhānena prāṇāyāmaṃ samācaret /
ārambhe prathame kuryāt kṣīrājyaṃ nityabhojanam /
madhyāhne caiva sāyāhne bhokjanadvayamāacaret //32//

According to the rules as specified above, one should begin *prāṇāyāma* practice. Before beginning *prāṇāyāma* practice, he should take food with milk and ghee daily and eat two meals a day, one at noon and the next in the evening. -32.

Purification of Nāḍī

कुशासने मृगाजिने व्याघ्राजिने च कम्बले ।
स्थलासने समासीनः प्राङ्मुखो वाप्युदङ्मुखः ।
नाडीशुद्धिं समासाद्य प्राणायामं समभ्यसेत् ॥ ३३॥

kuśāsane mṛgājine vyāghrājine ca kambale /
sthalāsane samāsīnaḥ prāṅmukho vāpyudaṅmukhaḥ /
nāḍīśuddhiṃ samāsādhya prāṇāyāmaṃ samabhyaset //33//

One should sit on a seat of *kuśa* (a sacred grass) or deer skin or a tiger skin or a blanket facing east or north. Having purified the *nāḍīs* first, he should do the practice of *prāṇāyāma*. -33.

चण्डकापालिरुवाच ।
नाडीशुद्धिं कथं कुर्यान्नाडीशुद्धिस्तु कीदृशी ।
तत्सर्वं श्रोतुमिच्छामि तद्वदस्व दयानिधे ॥ ३४॥

caṇḍakapāliruvāca /

nāḍīśuddhiṃ kathaṃ kuryānnāḍīśuddhistu kīḍṛśī /

tatsarvaṃ śrotumicchāmi tatvadasva dayānidhe //34//

Caṇḍakapāli asked: - How is purification of *nāḍīs* done? What is its form? I want to hear all about these. O ocean of kindness, please tell me about it. -34.

घेरण्ड उवाच ।

मलाकुलासु नाडीषु मारुतो नैव गच्छति ।

प्राणायामः कथं सिध्येत्तत्त्वज्ञानं कथं भवेत् ।

तस्मादादौ नडीशुद्धिं प्राणायामं ततोऽभ्यसेत् ॥ ३५॥

gheraṇḍa uvāca /

malākulāsu nāḍīṣu māruto naiva gacchati /

prāṇāyāmaḥ kathaṃ siddhayetatvajñānaṃ kathaṃ bhavet /

tasmādādau nāḍīśuddhiṃ prāṇāyāmaṃ tato'bhyaset //35//

Sage *Gheraṇḍa* replied: - The air cannot go through the *nāḍīs* when they are full of impurities. In this condition, how can *prāṇāyāma* be perfected? How can *tatvajñāna* (the real knowledge) arise? Therefore, first of all one must purify the *nāḍīs*, and then he should practice *prāṇāyāma*. -35.

नाडीशुद्धिर्द्विधा प्रोक्ता समनुर्निर्मनुस्तथा ।

बीजेन समनुं कुर्यान्निर्मनुं धौतिकर्मणा ॥ ३६॥

nāḍīśuddhirdvidhā proktā samanurnirmanustathā /

bījena samanuṃ kuryānnirmanuṃ dhautikarmaṇā //36//

Purification of *nāḍīs* is of two types. They are *samanu* and *nirmanu*. *Samanu* is performed with *bīja mantra*. *Nirmanu* is performed with the practice of *dhauti karma*. -36.

धौतिकर्म पुरा प्रोक्तं षट्कर्मसाधने यथा ।

शृणुष्व समनुं चण्ड नाडीशुद्धिर्यथा भवेत् ॥ ३७॥

dhautikarma purā proktaṃ ṣaṭkarmasādhane yathā /

śṛuṇuṣva samanuṃ caṇḍa nāḍīśuddhiryathā bhavet //37//

The *dhautikarma* has already been described in the practice of *ṣaṭkarma* sādhanā (the six yogic cleansing practices). O *Caṇḍa*, now listen to the *samanu* method through which the *nāḍīs* are purified. -37.

उपविश्यासने योगी पद्मासनं समाचरेत् ।
गुर्वादिन्यासनं कुर्याद्यथैव गुरुभाषितम् ।
नाडीशुद्धिं प्रकुर्वीत प्राणायामविशुद्धये ॥ ३८॥

upaviśyāsane yogī padmāsanaṃ samācaret /
gurvādinyāsanaṃ kuryād yathaiva gurubhāṣitam /
nāḍīśuddhiṃ prakurvīta prāṇāyāmaviśuddhaye //38//

After sitting on a seat, a yogi should assume *padmāsana* and perform *gurvādinyāsa* (invocation of the guru, etc., by rotating awareness on various parts of the body with specific *mantras*). Then according to the instructions of the guru, practice purification of the *nāḍīs* for attaining perfection in *prāṇāyāma*. -38.

वायुबीजं ततो ध्यात्वा धूम्रवर्णं सतेजसम् ।
चन्द्रेण पूरयेद्वायुं बीजषोडशकैः सुधीः ॥ ३९॥
चतुःषष्ट्या मात्रया च कुम्भकेनैव धारयेत् ।
द्वात्रिंशन्मात्रया वायुं सूर्यनाड्या च रेचयेत् ॥ ४०॥

vāyubījaṃ tato dhyātvā dhūmravarṇaṃ satejasam /
candreṇa pūrayedvāyuṃ vījaṃ ṣoḍaśakaiḥ śudhiḥ //39//
catuḥṣaṣṭyā mātrayā ca kumbhakenaiva dhārayet /
dvātrimśanmātrayā vāyuṃ sūryanāḍyā ca recayet //40//

Meditating on *vāyubīja mantra* '*yaṃ*' with its bright smoke color, perform *pūraka* (inhalation) through the *candra nāḍī* (left nostril) repeating the *bīja mantra* sixteen times. Thus, after inhalation perform *kumbhaka* (retention of breath) repeating the *mantra* sixty-four times. then perform *rechaka* (exhalation) through *sūryanāḍī* (right nostril) repeating the *mantra* thirty-two times. -39-40.

नाभिमूलाद्वह्निमुत्थाप्य ध्यायेत्तेजोऽवनीयुतम् ।
वह्निबीजषोडशेन सूर्यनाड्या च पूरयेत् ॥ ४१॥
चतुःषष्ट्या मात्रया च कुम्भकेनैव धारयेत् ।
द्वात्रिंशन्मात्रया वायुं शशिनाड्या च रेचयेत् ॥ ४२॥

nābhimūlādvahnimutthāpya dhyāyettejo'vanīyutam /
vahnibījaṣoḍaśena sūryanāadyā ca pūrayet //41//
catuḥṣaṣṭyā mātrayā ca kumbhakenaiva dhārayet /

dvātriśanmātrayā vāyuṃ śaśināḍyā ca recayet //42//

Raising the fire element from the navel center, concentrate on its light associated with the earth element. Repeating the *raṃ bīja* of fire element sixteen times, inhale through *sūryanāḍī* (right nostril), hold the breath through *kumbhaka* repeating it sixty-four times and then exhale through the *śaśi nāḍī* (left nostril) repeating the *mantra* thirty-two times. -41-42.

नासाग्रे शशधृग्बिम्बं ध्यात्वा ज्योत्स्नासमन्वितम् ।
ठं बीजं षोडशेनैव इडया पूरयेन्मरुत् ॥ ४३॥
चतुःषष्ट्या मात्रया च वं बीजेनैव धारयेत् ।
अमृतं प्लावितं ध्यात्वा नाडीधौतिं विभावयेत् ।
लकारेण द्वात्रिंशेन दृढं भाव्यं विरेचयेत् ॥ ४४॥

nāsāgre śaśadhṛgbimbaṃ dhyātvā jyotsnāsamanvitam /
ṭhaṃ bījaṃ ṣoḍaśenaiva iḍayā pūrayenmarut //43//
catuḥṣaṣṭyā mātrayā ca vaṃ bījenaiva dhārayet /
amṛtaṃ plāvitaṃ dhyātvā nāḍīdhautiṃ vibhāvayet /
lakāreṇa dvātrimśena dṛḍhaṃ bhāvyaṃ virecayet //44//

Concentrating on the image of the moon with its luminous reflection on the tip of the nose, inhale through the left nostril repeating the *bīja mantra* '*ṭhaṃ*' sixteen times. Hold the breath by *kumbhaka* repeating the *bīja mantra* '*vaṃ*' sixty-four times. Perceive the flow of nectar from the moon at the tip of the nose and purify all the *nāḍīs*. Then exhale through the right nostril by repeating the *bīja mantra* '*laṃ*' thirty-two times. -43-44.

एवंविधां नाडीशुद्धिं कृत्वा नाडीं विशोधयेत् ।
दृढो भूत्वाऽऽसनं कृत्वा प्राणायामं समाचरेत् ॥ ४५॥

evamvidhāṃ nāḍīśuddhiṃ kṛtvā nāḍīṃ viśodhayet /
dhṛḍhobhūtvā"sanaṃ kṛtvā prāṇāyāmaṃ samācaret //45//

Purify the *nāḍīs* through these specified methods. After purifying the *nāḍīs*, be firmly seated in an āsana and begin the practice of *prāṇāyāma*. -45.

Types of Kumbhaka

सहितः सूर्यभेदश्च उज्जायी शीतली तथा ।

भस्त्रिका भ्रामरी मूर्च्छा केवली चाष्टकुम्भकाः ॥ ४६॥

sahitaḥ sūryabhedaśca ujjāyī śītalī tathā /

bhastrikā bhrāmarī mūrcchā kevalī cāṣṭakumbhakā //46//

There are eight types of *prāṇāyāmas.* They are *sahita, sūrya bheda, ujjāyī, śītalī, bhastrikā, bhrāmarī, mūrcchā* and *kevalī.* -46.

Sahita Prāṇāyāma

सहितो द्विविधः प्रोक्तः सगर्भश्च निगर्भकः ।

सगर्भो बीजमुच्चार्य निगर्भो बीज वर्जितः ॥ ४७॥

sahita dvividhaḥ proktaḥ sagarbhśca nigarbhakaḥ /

sagarbho bījamuccārya nigarbho bīja varjitaḥ //47//

*Sahita prāṇāyāma*is of two types: *sagarbha* and *nigarbha. Bīja mantra* is repeated in *sagarbhaprāṇāyāma. Nigarbhaprāṇāyāma* is done without *bīja mantra.* -47.

Sagarbha Prāṇāyāma

प्राणायामं सगर्भं च प्रथमं कथयामि ते ।

सुखासने चोपविश्य प्राङ्मुखो वाऽप्युदङ्मुखः ।

ध्यायेद् विधिं रजोगुणं रक्तवर्णमवर्णकम् ॥ ४८॥

prāṇāyāmaṃ sagarbhaṃ ca prathamaṃ kathayāmi te /

sukhāsane copāviśya praṅmukho vā'pyudaṅmukhaḥ /

dhyāyed vidhiṃ rajoguṇaṃ raktavarṇamavarṇam //48//

First of all, I shall tell you about *sagarbha prāṇāyāma.* Sit in *sukhāsana* (easy pose) facing east or north and meditate on red colored *Brahmā,* full of *rajas guṇa* with the letter '*a*' as its *bīja mantra.* -48.

इडया पूरयेद्वायुं मात्रया षोडशैः सुधीः ।

पूरकान्ते कुम्भकाद्ये कर्तव्यस्तूड्डियानकः ॥ ४९॥

सत्त्वमयं हरिं ध्यात्वा उकारं कृष्णवर्णकम् ।

चतुःषष्ट्या च मात्रया कुम्भकेनैव धारयेत् ॥ ५०॥

तमोमयं शिवं ध्यात्वा मकारं शुक्लवर्णकम् ।

द्वात्रिंशन्मात्रया चैव रेचयेद्विधिना पुनः ॥ ५१॥

iḍayā pūrayedvāyuṃ mātrayā ṣoḍaśaiḥ sudhiḥ /

pūrakānte kumbhakādye kartavyastūḍḍiyānakaḥ //49//

satvamayaṃ hariṃ dhyātvā ukāraṃ kṛṣṇavarṇakam /

catuḥṣaṣṭyā ca mātrayā kumbhakenaiva dhārayet //50//
tamomayaṃ śivaṃ dhyātvā makāraṃ śuklavarṇakam /
dvātrimśanmātrayā caiva recayedvidhinā punaḥ //51//

Inhale through the left nostril repeating *bīja mantra* 'a' sixteen times. At the end of inhalation and before *kumbhaka*, perform *uḍḍiyāna bandha*. Then hold the breath repeating *bīja mantra* 'u' sixty-four times and meditate on dark colored *Hari* full of *sat-vaguṇa.* Then again exhale repeating the *bīja mantra* 'm' thirty-two times meditating on bright colored *Śiva* full of *tamas guṇa.* -49-51.

पुनः पिङ्गलयाऽऽपूर्य कुम्भकेनैव धारयेत् ।
इडया रेचयेत्पश्चात्तद्बीजेन क्रमेण तु ॥ ५२॥
अनुलोमविलोमेन वारं वारं च साधयेत् ।
पूरकान्ते कुम्भकान्तं धृतनासापुटद्वयम् ।
कनिष्ठाकानामिकाङ्गुष्ठैः तर्जनी मध्यमे विना ॥ ५३॥

punaḥ piṅgalayā"pūrya kumbhakenaiva dhārayet /
iḍayā recayetpaścāt tadbījena krameṇa tu //52//
anulomavilomena vāram vāraṃ ca sādhayet /
pūrakānte kumbhakāntaṃ dhṛtanāsāpuṭadvayam /
kaniṣṭhākānāmikāṅguṣṭhaiḥ tarjani madhyame vinā //53//

Again inhale through the right nostril, retain the breath and exhale through the left nostril repeating the *bīja mantras* in the same way/order as mentioned before. In this way, practice *anu-loma viloma* (alternate nostril breathing) again and again. After the end of inhalation till the end of *kumbhaka*, close both nostrils, the right (nostril) with the thumb and the left (nostril) with the ring finger and little finger without (using) the index and middle fingers. -52-53.

Nigarbha Prāṇāyāma

प्राणायामो निगर्भस्तु विना बीजेन जायते ।
वामजानूपरिन्यस्तं वामपाणितलं भ्रमेत् ।
एकादिशतपर्यन्तं पूरकुम्भकरेचनम् ॥ ५४॥

prāṇāyamo nigarbhastu vinā bījena jāyate /

vāmajānūparinyastaṃ vāmapāṇitalaṃ bhramet /
ekādiśataparyantaṃ pūrakumbhakarecanam //54//

Practice of *nigarbha prāṇāyāma* is done without *bīja mantras.* The left hand is moved around on the left knee (for the count) of *prāṇāyāma* during *pūraka, kumbhaka* and *recaka* (inhalation, retention and exhalation) from one to hundred. -54.

उत्तमा विंशतिर्मात्रा षोडशी मात्रा मध्यमा ।
अधमा द्वादशी मात्रा प्राणायामास्त्रिधा स्मृताः ॥ ५५॥

uttamā vimśatirmātrā ṣoḍaśī mātrā madhyamā /
adhamā dvādaśi mātrā prāṇāyāmāstridhā smṛtā //55//

The highest *prāṇāyāma* has twenty *mātrās* (i.e. the ratio of counts is 20:80:40), the medium has sixteen *mātrās* (i.e. the ratio of counts is 16:64:32) and the lowest has twelve *mātrās* (i.e. the ratio of counts is 12:48:24). Thus, *prāṇāyāma* is considered of three types. -55.

अधमाज्जायते घर्मो मेरुकम्पश्च मध्यमात् ।
उत्तमाच्च भूमित्यागस्त्रिविधं सिद्धिलक्षणम् ॥ ५६॥

adhamājjāyate gharmo merukampaśca madhyamāt /
uttamācca bhūmityāgastrividhaṃ siddhilakṣaṇam //56//

The lowest type of *prāṇāyāma* produces heat or perspiration in the body. The medium type of *prāṇāyāma* causes trembling of the spinal column. By the highest type of *prāṇāyāma*, one gives up the ground (levitates). These three results (of *prāṇāyāma* practice) are considered as signs of perfection. -56.

प्राणायामात् खेचरत्वं प्राणायामात् रोगनाशनम् ।
प्राणायामात् बोधयेच्छक्तिं प्राणायामात् मनोन्मनी ।
आनन्दो जायते चित्ते प्राणायामी सुखी भवेत् ॥ ५७॥

prāṇāyāmāt khecaratvaṃ prāṇāyāmāt roganaśanam /
prāṇāyāmāt bodhayecchaktiṃ prāṇāyāmāt manonmanī /
ānando jāyate citte prāṇāyāmī sukhī bhavet //57//

Through the practice of *prāṇāyāma,* travelling ability in space is attained. Diseases are destroyed by the *prāṇāyāmā. Kuṇḍalinī śakti* is awakened through the practice of *prāṇāyāma. Manon-*

manī (a blissful state of mind) is achieved by the *prāṇāyāma*. Through *prāṇāyāma* practice, mind becomes *ānanda* (joyful). One who practices *prāṇāyāma* becomes happy. -57.

Sūryabheda Prāṇāyāma

कथितं सहितं कुम्भं सूर्यभेदनकं शृणु ।
पूरयेत्सूर्यनाड्या च यथाशक्ति बहिर्मरुत् ॥ ५८॥
धारयेद्बहुयत्नेन कुम्भकेन जलन्धरैः ।
यावत्स्वेदं नखकेशाभ्यां तावत्कुर्वन्तु कुम्भकम् ॥ ५९॥

kathitaṃ sahitaṃ kumbhaṃ sūryabhedanakaṃ śṛuṇu /
pūrayet sūryanāḍyā ca yathāśaktiṃ bahirmarut //58//
dhārayedbahuyatnena kumbhakena jalandharaiḥ /
yāvatsvedaṃ nakhakeśabhyaṃ tavatkurvantu kumbhakam //59//

Sahita kumbhaka has already been explained. Now pay attention to *sūryabheda*. Inhale deeply as far as possible through the right nostril and hold the breath with all the effort performing *jālandhara bandha* until the body perspires from the nails to the hairs on the head. -58-59.

Prāṇa Vāyus

प्राणोऽपानः समानश्चोदानव्यानौ तथैव च ।
नागः कूर्मश्च कृकरो देवदत्तो धनञ्जयः ॥ ६०॥

prāṇo'pānaḥ samānaścodānavyānau tathaiva ca /
nāgaḥ kūrmaśca kṛkaro devadatto dhanañjayaḥ //60//

There are ten *prāṇa vāyus*. They are *prāṇa, apāna, samāna, udāna, vyāna, nāga, kūrma, kṛkara, devadatta* and *dhanañjaya*. -60.

Locations of Prāṇa Vāyus

हृदि प्राणो वहेन्नित्यमपानो गुदमण्डले ।
समानो नाभिदेशे तु उदानः कण्ठमध्यगः ॥ ६१॥
व्यानो व्याप्य शरीरे तु प्रधानाः पञ्च वायवः ।
प्राणाद्याः पञ्च विख्याता नागाद्याः पञ्च वायवः ॥ ६२॥

hṛdi prāṇo vahennityamapāno gudamaṇḍale /
samāno nābhideśe tu udānaḥ kaṇṭhamadhyagaḥ //61//

vyāno vyāpya śarīre tu pradhānāḥ pañca vāyavaḥ /
prāṇādyāḥ pañca vikhyātā nāgādyāḥ pañca vāyavaḥ //62//

Prāṇa always flows in the heart, *apāna* in the region of the anus, *samāna* in the navel region, *udāna* in the middle of the throat and *vyāna* is pervasive in the whole body. These five are known as the main *prāṇas. Nāga*, etc., are the five sub-*prāṇa vayus.* -62.

तेषामपि च पञ्चानां स्थानानि च वदाम्यहम् ।
उद्गारे नाग आख्यातः कूर्मस्तून्मीलने स्मृतः ॥ ६३॥
कृकरः क्षुत्कृते ज्ञेयो देवदत्तो विजृम्भणे ।
न जहाति मृते क्वाऽपि सर्वव्यापी धनञ्जयः ॥ ६४॥

teṣāmapi ca pañcānāṃ sthānāni ca vadāmyaham /
udgāre nāga ākhyātaḥ kūrmastūnmīlane smṛtaḥ //63//
kṛkaraḥ kṣutkṛte jñeyo devadatto vijṛmbhaṇe /
na jahāti mṛte kvāpi sarvavyāpī dhanañjayaḥ //64//

Now I tell you the places of these five sub-*prāṇa vayus.* It is considered that *Nāga* presents in belching, *kūrma* in opening the eyes, *kṛkara* in sneezing; *devadatta* in yawning and *dhanañjaya*, all pervasive one, does not leave the body even after death. -63-64.

नागो गृह्णाति चैतन्यं कूर्मश्चैव निमेषणम् ।
क्षुत्तृषं कृकरश्चैव जृम्भणं चतुर्थेन तु ।
भवेद्धनञ्जयाच्छब्दं क्षणमात्रं न निःसरेत् ॥ ६५॥

nāgo gṛhṇāti caitanyaṃ kūrmaścaiva nimeṣaṇam /
kṣuttṛṣaṃ kṛkaraścaiva jṛmbhaṇaṃ caturthena tu /
bhaveddhanañjayācchabdaṃ kṣaṇamātraṃ na niḥsaret //65//

From *nāga* consciousness, from *kūrma* blinking (of the eyes), from *kṛkara* hunger and thirst and from *devadatta* yawning are produced. Sound is produced through *dhanañjaya* which does not leave the body even for a moment. -65.

सर्वे ते सूर्यसम्भिन्ना नाभिमूलात्समुद्धरेत् ।
इडया रेचयेत्पश्चाद्धैर्येणाखण्डवेगतः ॥ ६६॥
पुनः सूर्येण चाकृष्य कुम्भयित्वा यथाविधि ।

रेचयित्वा साधयेत्तु क्रमेण च पुनः पुनः ॥ ६७॥

sarve te sūryasambhinnā nābhimūlāt samuddharet /
iḍaya recayet paścād dhairyeṇākhaṇḍavegataḥ //66//
punaḥ sūryeṇa cākṛsya kumbhayitvā yathāvidhi /
recayitvā sādhayettu krameṇa ca punaḥ punaḥ //67//

Seperating these *prāṇa vayus* with the help of *sūryanāḍī* during practice, raise *samāna vāyu* which comes from the root of the navel. Then exhale slowly and continuously through the left nostril with patience. Again inhale through the right nostril, hold the breath as per the specified method, and exhale through left nostil. Repeat this process of practice again and again. -66-67.

कुम्भकः सूर्यभेदस्तु जरामृत्युविनाशकः ।
बोधयेत्कुण्डलीं शक्तिं देहानलविवर्धनम् ।
इति ते कथितं चण्ड सूर्यभेदनमुत्तमम् ॥ ६८॥

kumbhakaḥ sūryabhedastu jarāmṛtyuvināśakaḥ /
bodhayetkuṇḍalīṃ śaktiṃ dehānalavivardhanam /
iti te kathitaṃ caṇḍa sūryabhedanamuttamam //68//

This is *sūryabheda kumbhaka*, the destroyer of old age and death. It awakens the *kuṇḍalinī śakti* and increases the fire in the body. O *Caṇḍa*! I have told/taught you the excellent *prāṇāyāma* called *sūrya bheda*. -68.

Ujjāyī Prāṇāyāma

नासाभ्यां वायुमाकृष्य मुखमध्ये च धारयेत् ।
हृद्गलाभ्यां समाकृष्य वायुं वक्त्रे च धारयेत् ॥ ६९॥
मुखं प्राक्षल्य सम्वन्द्य कूर्याज्जालन्धरं ततः ।
आशक्ति कुम्भकं कृत्वा धारयेदविरोधतः ॥ ७०॥

nāsābhyāṃ vāyumākṛsya mukhamadhye ca dhārayet /
hṛdgalābhyāṃ samākṛṣya vāyuṃ vaktre ca dhārayet //69//
mukhaṃ prakṣālya samvandya kuryājjālandharaṃ tataḥ /
āśakti kumbhakaṃ kṛtvā dhārayedavirodhataḥ //70//

Inhaling the air through both nostrils, pull the internal air from the heart and throat and hold it in the mouth. After washing the mouth (with the air), perform *jālandhara bandha.* Hold the breath with *kumbhaka* according to capacity without causing any hindrance. -69-70.

उज्जायी कुम्भकं कृत्वा सर्वकार्याणि साधयेत् ।
न भवेत्कफरोगश्च क्रूरवायुरजीर्णकम् ॥ ७१॥
आमवातः क्षयः कासो ज्वरः प्लीहा न विद्यते ।
जरामृत्युविनाशाय चोज्जायीं साधयेन्नरः ॥ ७२॥

ujjāyī kumbhakaṃ kṛtvā sarvakāryaṇī sādhayet /
na bhavet kapharogaśca krūravāyurajīrṇakam //71//
āmavātaḥ kṣayaḥ kāso jvaraḥ plīhā na vidyate /
jarāmṛtyuvināśāya cojjāyīṃ sādhayennaraḥ //72//

All works are accomplished by the practice of *ujjāyī kumbhaka. Kapha* (phlegm), *krūra vāyu* (air or nervous related disorders) and digestive disorders do not occur. Dysentery, tuberculosis, cough, fever and spleen disorders do not exist. A person should perfect *ujjāyī kumbhaka* in order to destroy old age and death. -71-72.

Śītalī Prāṇāyāma

जिह्वया वायुमाकृष्य उदरे पूरयेच्छनैः ।
क्षणं च कुम्भकं कृत्वा नासाभ्यां रेचयेत्पुनः ॥ ७३॥

jihvayā vāyumākṛṣya udare purayecchanaiḥ /
kṣaṇaṃ ca kumbhakaṃ kṛtvā nāsābhyāṃ recayet punaḥ //73//

Pulling in the air through the tongue (rounded), slowly fill up the abdomen. Holding the breath for a short time, exhale it through both nostrils. -73.

सर्वदा साधयेद्योगी शीतलीकुम्भकं शुभम् ।
अजीर्णं कफपित्तं च नैव तस्य प्रजायते ॥ ७४॥

sarvadā sādhayedyogī śītalīkumbhakaṃ śubham /
ajirṇaṃ kaphapittaṃ ca naiva tasya prajāyate //74//

A yogi should always practice this auspicious *śītalī kumbhaka.* By doing this practice, digestive disorders and *kapha* (phlegm) and *pitta* (bile) disorders do not appear. -74.

Bhastrikā Prāṇāyāma

भस्त्रैव लोहकाराणां यथाक्रमेण सम्भ्रमेत् ।
तथा वायुं च नासाभ्यामुभाभ्यां चालयेच्छनैः ॥ ७५॥

bhastraiva lauhakārāṇāṃ yathākrameṇa sambhramet /
tathā vāyuṃ ca nāsābhyāmubhābhyāṃ cālayecchanaiḥ //75//

Just like the (expanding and contracting) movements of the bellows of a blacksmith, inhale slowly and then exhale slowly through both nostrils. -75.

एवं विंशतिवारं च कृत्वा कुर्याच्च कुम्भकम् ।
तदन्ते चालयेद्वायुं पूर्वोक्तं च यथाविधि ॥ ७६॥
त्रिवारं साधयेदेनं भस्त्रिकाकुम्भकं सुधीः ।
न च रोगो न च क्लेश आरोग्यं च दिने दिने ॥ ७७॥

evam vimśativāraṃ ca kṛtvā kuryācca kumbhakam /
tadante calayedvāyuṃ pūrvoktaṃ ca yathāvidhi //76//
trivāraṃ sādhayedenaṃ bhastrikākumbhakaṃ śudhīḥ //
na ca rogo na ca kleśa arogyaṃ ca dine dine //77//

After repeating it twenty times, hold the breath and then practice this breath movement as per the prescribed method explained above. A wise yogi should practice this *bhastrikā kumbhaka* three rounds. Through its practice, diseases and afflictions do not appear and good health is attained everyday. -76-77.

Bhrāmarī Prāṇāyāma

अर्धरात्रे गते योगी जन्तूनां शब्दवर्जिते ।
कर्णौ पिधाय हस्ताभ्यां कुर्यात्पूरककुम्भकम् ॥ ७८॥

ardharātre gate yogī jantūnāṃ śabdavarjite /
karṇau pidhāya hastābhyāṃ kuryātpurakakumbhakam //78//

After midnight, in a place where there are not any sounds of living beings, a yogi should practice *pūraka* (inhalation) and *kumbhaka* (retention) closing the ears with the hands. -78.

शृणुयाद्दक्षिणे कर्णे नादमन्तर्गतं शुभम् ।
प्रथमं झिञ्झिनादं च वंशीनादं ततः परम ॥ ७९॥
मेघझर्झरभ्रामरी घण्टाकास्यं ततः परम् ।
तुरीभेरीमृदङ्गादि निनादानेकदुन्दुभिः ॥ ८०॥

śṛṇuyāddakṣiṇe karṇe nādamantargataṃ śubham /

prathamaṃ jhiñjhinādaṃ ca vamśinādaṃ tataḥ param //79//
meghajharjharabhrāmarī ghanṭākāsyaṃ tataḥ param /
turībherīmṛdaṅgādi ninādānekadundubhiḥ //80//

He then hears auspicious internal sounds in his right ear. First the sound of a cricket (grasshopper), then the sound of a flute, then the thundering sound of clouds, then the sound of a drum, then of a bee, then of bell, then of big metal gongs, then of a trumpet, a kettle drum, a drum and other kinds of drums. -79-80.

एवं नानाविधो नादो जायते नित्यमभ्यसात् ।
अनाहतस्य शब्दस्य तस्य शब्दस्य यो ध्वनिः ॥ ८१॥
ध्वनेरन्तर्गतं ज्योतिर्ज्योतिरन्तर्गतं मनः ।
तन्मनो विलयं याति तद्विष्णोः परमं पदम् ।
एवं भ्रामरीसंसिद्धिः समाधिसिद्धिमाप्नुयात् ॥ ८२॥

evaṃ nānāvidho nādo jāyate nityamabhyāsāt /
anāhatasya śabdasya tasya śabdasya yo dhvaniḥ //81//
dhvanerantargataṃ jyotirjyotirantargataṃ manaḥ /
tanmano vilayaṃ yāti tadviṣṇoḥ paramaṃ padam /
evaṃ bhrāmarīsamsiddhiḥ samādhisiddhimāpnuyāt //82//

Thus, one hears various sounds through regular practice. The sound that comes from *anāhata* has its resonance. In that resonance there is a light. The mind should be absorbed in that light. When the mind is dissolved into it, one attains the supreme seat of *Viṣṇu*. So by duly perfecting *bhrāmarī kumbhaka*, one achieves *siddhi* (perfection) in *samādhi*. -81.82.

Mūrcchā Prāṇāyāma

सुखेन कुम्भकं कृत्वा मनश्च भ्रुवोरन्तरम् ।
सन्त्यज्य विषयान्सर्वान्मनोमूर्च्छा सुखप्रदा ।
आत्मनि मनसो योगादानन्दो जायते ध्रुवम् ॥ ८३॥

sukhena kumbhakaṃ kṛtvā manaśca bhruvorantaram /
santyajya viṣayānsarvānmanomūrcchā sukhapradā /
ātmani manaso yogādānando jāyate dhruvam //83//

Holding the breath with *kumbhaka* comfortably, withdraw the mind from all sense-objects and fix it in the middle of the eyebrows. This causes *manomūrcchā* (literally, a fainted or an absent state of the mind, a state similar to *Samādhi*) and bestows happiness. By the yoga of joining the mind with the *Ātman*, a blissful state is certainly attained. -83.

Kevalī Prāṇāyāma

हङ्कारेण बहिर्याति सःकारेण विशेत्पुनः ।
षट्शतानि दिवारात्रौ सहस्राण्येकविंशतिः ।
अजपां नाम गायत्रीं जीवो जपति सर्वदा ॥ ८४॥

haṅkāreṇa bahiryāti saḥkāreṇa viśetpunaḥ /
ṣaṭśatāni divārātrau sahasrāṇyekavimśatiḥ /
ajapāṃ nāma gāyatrīṃ jīvo japati sarvadā //84//

A *jīva* (living being) exhales with *ham* sound and inhales with *sa* sound in every breath. There are twenty-one thousand six hundred breaths throughout a day and a night. This (repetition of *haṃsa* or *soham*) is called *Ajapā Gāyatrī*. The *jīva* always repeats it. -84.

मूलाऽऽधारे यथा हंसस्तथा हि हृदि पङ्कजे ।
तथा नासापुटद्वन्द्वे त्रिभिर्हंससमागमः ॥ ८५॥

mūlādhāre yathā haṃsastathā hi hṛdi paṅkaje /
tathā nāsāpuṭadvandve tribhirhaṃsasamāgamaḥ //85//

There are three places of in and out movements of the air (while repeating *haṃsa*). They are *mūlādhāra*, *anāhata*, and *nāsāpuṭa* (the two nostrils) which are the meeting points of *haṃsa*. -85.

षण्णवत्यङ्गुलीमानं शरीरं कर्मरूपकम् ।
देहाद्बहिर्गतो वायुः स्वभावात् द्वादशाङ्गुलिः ॥ ८६॥
गायने षोडशाङ्गुल्यो भोजने विंशतिस्तथा ।
चतुर्विंशाङ्गुलिः पन्थे निद्रायां त्रिंशदङ्गुलि ।
मैथुने षट्त्रिंशदुक्तं व्यायामे च ततोऽधिकम् ॥ ८७॥

ṣaṇṇavatyaṅgulīmānaṃ śarīraṃ karmarūpakam /
dehādvahirgato vāyuḥ svabhāvāt dvādśāṅguliḥ //86//
gāyane ṣoḍaśāṅgulyao bhojane vimśatistathā /

caturvimśāṅguli panthe nidrāyāṃ triśadaṅguliḥ /

maithune ṣaṭtrimśaduktaṃ vyāyāme ca tato'dhikam //87/

The physical body has the length of ninety-six *aṅgulas* (*aṅgula,* a measure of thumb's width) according to one's karma. The length of the out going air is normally twelve *aṅgulas*. During singing it is sixteen *aṅgulas* long. During eating it is twenty *aṅgulas* long. During walking it is twenty-four *aṅgulas* long. During sleep it is thirty *aṅgulas* long. During sexual intercourse it is thirty-six *aṅgulas* long and during physical exercise it is significantly longer than that. -86-87.

स्वभावेऽस्य गतेर्न्यूने परमायुः प्रवर्धते ।

आयुःक्षयोऽधिके प्रोक्तो मारुतेचान्तराद्गते ॥ ८८॥

तस्मात्प्राणे स्थिते देहे मरणं नैव जायते ।

वायुना घटसम्बन्धे भवेत्केवलकुम्भकम् ॥ ८९॥

svabhāve'sya gaternyūne paramāyuḥ pravardhate /

āyuḥkṣayo'dhike prokto mārutecāntarādgate //88//

tasmātprāṇe sthite dehe maraṇaṃ naiva jāyate /

vāyunā ghaṭasambandhe bhavet kevalakumbhakaḥ //89//

When the length of the out going breath is naturally decreased, longevity is increased. It is said that longevity decreases when there is a greater outward flow of *maruta* or *prāṇa*. Therefore, as long as *prāṇa* exists in the body, there is no death. When *prāṇa* is naturally restrained within the body, this is called *kevala kumbhaka*. -88-89.

यावज्जीवं जपेन्मन्त्रम् अजपासङ्ख्यकेवलम् ।

अद्यावधि धृतं सङ्ख्याविभ्रमं केवली कृते ॥ ९०॥

अत एव हि कर्तव्यः केवलीकुम्भको नरैः ।

केवली चाजपासङ्ख्या द्विगुणा च मनोन्मनी ॥ ९१॥

yāvajjīvaṃ japenmantraṃ ajapāsaṅkhyakevalam /

adhyāvadhi dhṛtaṃ saṅkhyāvibhramaṃ kevalī kṛte //90//

ata eva hi kartavyaḥ kevalīkumbhako naraiḥ /

kevalī cājapāsaṅkhyā dviguṇā ca manonmanī //91//

All *jīvas* are normally repeating certain numbers of *ajapā man-*

tra daily. As long as body exists, one should continue repeating *ajapā mantra* with counts while performing *kevalī kumbhaka*. When *kevalī* is done or twenty-one thousands six hundred repetitions are completed, the rate of respiration decreases and longevity increases. When the number of repetitions of *ajapā mantra* is doubled, there remains *kevalī* alone and a blissful state is achieved. Therefore, it is certainly a task of yogis to practice *kevalī kumbhaka*. -90-91.

नासाभ्यां वायुमाकृष्य केवलं कुम्भकं चरेत् ।
एकादिकचतुः षष्टिं धारयेत् प्रथमे दिने ॥ ९२॥

nāsābhyāṃ vāyumākṛṣya kevalaṃ kumbhakaṃ caret /
ekādikacatuḥ ṣaṣṭiṃ dhārayet prathame dine //92//

Inhaling air through both nostrils, naturally hold the breath by *kevalī kumbhaka*. Hold the breath (by this *kumbhaka*) from one to sixty-four times on the first day. -92.

केवलीमष्टधा कुर्याद्यामे यामे दिने दिने ।
अथवा पञ्चधा कुर्याद्यथा तत्कथयामि ते ॥ ९३॥
प्रातर्मध्याह्नसायाह्ने मध्ये रात्रिचतुर्थके ।
त्रिसन्ध्यमथवा कुर्यात्सममाने दिने दिने ॥ ९४॥

kevalīmaṣṭadhā kuryādyāme yāme dine dine /
athavā pañcadhā kuryādyathā tat kathayāmi te //93//
prātarmadhyāhnasāyāhne madhye rātricaturthake /
trisandhyamathavā kuryātsamamāne dine dine //94//

Kevalī kumbhaka should be practiced eight times, once every three hours a day or it should be practiced five times a day, as I explain: - in early morning, at noon, in twilight, at midnight and in the fourth quarter of the night. Or it should be practiced in *samamāna* (equal duration/length of time) three times a day at the *trisandhyās* (the three times of transitions or sunrise, noon and sunset). -93-94.

पञ्चवारं दिने वृद्धिर्वारैकं च दिने तथा ।
अजपापरिमाणं च यावत्सिद्धिः प्रजायते ॥ ९५॥
प्राणायामं केवलीं च तदा वदति योगवित् ।
केवलीकुम्भके सिद्धे किं न सिध्यति भूतले ॥ ९६॥

pañcavāraṃ dine vṛddhirvāraikaṃ ca dine tathā /
ajapāparimāṇaṃ ca yāvat siddhiḥ prājayate //95//
prāṇāyāmaṃ kevalīṃ ca tadā vadati yogavit /
kevalīkumbhake siddhe kiṃ na sidhyati bhūtale //96//

One should go on increasing the period/length of *ajapā japa* practice five times every day until the result of perfection is not achieved. One who knows *prāṇāyāma* and *kevalī* is called the knower of yoga. One who has gained mastery over *kevalī kumbhaka*, what cannot he achieve in this earth? -96.

इति श्रीघेरण्डसंहितायां घेरण्डचण्डसंवादे
प्राणायामप्रयोगो नाम पञ्चमोपदेशः ॥

iti śrīgheraṇḍasamhitāyāṃ gheraṇḍacaṇḍasamvāde
prāṇāyāmaprayogo nāma pañcamopadeśaḥ /

Thus ends the Fifth Chapter of *Gheraṇḍa Samhitā* entitled *Prāṇāyāma* Practice.

CHAPTER SIX

Discourse On Dhyāna

घेरण्ड उवाच ।
स्थूलं ज्योतिस्तथा सूक्ष्मं ध्यानस्य त्रिविधं विदुः ।
स्थूलं मूर्तिगयं प्रोक्तं ज्योतिस्तोजोमयं तथा ।
सूक्ष्मं बिन्दुमयं ब्रह्म कुण्डलीपरदेवता ॥ १॥

gheraṇḍa uvāca /
sthūlaṃ jyotistathā sūkṣmam dhyānasya trividhaṃ viduḥ /
sthūlaṃ mūrtimayaṃ proktaṃ jyotistejomayaṃ tathā /
sūkṣmaṃ vindumayaṃ brahma kuṇḍalī paradevatā //1//

Sage *Gheraṇḍa* said: - *Sthūla* (gross), *jyoti* (light) and *sūkṣma* (subtle) are known three types of *dhyāna* (meditation). It is called *Sthūla dhyāna* (gross meditation) when one meditates on the physical form (of a guru, *devatā* or deity). It is *jyoti dhyāna* (meditation on light) when one meditates on the radiant form of *Brahma*, full of light. It is *sūkṣma dhyāna* (subtle meditation) when one meditates on *Brahma* in the form of *bindu* and *kuṇḍalī śakti*, the divine power. -1.

Sthūla Dhyāna

स्वकीयहृदये ध्यायेत्सुधासागरमुत्तमम् ।
तन्मध्ये रत्नद्वीपं तु सुरत्नवालुकामयम् ॥ २॥
चतुर्दिक्षु नीपतरुं बहुपुष्पसमन्वितम् ।
नीपोपवनसङ्कुलैर्वेष्टितं परिखा इव ॥ ३॥
मालतीमाल्लिकाजातीकेसरैश्चम्पकैस्तथा ।
पारिजातैः स्थलपद्मैर्गन्धामोदितदिङ्मुखैः ॥ ४॥

svakīyahṛdaye dhyāyet sudhāsāgaramuttamam /

tanmadhye ratnadvīpaṃ tu suratnavālukāmayam //2//
caturdikṣu nīpataruṃ bahupuṣpasamanvitam /
nipopavanasaṅkulairveṣṭitaṃ parikhā iva //3//
mālatīmallikājātikeśaraiścampakaistathā /
pārijātaiḥ sthalapadmairgandhāmoditadiṅmukhaiḥ //4//

Contemplate a magnificent ocean of nectar in the heart. In the middle of it, there is an island of precious jewels and the sand is made of the dust of diamonds and jewels. On all four sides *nīpataru* (a kind of tree, its flowers and fruits) trees are laden with many flowers. On the island these trees are surrounded like ditches by many varieties of flowering trees like *mālatī, mallikā, jāti, keśara, campaka, pārijāta* and *padma* (these are name of flowers), and their fragrance spreads every direction all over the island. -2-4.

तन्मध्ये संस्मरेद्योगी कल्पवृक्षं मनोहरम् ।
चतुःशाखाचतुर्वेदं नित्यपुष्पफलान्वितम् ॥ ५॥
भ्रमराः कोकिलास्तत्र गुञ्जन्ति निगदन्ति च ।
ध्यायेत्तत्र स्थिरो भूत्वा महामाणिक्यमण्डपम् ॥ ६॥
तन्मध्ये तु स्मरेद्योगी पर्यङ्कं सुमनोहरम् ।
तत्रेष्टदेवतां ध्यायेद्यद्ध्यानं गुरुभाषितम् ॥ ७॥
यस्य देवस्य यद्रूपं यथा भूषणवाहनम् ।
तद्रूपं ध्यायते नित्यं स्थूलध्यानमिदं विदुः ॥ ८॥

tanmadhyesamsmaredyogī kalpavṛkṣaṃ manoharam /
catuhśākhācaturvedaṃ nityapuṣpaphalānvitam //5//
bhramarāḥ kokilāstatra guñjanti nigadanti ca /
dhyāyettatra sthiro bhūtvā mahāmāṇikyamaṇḍapam //6//
tanmadhye tu smaredyogī paryaṅkaṃ sumanoharam /
tatreṣṭadevatāṃ dhyāyet yatdhyānaṃ gurubhāṣitam //7//
yasya devasya yadrūpaṃ yathā bhūṣaṇavāhanam /
tadrūpaṃ dhyāyate nityaṃ sthuladhyānamidaṃ viduḥ //8//

A yogi should contemplate that in the middle of this island there is a beautiful *kalpa vṛkṣa* (wish fulfilling tree). The four branches of this tree represent the four *Vedas.* It is always laden with flowers and fruits. Wild bees make humming sounds and cuckoos sing with melodious voice there. There is a great pavilion made of precious gems and a throne decorated with jewels. On this throne contemplate the *deva* (deity) as per the teaching of the guru and always meditate on the form, jewelry and vehicle of the deity. This is called *sthula dhyāna*. -5-8.

Another Method

सहस्रारे महापद्मे कर्णिकायां विचिन्तयेत् ।
विलग्नसहितं पद्मं द्वादशैर्दलसंयुतम् ॥ ९॥
शुक्लवर्णं महातेजो द्वादशैर्बीजभाषितम् ।
हसक्षमलवरयुं हसखफ्रें यथाक्रमम् ॥ १०॥
तन्मध्ये कर्णिकायां तु अकथादिरेखात्रयम् ।
हलक्षकोणसंयुक्तं प्रणवं तत्र वर्तते ॥ ११॥

sahasrāre mahāpadme karṇikayaṃ vicintayet /
vilagnasahitaṃ padmaṃ dalairdvādaśabhiryutam //9//
śuklavarṇaṃ mahātejo dvādaśairbījabhāṣitam /
hasakṣamalavarayuṃ hasakhapreṃ yathākramam //10//
tanmadhye karṇikāyāṃ tu akathādi rekhātrayam /
halakṣakoṇasamyuktaṃ praṇavaṃ tatra vartate //11//

Imagine that in the region of *sahasrāra* there is a great lotus with a thousand petals and in its center there is a small lotus with twelve petals. Its petals are white and full of radiance with the twelve shining *bīja mantras* located on them: *ha, sa, ksa, ma, la, va, ra, yum, ha, sa, kha* and *phrem*. In the center of this small lotus there are three lines *a, ka* and *tha* forming a triangle. This triangle has three angles with their symbols *ha, la* and *kṣa*. The *praṇava* (OM) is situated in the middle of this triangle. -9-11.

नादबिन्दुमयं पीठं ध्यायेत्तत्र मनोहरम् ।
तत्रोपरि हंसयुग्मं पादुका तत्र वर्तते ॥ १२॥

nādavindumayaṃ pīṭhaṃ dhyāyettatra manoharam /
tatropari haṃsayugmaṃ pādukā tatra vartate //12//

Contemplate that in that thousand petalled lotus there is a beautiful seat with *nāda* (sound) and *bindu* (light). There are two swans (as symbol of *nāda* and *bindu*) and a pair of sandals on it (as symbol of the guru). -12.

ध्यायेत्तत्र गुरुं देवं द्विभुजं च त्रिलोचनम् ।
श्वेताम्बरधरं देवं शुक्लगन्धानुलेपनम् ॥ १३॥
शुक्लपुष्पमयं माल्यं रक्तशक्तिसमन्वितम् ।
एवंविधगुरुध्यानात्स्थूलध्यानं प्रसिध्यति ॥ १४॥

dhyāyettatra guruṃ devaṃ dvibhujaṃ ca trilocanam /
svetāmbaradharaṃ devaṃ śuklagandhānulepanam //13//
śuklapuṣpamayaṃ mālyaṃ raktaśaktisamanvitam /
evamvidhagurudhyānāt sthūladhyānaṃ prasidhyati //14//

Now contemplate on the guru *deva*, having two arms and three eyes, wearing white clothes, a garland of whilte flowers and anointed with aromatic white sandalwood paste. On his left side there is his *śakti* in red color. By meditating on the guru in this way, perfection is attained in *sthūla dhyāna.* -13-14.

Jyoti Dhyāna

घेरण्ड उवाच ।
कथितं स्थूलध्यानं तु तेजोध्यानं श्रृणुष्व मे ।
यद्ध्यानेन योगसिद्धिरात्मप्रत्यक्षमेव च ॥ १५॥

gheraṇḍa uvāca /
kathitaṃ sthūla dhyānaṃ tu tejodhyānaṃ śṛuṇuṣva me /
yaddhyānena yogasiddhirātmapratyakṣameva ca //15//

Sage *Gheraṇḍa* said: - I have described you *sthūla dhyāna.* Now listen to *tejodhyāna* (the meditation on light). By this meditation one attains *yogasiddhi* (perfection in yoga) and gains a direct knowledge of the Self. -15.

मूलाधारे कुण्डलिनी भुजङ्गाकाररूपिणी ।
तत्र तिष्ठति जीवात्मा प्रदीपकलिकाकृतिः ।
ध्यायेत्तेजोमयं ब्रह्म तेजोध्यानं परात्परम् ॥ १६॥

mūlādhāre kuṇḍalinī bhujaṅgākārarūpiṇīḥ /
tatra tiṣṭhati jīvātmā pradīpakalikākṛti /
dhyāyettejomayaṃ brahma tejodhyānaṃ parātparam //16//

Kuṇḍalinī rests in *mūlādhāra* in the form of a serpent. *Jīvātmā* (the embodied Self) remains there like the flame of a lamp.

Meditate on the luminous *Brahma* there. This is the supreme *tejodhyāna* or *jyoti dhyāna* (meditation on light).-16.

भ्रुवोर्मध्ये मनोर्ध्वे च यत्तेजः प्रणवात्मकम् ।
ध्यायेत् ज्वालावलीयुक्तं तेजोध्यानं तदेव हि ॥ १७॥

bhruvormadhye manordve yattejaḥ praṇavātmakam /
dhyāyet jvālāvalīyuktaṃ tejodhyānaṃ tadeva hi //17//

Between the eyebrows, above the area of *manas* (the mind) there is light in the form of *praṇava* (OM). Meditate on this flaming light. This is verily called *tejodhyāna*. -17.

Sūkṣma Dhyāna

घेरण्ड उवाच ।
तेजोध्यानं श्रृतं चण्ड सूक्ष्मध्यानं श्रृणुष्व मे ।
बहुभाग्यवशाद्यस्य कुण्डली जाग्रती भवेत् ॥ १८॥
आत्मना सह योगेन नेत्ररन्ध्राद्विनिर्गता ।
विहरेद्राजमार्गे च चञ्चलत्वान्न दृश्यते ॥ १९॥

gheraṇḍa uvāca /
tejodhyānaṃ śrutaṃ caṇḍa sūkṣmadhyānaṃ śṛuṇuṣva me /
bahubhāgyavaśādyasya kuṇḍalī jāgrati bhavet //18//
ātmanā saha yogena netrarandhrādvinirgatā /
viharedrājamārge ca cañcalatvānna dṛśyate //19//

Sage *Gheraṇḍa* said: O *Caṇḍa*, you have heard the *tejodhyāna*, now listen to *sūkṣma dhyāna* (subtle meditation). One whose *kuṇḍalinī śhakti* is awakened by the power of great fortune, it unites with *Ātmā* and goes upward through *netra randhra* (the holes/openings of the eyes) and roams on the *rajamārga* (high way). It is not visible because of its (subtle) restlessness. 18-19.

शाम्भवीमुद्रया योगी ध्यानयोगेन सिध्यति ।
सूक्ष्मध्यानमिदं गोप्यं देवानामपि दुर्लभम् ॥ २०॥

śāmbhavīmudrayā yogī dhyānayogena sidhyati /
sūkṣmadhyānamidaṃ gopyaṃ devānāpi durlabham //20//

A yogi attains *siddhi* (perfection) through the practice of *śāmbhavī mudrā* and *dhyāna yoga* (meditation on *kuṇḍalinī śhakti*). This is called *sūkṣma dhyāna* which is secret. It is difficult to obtain even by gods. -20.

स्थूलध्यानाच्छतगुणं तेजोध्यानं प्रचक्षते ।
तेजोध्यानाल्लक्षगुणं सूक्ष्मध्यानं परात्परम् ॥ २१॥

sthūladhyānācchataguṇaṃ tejodhyānaṃ pracakṣate /
tejodhyānāllakṣaguṇaṃ sūkṣmadhyānaṃ parātparam //21//

Tejodhyāna (meditation on light) is a hundred times superior to *sthūla dhyāna* (meditation on form) and *sūkṣma dhyāna* (subtle meditation) is a hundred thousand times superior to *tejodhyānā*. -21.

इति ते कथितं चण्ड ध्यानयोगं सुदुर्लभम् ।
आत्मा साक्षात् भवेद्यस्मात्तस्माद्ध्यानं विशिष्यते ॥ २३॥

iti te kathitaṃ caṇḍa dhyānayogaṃ sudurlabham /
ātmasākṣād bhaved yasmāttasmāddhyānaṃ viśiṣyate //22//

O *Caṇḍa*! Thus, I have told you the *dhyānayoga* which is extremely difficult to obtain. Knowledge of the Self becomes direct by its practice. Therefore, this *dhyānayoga* is uniquely admired. -22.

इति श्रीघेरण्डसंहितायां घेरण्डचण्डसंवादे
ध्यानयोगो नाम षष्ठोपदेशः ॥

iti śrīgheraṇḍasamhitāyāṃ gheraṇḍacaṇḍasamvāde
dhyānayogo nāma ṣaṣṭhopadeśaḥ /

Thus ends the Sixth Chapter of *Gheraṇḍa Samhitā*
entitled Dhyānayoga.

CHAPTER SEVEN

Discourse On Samādhi

घेरण्ड उवाच ।
समाधिश्च परो योगो बहुभाग्येन लभ्यते ।
गुरोः कृपाप्रसादेन प्राप्यते गुरुभक्तितः ॥ १॥

gheraṇḍa uvāca /
samādhiśca paro yogo bahubhāgyena labhyate /
guroḥ kṛpāprasādena prāpyate gurubhaktitaḥ //1//

Sage *Gheraṇḍa* said: - *Samādhi* is the supreme yoga and is attained by great fortunate. It is received through the compassion and grace of the gurus by earnest devotion to them. -1.

विद्याप्रतीतिः स्वगुरुप्रतीतिः
रात्मप्रतीतिर्मनसः प्रबोधः ।
दिने दिने यस्य भवेत्स योगी
सुशोभनाभ्यासमुपैति सद्यः ॥ २॥

vidyāpratītiḥ svagurupratītiḥ
ātmapratītirmanasaḥ prabodhaḥ /
dine dine yasya bhavetsa yogī
suśobhanābhyāsamupaiti sadyaḥ //2//

The yogi is quickly endowed with this auspicious practice of *Samādhi* who has the insight of knowledge, has faith in his guru, has faith in his Self and has an awakening mind everyday. -2.

घटाद्भिन्नं मनः कृत्वा ऐक्यं कुर्यात्परात्मनि ।
समाधिं तं विजानीयात् मुक्तसंज्ञो दशादिभिः ॥ ३॥

ghaṭādbhinnaṃ manaḥ kṛtvā
aikyaṃ kuryātparamātmani /

samādhiṃ taṃ vijānīyān
muktasañjñyo daśādibhi //3//

A yogi should separate his mind from the body and unite it with *paramātmā* (the Supreme Soul). This should be known as *Samādhi*, a free state of consciousness from all conditions. -3.

अहं ब्रह्म न चान्योऽस्मि ब्रह्मैवाहं न शोकभाक् ।
सच्चिदानन्दरूपोऽहं नित्यमुक्तः स्वभाववान् ॥ ४॥

ahaṃ brahma na cānyo'smi
brahmaivāhaṃ na śokabhāk /
saccidānandarūpo'haṃ
nityamuktaḥ svabhāvavān //4//

I am *Brahma*. I am not anything else. I am *Brahma* alone. I am not the possessor of sorrow. I am the form of *Sat, Cit* and *Ānanda* (*Saccidānanda* – Truth-Consciousness-Bliss). I am ever free and exist in my own nature. -4.

शाम्भव्या चैव भ्रामर्या खेचर्या योनिमुद्रया ।
ध्यानं नादं रसानन्दं लयसिद्धिश्चतुर्विधा ॥ ५॥
पञ्चधा भक्तियोगेन मनोमूर्च्छा च षड्विधा ।
षड्विधोऽयं राजयोगः प्रत्येकमवधारयेत् ॥ ६॥

śambhavyā caiva bhrāmaryā khecaryā yonimudrayā /
dhyānaṃ nādaṃ rasānandaṃ layasiddhiścaturvidhā //5//
pañcadhā bhaktiyogena manomūrcchā ca ṣaḍvidhā /
ṣaḍvidho'yaṃ rājayogaḥ pratyekamavadhārayet //6//

The four types of *samādhi: dhyāna, nāda, rasānanda* and *laya* are accomplished by *śambhavī, khecari, bhrāmari* and *yoni mudrās. Bhaktiyoga* (yoga of devotion) *samādhi* is the fifth and *manomūrcchā samādhi* is the sixth. These are the six types of *samādhis* in *Rajayoga.* On should practice each of them in order. -5-6.

Dhyānayoga Samādhi

शाम्भवीं मुद्रिकाः कृत्वा आत्मप्रत्यक्षमानयेत् ।
बिन्दु ब्रह्ममयं दृष्ट्वा मनस्तत्र नियोजयेत् ॥ ७॥

śāmbhavīṃ mudrikāḥ kṛtvā ātmapratyakṣamānayet /

bindubrahmamayaṃ dṛṣṭvā manastatra niyojayet //7//

Assuming *śāmbhavī mudrā*, perceive the Self. Having seen the *bindu* in the form of *Brahma*, concentrate the mind there. -7.

खमध्ये कुरु चात्मानमात्ममध्ये च खं कुरु ।
आत्मानं खमयं दृष्ट्वा न किञ्चिदपि बुध्यते ।
सदानन्दमयो भूत्वा समाधिस्थो भवेन्नरः ॥ ८॥

khamadhye kurucātmānamātmamadhye ca khaṃ kuru /
ātmānaṃ khamayaṃ dṛtvā na kiñcidapi budhyate /
sadānandamayo bhūtvā samādhistho bhavennaraḥ //8//

Dissolve the Self in the eternal space and the space in the Self. Perceiving the *Ātmā* full of space or *Brahma,* nothing else is seen (except *Brahma*). Being ever full of bliss, a person is established in *samādhi.* -8.

Nādayoga Samādhi

अनिलं मन्दवेगेन भ्रामरीकुम्भकं चरेत् ।
मन्दं मन्दं रेचयेद्वायुं भृङ्गनादं ततो भवेत् ॥ ९॥
अन्तःस्थं भ्रमरीनादं श्रुत्वा तत्र मनो नयेत् ।
समाधिर्जायते तत्र आनन्दः सोऽहमित्यतः ॥ १०॥

anilaṃ mandavegena bhrāmarīkumbhakaṃ caret /
mandaṃ mandaṃ recayedvāyuṃ bhṛṅganādaṃ tato bhavet //9//
antaḥsthaṃ bhramarīnādaṃ śrutvā tatra mano nayet /
samādhirjāyate tatra cānandaḥ so'hamityataḥ //10//

Inhaling the air in a slow speed, perform *bhrāmarī kumbhaka.* Exhale the air slowly and slowly. This slow exhalation creates a sound of a wild bee. Listening to this internal sound of *bhramara* (the wild bee), focus the mind there. By this, a *samādhi* with a blissful state occurs there with the knowledge of 'I am That'. -9-10.

Rasanānanda Samādhi

खेचरीमुद्रासाधनात् रसनोर्ध्वगता यदा ।
तदा समाधिसिद्धिः स्याद्धित्वा साधारणक्रियाम् ॥ ११॥

khecarimudrāsādhanāt rasanordvagatā yadā /

tadā samādhisiddhiḥ syāddhitvā sadhāraṇakriyām //11//

When the tongue is turned upward through the perfection of *khecari mudrā*, then by this simple yogic practice one attains *siddhi* in *samādhi*. -11.

Layasiddhi Samādhi

योनिमुद्रां समासाद्य स्वयं शक्तिमयो भवेत् ।
सुश्रृङ्गाररसेनैव विहरेत्परमात्मनि ॥ १२॥
आनन्दमयः सम्भूत्वा ऐक्यं ब्रह्मणि सम्भवेत् ।
अहं ब्रह्मेति चाद्वैतसमाधिस्तेन जायते ॥ १३॥

yonimudrāṃ samāsadya svayaṃ śaktimayo bhavet /
suśṛṅgārarasenaiva viharetparamātmani //12//
ānandamayaḥ sambhūtvā ekyaṃ brahmaṇi sambhavet /
ahaṃ brahmeti cādvaitasamādhistena jāyate //13//

After properly perfecting *yoni mudrā*, a yogi should imagine that he himself is full of *Śakti* and *Paramātmā*. Then again feel that in him and in *Paramātmā* (the Supreme Soul) *Śakti* and *Puruṣa* are roaming joyfully. After being established in a blissful oneness, he becomes united with *Brahma* and declares that 'I am *Brahma*'. This is called *advaita* (non-dual) *samādhi* or *laya siddhi samādhi*. -12-13

Bhaktiyoga Samādhi

स्वकीयहृदये ध्यायेदिष्टदेव स्वरूपकम् ।
चिन्तयेद्भक्तियोगेन परमाह्लादपूर्वकम् ॥ १४॥
आनन्दाश्रुपुलकेन दशाभावः प्रजायते ।
समाधिः सम्भवेत्तेन सम्भवेच्च मनोन्मनी ॥ १५॥

svakīyahṛdaye dhyāyediṣṭadeva svarūpakam /
cintayedbhaktiyogena paramāhlādapūrvakam //14//
ānandāśrupulakena daśābhāvaḥ prajāyate /
samādhiḥ sambhavettena sambhavecca manonmanī //15//

Imagine the form of *iṣṭadeva* (the favorable god) in the heart and meditate on it with supreme joy and highest devotion. This brings a state of bliss with tears and a sign of rapture (with erection of hairs) in the body. This gives rise to *samādhi* and *manon-*

manī (a state similar to *samādhi*). -14-15.

Manomūrcchā Samādhi

मनोमूर्च्छां समासाद्य मन आत्मनि योजयेत् ।
परात्मनः समायोगात्समाधिं समवाप्नुयात् ॥ १६॥

manomūrcchāṃ samāsādya mana ātmani yojayet /
paramātmanaḥ samāyogātsamādhiṃ samavāpnuyāt //16//

After perfecting *manomūrcchā kumbhaka*, one should meditate on *Ātmā*. By means of this, union with the *Paramātmā* is attained in *samādhi*. -16.

Greatness of Samādhi Yoga

इति ते कथितं चण्ड समाधिर्मुक्तिलक्षणम् ।
राजयोगः समाधिः स्यादेकात्मन्येव साधनम् ।
उन्मनी सहजावस्था सर्वे चैकात्मवाचकाः ॥ १७॥

iti te kathitaṃ caṇḍa samādhirmuktilakṣaṇam /
rājayogasamādhiḥ syādekātmanyeva sādhanam /
unmanī sahajāvasthā sarvecaikātmavācakā //17//

O *Caṇḍa*! I have explained you *samādhi* as a sign of *mukti* (liberation). This *Rājayoga samādhi* is one of the means of self-realization. *Unmanī* and *sahaja avasthā* are the same states of *samādhi* like *Rājayoga samādhi* with regard to the achievement of union with *Ātmā* (the Self). So, they are all synonymous. -17.

जले विष्णुः स्थले विष्णुर्विष्णुः पर्वतमस्तके ।
ज्वालामालाकुले विष्णुः सर्वं विष्णुमयं जगत् ॥ १८॥

jale viṣṇuḥ sthale viṣṇurviṣṇuḥ parvatamastake /
jvālāmālākule viṣṇuḥ sarva viṣṇumayaṃ jagat //18//

Lord *Viṣṇu* is in the water, Lord *Viṣṇu* is on land, Lord *Viṣṇu* is on the top of mountain, and Lord *Viṣṇu* is in the flames of fire. So, this whole universe is composed of Lord *Viṣṇu*. -18.

भूचराः खेचराश्चामी यावन्तो जीवजन्तवः ।
वृक्षगुल्मलतावल्लीतृणाद्या वारिपर्वताः ।
सर्वं ब्रह्म विजानीयात्सर्वं पश्यति चात्मनि ॥ १९॥

bhūcarāḥ khecarāścāmī yāvanto jīvajantavaḥ /
vṛkṣagulmalatāvallītṛṇādyāḥ vāri parvatāḥ /

sarvaṃ brahma vijānīyātsarvaṃ paśyati cātmani //19//

All living creatures on earth, in air, trees, bushes, creepers, grass, oceans, mountains should be known as *Brahma*. One should see all in *Ātmā* (the Self) and *Ātmā* (the Self) in all. -19.

आत्मा घटस्थचैतन्यमद्वैतं शाश्वतं परम् ।
घटाद्विभिन्नतो ज्ञात्वा वीतरागं विवासनम् ॥ २०॥

ātmā ghaṭasthacaitanyamadvaitaṃ śāśvataṃ param /
gaṭādvibhinnato jñātvā vītarāgaṃ vivāsanam //20//

One should consider that *Caitanya* (the Conscious Self) based in the body is non-dual (without a second), eternal and supreme. Knowing that *Ātmā* (the Self) or *Caitanya* (the Conscious Self) is separate from the body, one should be detached from worldly attachments and passions. -20.

एवं मिथः समाधिः स्यात्सर्वसङ्कल्पवर्जितः ।
स्वदेहे पुत्रदारादिबान्धवेषु धनादिषु ।
सर्वेषु निर्ममो भूत्वा समाधिं समवाप्नुयात् ॥ २१॥

evaṃ mithaḥ samādhiḥ syātsarvasaṅkalpavarjitaḥ /
svadehe putradārādibāndhaveṣu dhanādiṣu /
sarveṣu nirmamo bhūtvā samādhi samavāpnuyāt //21//

Thus, *samādhi* should be attained departing from all desires and attachments of the body, son, spouse, relatives, wealth and treasure, etc. Keeping the mind free from all worldly desires, try to achieve *samādhi*. -21.

तत्त्वं लयामृतं गोप्यं शिवोक्तं विविधानि च ।
तेषां सङ्क्षेपमादाय कथितं मुक्तिलक्षणम् ॥ २२॥

tattvaṃ layāmṛtaṃ gopyaṃ śivoktaṃ vividhāni ca /
teṣāṃ saṅkṣepamādāya kathitaṃ muktilakṣaṇam /22//

A variety of this secret *Laya Amṛta Tattva* (essence of absorption in nectar) has been expounded by Lord *Śiva*. I have explained you briefly with regard to it as a sign of liberation. -22.

इति ते कथितं चण्ड समाधि दुर्लभः परः ।
यं ज्ञात्वा न पुनर्जन्म जायते भूमि मण्डले ॥ २३॥

iti te kathitaṃ caṇḍa samādhi durlabhaḥ paraḥ /

yaṃ jñātvā na punarjanma jāyate bhūmi maṇḍale //23//

O *Caṇḍa*! Thus I have told you about *samādhi* which is supreme and difficult to attain. By knowing this, one is not born again in this terrestrial world. -23.

इति श्रीघेरण्डसंहितायां घेरण्डचण्डसंवादे
समाधियोगो नाम सप्तमोपदेशः समाप्तः ॥

iti śrīgheraṇḍasamhitāyāṃ gheraṇḍacaṇḍasaṃvāde
samādhiyogo nāma saptamopadeśaḥ /

Thus ends the Seventh Chapter of *Gheraṇḍa Samhitā* entitled *Samādhi Yoga.*

GORAKSHA SAMHITA

Also Known As

Goraksha Paddhati

गोरक्षसंहिता

Book Two

English Translation Accompanied by Sanskrit Text in Roman Transliteration

Translated into English by
Swami Vishnuswaroop

Published by
Divine Yoga Institute
Kathmandu, Nepal

INTRODUCTION

Gorakśa Samhitā is composed by the great *Yogī Gorakśanātha*. Renowned spiritual masters in the East have highly acknowledged and honored him as a *Siddha Yogī* for many centuries. His name is mentioned by *Svāmi Svātmārāma* in his classical text *Hatha Yoga Pradipikā* (Chapter One, Verses 4 and 5). He is also one of the Masters mentioned in the *Purānas* and yogic texts. He is well known as Guru *Gorakhanātha*, and a highly respected, revered and worshipped spiritual master in India and Nepal. The followers of the *Nātha* Tradition worship him as the incarnation of Lord *Śiva*, and say that the nine *Nāthas* and eighty-four *Siddhas* belong to *Adinātha*, Lord *Śiva*. So, he is also called *Śiva Gorakśa*, the founder of the *Natha Siddha* tradition.

It is said that *Gorakśanātha* was an Eighth Century *Siddha Yogī*. But some say that his physical presence occurred somewhere from the 8th to 11th century. According to the *Natha Siddha* tradition, Guru *Gorakhnātha* is an immortal sage and takes care of human beings and their welfare.

Gorkha, a historic district of Nepal, was named after *Gorakhanātha*, and its inhabitants were called Gorkhāli according to the legend. There is a cave of Guru *Gorakhnātha* which lies next to the famous *Gorakhakāli* Temple. Like Gorkha, the district of Gorakhapur in North Bihar of India, was also named after him. There is also a famous temple of *Gorakhanātha* in Gorakhapur.

It is said that *Hatha Yogī Mastsyendranāth* was the Guru of *Gorakśanatha*. *Yogı Mastsyendranāth* received Yoga *Vidyā* (knowledge/wisdom) directly from the mouth of Lord *Śiva* through *Parvati*. It was Guru *Gorakśanātha* who summarized the yogic subject matter in two hundred verses, which he had received from his Guru *Mastsyendranāth*, based on the teachings of *Śri Ādinātha* (Lord *Śiva*). This summarized text by *Gorakśanātha* is called *Gorakśa Samhitā* (compendium) which is also known as *Gorakśa Paddhati*: *Yogic* Path of *Guru Gorakhanātha*.

Gorakśa Samhitā highly emphasizes the purification of the body, *prāna* and the mind. It is believed that total purification of all impurities on both the physical and *prānic* levels is absolutely necessary in order to purify the mind. When these impurities are eliminated from the body and the energy blocks are removed, then the foundation for the awakening of the *Śakti* is prepared.

Therefore, *Guru Gorakhanātha* in *Gorakśa Samhitā* clearly outlines the various aspects of the *Hatha Yoga* practices e.g. *āsana*, *prānāyāma*, *mudrā*, *bandha* and *dhyāna*, etc., which serve as a solid foundation for the preparation and practice of *Raja Yoga*. Originally, the science of *Hatha Yoga* was discovered for the expansion and evolution of human consciousness, and for the accomplishment of the ultimate goal of human life, *mokśa* (liberation) through *samādhi* (the super conscious state).

According to *Gorakśa Samhitā*, the objective of *Hatha Yoga* is to create a harmonious balance between the physical body, *prāna* (the vital energy) and the mind. It is said that when the impulses generated by this harmonious balance stimulate the awakening of the *Kuṇḍalī Śakti*, only then is the evolution of consciousness or union between *Śiva* and *Śakti* possible. This accomplishment is the sole objective of the teaching of *Gorakśa Samhitā* by *Guru Gorakśanātha*.

It should be noted that the original Sanskrit Text is in Devanagari along with its Roman transliteration. All the Sanskrit words/phrases that appear in the English translation are given in the transliterated Roman alphabets.

It is hoped that this compilation will be helpful to all yoga lovers, yoga *sādhakas*, yoga teachers and yoga professionals to understand the traditional yoga, its objective and practice for the human welfare.

Publisher

CHAPTER TOPICS

Pūrva Śatakam

Part One

Salutation to Guru - Objective of Gorakṣa Samhitā - Taking Refuge in Yoga - Description of Āsanas: Siddhāsana, Padmāsana - Six Limbs of Yoga - Bodily Organs to Be Known -Description of Six Cakras - The Supreme Light - Description of Ten Nādis - Other Various Nādis - The Ten Vāyus - Need of Prānāpāna Practice - Haṃsa Mantra and Ajapā Gāyatri Awakening of Kuṇḍalī Śakti - Śakticālini Mudrā - Daily Routine of a Yogī - Description of Mudrās: Mahāmudrā, Results of Mahāmudrā - Khecari Mudrā, Results of Khecari Mudrā - Making the Bindu Stable in Its Place - Supreme State: Unity of Bindu and Raja - Harmony of the Sun and the Moon - Descriptions of Bandhas: Uḍḍīyāna Bandha, Jālandhara Bandha, Mūlabandha - Practice of Praṇava - Practice of Breath Control - Haṃsa: Form of Prānāpāna Vāyu - Nādi Śodhana Prānāyāma - Iḍa and Piṅgalā Prānāyāma - The Results of Nādi Śodhana

Pūrva Śatakam

Part Two

Description of Prānāyāma - Three Types of Prānāyāma, Methods of Prānāyāma, Kumbhaka Prānāyāma, Results of Prānāyāma - The Nature of Samādhi   The Signs of Yogasiddhi - Destruction of Diseases by Prānāyāma - Description of Pratyāhāra - Three Divisions of the Day - Pratyāhāra of Likes and Dislikes - Pratyāhāra of the Nectar - Various Types of Pratyāhāra - Pratyāhāra Through Hatha Yoga - Viparītakaraṇi Mudrā - Anāhata Cakra - Kāki Mudrā - Viśuddha Cakra - Depriving the Mouth of the Sun - Drinking of the Lunar Nectar - Experience of the Nectar Juice - Description of Dhāraṇā: Dhāraṇā on Earth Element, Dhāraṇā on Water Element, Dhāraṇā on Fire Element, Dhāraṇā on Air Element, Dhāraṇā on Ether Element - Description of Dhyāna - Elimination of Sins Through Dhyāna - Achievement of Strength Through Dhyāna - Immortality Through Atmā Dhyāna

- Attainment of Liberation through Dhyāna - Attainment of Siddhis Through Dhyāna - Kundalini: Union with Śiva - Supremacy of Dhyāna Yoga - Description of Samādhi - Distinction between Dhyāna and Samādhi - Instances Relating to Samādhi - Absence of Objective World in Samādhi - Attainment of Beatific State through Yoga - Fulfillment of Ultimate Goal by Yoga Śāstra

PŪRVA ŚATAKAM

Part One

Salutation to Guru

श्रीगुरुं परमानन्दं वन्दे स्वानन्दविग्रहम् ।
यस्य संनिध्यमात्रेण चिदानन्दायते तनुः ।।१।।

śrīgurum paramānandam vande svānandavigraham /
yasya sannidhyamātreṇa cidānandāyate tanuḥ //1//

I salute the teacher, who is in *paramānanda* (supreme bliss), and an embodiment of *svānanda* (self-bliss). Just by being near him, I find myself in a state of bliss. -1.1

नमस्कृत्य गुरुं भक्त्या गोरक्षो ज्ञानमुत्तमम् ।
अभीष्टं योगिनां ब्रूते परमानन्दकारकम् ।।२।।

namaskṛtya guruṃ bhaktyā gorakṣo jñānamuttamam /
abhīṣṭaṃ yogināṃ brūte paramānandakārakam //2//

Having expressed his devotion by saluting his Guru, *Gorakṣa* imparts the supreme knowledge, which is beneficial for all yogīs, and bestows ultimate bliss. -1.2

Objective of Gorakṣa Samhitā

गोरक्षसंहितां वक्ति योगिनां हितकाम्यया ।
ध्रुवं यस्यावबोधेन जायते परमं पदम् ।।३।।

gorakṣasaṃhitāṃ vakti yogināṃ hitakāmyayā /
dhruvaṃ yasyavabodhena jāyate paramaṃ padam //3//

He will now expound the *Gorakṣa Samhitā* with his good wishes for the benefit of all yogīs. By understanding it, one will certainly attain *paraṃpada* (the supreme state). -1.3

एतद् विमुक्तिसोपानमेतत् कालस्य वञ्चनम् ।
यद् व्यावृत्तं मनो भोगादासक्तं परमात्मनि ।।४।।

etad vimuktisopānametat kālasya vañcanam /
yad vyāvṛttaṃ mano bhogādāsaktaṃ paramātmani //4//

This *Samhitā* is a ladder of liberation, and a way to deceive death.

It turns the mind away from the attachment of *bhoga* (worldly pleasures) towards *Paramātma* (the Supreme Self). -1.4

Taking Refuge in Yoga

द्विजसेवितशाखस्य श्रुतिकल्पतरोः फलम् ।
शमनं भवतापस्य योगं भजत सत्तमाः ।।५।।

dvijasevitaśākhasya śrutikalpataroḥ phalam /
śamanaṃ bhavatāpasya yogaṃ bhajata sattamāḥ //5//

The most exceptional ones take refuge in yoga to relieve their worldly pains and sufferings. This branch of revelation (*śruti*) which is served by the *dvija* (literally, twice-born) yields the fruit of *kalpataru* (a heavenly tree that fulfills all one's wishes). -1.5

Six Limbs of Yoga

आसनं प्राणसंरोधः प्रत्याहारश्च धारणा ।
ध्यानं समाधिरेतानि योगाङ्गानि वदन्ति षट् ।।६।।

āsanaṃ prāṇasaṃrodhaḥ pratyāhāraśca dhāraṇā /
dhyānaṃ samādhiretāni yogāṅgāni vadanti ṣaṭ //6//

Āsana, control over *prāna*, *pratyahāra*, *dhārana*, *dhyāna* and *samādhi* are said to be the six limbs of yoga. -1.6

आसनानि च तावन्तो यावन्तो जीवजान्तवः ।
एतेषामखिलान् भेदान् विजानाति महेश्वरः ।।७।।

āsanāni ca tāvanto yāvanto jīvajāntavaḥ /
eteṣāmakhilān bhedān vijānāti maheśvaraḥ //7//

There are as many postures as there are sentient beings. *Maheśvara* (Lord *Śiva*) alone knows all their many forms. -1.7

Descriptions of Āsanas

चतुराशीतिलक्षाणामेकैकं समुदाहृतम् ।
ततः शिवेन पीठानां षोडेशानं शतं कृतम् ।।८।।

caturāśītilakṣāṇāmekaikaṃ samudāhṛtam /
tataḥ śivena pīṭhānāṃ ṣoḍeśānaṃ śataṃ kṛtam //8//

Of the eighty four hundred thousand āsanas, one hundred thousand have been mentioned. Thus Lord *Śiva* created eighty-four āsanas (*pithas*). -1.8

आसनेभ्यः समस्तेभ्यो द्वयमेतदुदाहृतम् ।
एकं सिद्धासनं प्रोक्तं द्वितीयं कमलासनम् ।।९।।

āsanebhyaḥ samastebhyo dvayametadudāhṛtam /
ekaṃ siddhāsanaṃ proktaṃ dvitīyaṃ kamalāsanam //9//

Among all the āsanas, two are mentioned specifically. The first is called *siddhāsana*, and the second is *kamalāsana* (i.e. *padmāsana*). -1.9

Siddhāsana

योनिस्थानकमङ्घ्रिमूलघटितं कृत्वा दृढं विन्यसेन्
मेढ्रे पादमथैकमेव हृदये कृत्वा हनुं सुस्थिरम् ।
स्थाणुः संयमितेन्द्रियो चलदृशा पश्येद् भ्रुवोरन्तरम्
ह्येतन्मोक्षकवाटभेदजनकं सिद्धासनं प्रोच्यते ।।१०।।

yonisthānakamaṅghrimūlaghaṭitaṃ kṛtvā dṛḍhaṃ vinyasen
meḍhre pādamathaikameva hṛdaye kṛtvā hanuṃ susthiram /
sthāṇuḥ saṃyamitendriyo caladṛśā paśyed bhruvorantaram
hyetanmokṣakavāṭabhedajanakaṃ siddhāsanaṃ procyate //10//

A yogī should firmly place his heel against *yonisthāna* (the perineum i.e. the base of urethra), while placing the other heel above the penis and pressing the chin against *hṛdaya* (the chest). With his senses restrained, the yogī should direct a steady gaze between the eyebrows. This is called *siddhāsana*, which breaks open the door to liberation. -1.10

Padmāsana

वामोरूपरि दक्षिणं चे चरणं संस्थाप्य वामं तथा
दक्षोरूपरि पश्चिमेनविधिना धृत्वा कराभ्यां दृढम् ।
अङ्गुष्ठौ हृदये निधाय चिबुकं नासाग्रमालोकयेद्
एतद् व्याधिविकारनाशनकरं पद्मासनं प्रोच्यते ।।११।।

vāmorūpari dakṣiṇaṃ ce caraṇaṃ saṃsthāpya vāmaṃ tathā
dakṣorūpari paścimena vidhinā dhṛtvā karābhyāṃ dṛḍham /
aṅguṣṭhau hṛdaye nidhāya cibukaṃ nāsāgramālokayed
etad vyādhivikāranāśanakaraṃ padmāsanaṃ procyate //11//

One should place the right foot and leg on top of the left thigh and the left foot and leg on top of the right thigh. Then, crossing the hands behind the back, grasp the big toes properly. After placing the chin on the chest in the heart region, fix the gaze at the tip of the nose. This is called *padmāsana*, which destroys all types of diseases and health disorders. -1.11

Bodily Organs to Be Known

षट्चक्रं षोडशाधारं द्विलक्ष्य् व्योमपञ्चकम् ।
स्वदेहे ये न जानन्ति कथं सिद्ध्यन्ति योगिनः ।।१२।।

ṣaṭcakraṃ ṣoḍaśādhāraṃ dvilakṣyaṃ vyomapañcakam /
svadehe ye na jānanti kathaṃ siddhyanti yoginaḥ //12//

How can yogīs achieve perfection if they do not know the six *chakras* (energy centers), the sixteen supports of the body, the two objects of concentration and the five elements located within their own bodies? -1.12

एकस्तम्भं नवद्वारं गृहं पञ्चाधिदैवतम् ।
स्वदेहे ये न जानन्ति कथं सिद्ध्यन्ति योगिनः ।।१३।।

ekastambhaṃ navadvāraṃ gṛhaṃ pañcādhidaivatam /
svadehe ye na jānanti kathaṃ siddhyanti yoginaḥ //13//

How can yogīs be successful if they do not know that their own body is made from a single pillar, a home having nine doors and containing five *adhidevatā* (i.e. *ishtadevatā*, deities who fulfill one's desires)? -1.13

Description of Six Cakras

चतुर्दलं स्यादाधारः स्वाधिष्ठानं च षट्दलम् ।
नाभौ दशदलं पद्मं सूर्यसङ्ख्यदलं हृदि ।।१४।।

caturdalaṃ syādādhāraṃ svādhiṣṭhānaṃ ca ṣaṭdalam /
nābhau daśadalaṃ padmaṃ sūryasaṅkhyadalaṃ hṛdi //14//

The *ādhāra* (*mūladhāra*) *cakra* has four petals, and the *svādhiṣṭhāna cakra* has six. At the navel is a lotus with ten petals; at the heart, a lotus with twelve petals (*sūrya saṅkhya dalaṁ*, i.e. representing the twelve solar months). -1.14

कण्ठे स्यात् षोडशदलं भ्रूमध्ये द्विदलं तथा ।
सहस्रदलम् आख्यातं ब्रह्मरन्ध्रे महापथे ।।१५।।

kaṇṭhe syāt ṣoḍaśadalaṃ bhrūmadhye dvidalaṃ tathā /
sahasradalamākhyātaṃ brahmarandhre mahāpathe //15//

At the throat is a sixteen-petalled lotus; between the eyebrows, a lotus with two petals. At the *brahmarandhra* (literally, the hole or way to *Brahma*), which is also called *mahāpatha* (the supreme way), there is a lotus with a thousand petals. 1.15

आधारः प्रथमं चक्रं स्वाधिष्ठानं द्वितीयकम् ।
योनिस्थानं द्वयोर्मध्ये कामरूपं निगद्यते ।।१६।।

ādhāraṃ prathamaṃ cakraṃ svādhiṣṭhānaṃ dvitīyakam /
yonisthānaṃ dvayormadhye kāmarūpaṃ nigadyate //16//

The first energy center is *mūlādhāra*, and the second is *svādhiṣṭhāna*. Located between those two centers is the yoni (literally, source or origin), which is known as the seat of *kāma* (sensual desires). -1.16

आधाराख्यं गुदस्थानं पङ्कजं च चतुर्दलम् ।
तन्मध्ये प्रोच्यते योनिः कामाक्षा सिद्धवन्दिता ।।१७।।

ādhārākhyaṃ gudasthānaṃ paṅkajaṃ ca caturdalam /

tanmadhye procyate yoniḥ kāmākṣā siddhavanditā //17//

The lotus called *ādhārā* has four petals, and is located at the anus. It is said that in the middle of this lotus is the yoni *kāmākṣā*, which is greatly admired by the *siddhas*. – 1.17

The Supreme Light

योनिमध्ये महालिङ्गं पश्चिमाभिमुखस्थितम् ।

मस्तके मणिवद् बिम्बं यो जानाति स योगवित् ।।१८।।

yonimadhye mahāliṅgaṃ paścimābhimukhasthitam /

mastake maṇivad bimbaṃ yo jānāti sa yogavit //18//

In the middle of that yoni is a *mahāliṅga* (the great symbol of *Śiva*), which is facing backward. Its radiance is like a jewel on top of a head. One who knows it, knows Yoga. -1.18

तप्तचामीकराभासं तडिल्लेखेव विस्फुरत् ।

त्रिकोणं तत्पुरं वह्नरधो मेढ्रात्प्रतिष्ठितम् ।।१९।।

taptacāmīkarābhāsaṃ taḍillekheva visphurat /

trikoṇaṃ tatpuraṃ vahniradho meḍhrātpratiṣṭhitam //19//

The city of fire, which is in the shape of a triangle, is situated below the penis, and emanates flashes like lightning bolts, in the color of melted gold. -1.19

यत् समाधौ परं ज्योतिरनन्तं विश्वतोमुखम् ।

तस्मिन् दृष्टे महायोगे यातायातन्न विन्दते ।।२०।।

yat samādhau paraṃ jyotiranantaṃ viśvatomukham /

tasmin dṛṣṭe mahāyoge yātayatanna vindate //20//

One who sees this Supreme Infinite Light, the form of the universe, in his *samādhi*, is the supreme yoga. After having seen that Great Light, he does not know his *yātāyātaṁ* (literally, going and coming; i.e. he becomes liberated from the cycle of death and birth). -1.20

स्वशब्देन भवेत्प्राणः स्वाधिष्ठानं तदाश्रयः ।

स्वाधिष्ठानात्पदादस्मान्मेढ्रमेवाभिधीयते ।।२१।।

svaśabdena bhavetprāṇaḥ svādhiṣṭhānaṃ tadāśrayaḥ /

svādhiṣṭhānātpadādasmānmeḍhramevābhidhīyate //21//

The life force arises with the sound '*sva*', and its abode is the *svādhiṣṭhāna cakra.* This is thus called *meḍhra* (*liṅga*), as it takes refuge at *svādhiṣṭhāna*. 1.21

तन्तुना मणिवत्प्रोतो यत्र कन्दः सुषुम्णया ।

तन्नाभिमण्डलं चक्रं प्रोच्यते मणिपूरकम् ।।२२।।

tantuna maṇivatproto yatra kandaḥ suṣumṇayā /

tannābhimaṇḍalaṃ cakraṃ procyate maṇipūrakam //22//

The *chakra* located in the navel region is called *maṇipūra cakra*, where the *kanda* (bulbous root) is woven onto the *suṣumṇā* like a jewel on a thread. -1.22

द्वादशारे महाचक्रे पुण्यपापविवर्जिते ।
तावज् जीवो भ्रमत्य एव यावत् तत्त्वं न विन्दति ।। २३।।

dvādaśāre mahācakre puṇyapāpavivarjite /
tāvajjīvo bhramatya eva yāvat tattvaṃ na vindati //23//

As long as *jīva* (the embodied self) wanders alone at the *mahācakra* (literally, great center) with twelve petals (the *manipura cakra*, located at the heart), which is free from *puṇya* (merit) and *pāpa* (demerit), the *jīva* does not know Reality. -1.23

Description of Ten Nādis

ऊर्ध्वं मेढ्रादधोनाभेः कन्दो योनिः खगाण्डवत् ।
तत्र नाड्यः समुत्पन्नाः सहस्राणां द्विसप्ततिः ।।२४।।

ūrdhvaṃ meḍhrādadhonābheḥ kando yoniḥ khagāṇḍavat /
tatra nāḍyaḥ samutpannāḥ sahasrāṇāṃ dvisaptatiḥ //24//

The *kanda yoni*, similar to a bird's egg, is located above the penis and below the navel. Seventy-two thousand *nāḍis* (subtle *prānic* channels) originate there. -1.24

तेषु नाडिसहस्रेषु द्विसप्ततिरुदाहृताः ।
प्रधानः प्राणवाहिन्यो भूयस्तासु दशस्मृताः ।।२५।।

teṣu nāḍisahasreṣu dvisaptatirudāhṛtāḥ /
pradhānāḥ prāṇavāhinyo bhūyastāsu daśasmṛtāḥ //25//

Among these thousands of *prānic* channels, seventy-two have been mentioned. Furthermore, among those seventy-two, ten are known as the most important carriers of *prāṇa*. -1.25

इडा च पिङ्गला चैव सुषुम्णा च तृतीयका ।
गान्धारी हस्तिजिह्वा च पूषा चैव यशस्विनी ।।२६।।

iḍā ca piṅgalā caiva suṣumṇā ca tṛtīyakā /
gāndhārī hastijihvā ca pūṣā caiva yaśasvinī //26//

Those channels called *iḍā* and *piṅgalā*, with *suṣumṇā* being the third one, *gāndhārī* and *hastijihvā*, *pūṣā* and *paśasvinī*. -1-26

अलम्बुषा कुहूश्चैव शङ्खिनी दशमी स्मृता ।
एतन्नाडिमयं चक्रं ज्ञातव्यं योगिभिः सदा ।।२७।।

alambuṣā kuhūścaiva śaṅkhinī daśamī smṛtā /
etannāḍimayaṃ cakraṃ jñātavyaṃ yogibhiḥ sadā //27//

The other channels are *alambuṣā* and *kuhūśa*, followed by *śaṅkhinī*, which is tenth. Yogīs should always have knowledge of each *cakra*, which is filled with these *prānic* channels. -1.27

Other Various Nādis

इडा वामे स्थिता भागे पिङ्गला दक्षिणे स्थिता ।

सुषुम्णा मध्यदेशे तु गान्धारी वामचक्षुषि ।।२८।।

iḍā vāme sthitā bhāge piṅgalā dakṣiṇe sthitā /

suṣumṇā madhyadeśe tu gāndhārī vāmacakṣuṣi //28//

Iḍā is situated on the left side and *piṅgalā* is on the right, while *suṣumṇā* is in the middle, while the *gāndhārī* is in the left eye. -1.28

दक्षिणे हस्तिजिह्वा च पूषा कर्णे च दक्षिणे ।

यशस्विनी वामकर्णे ह्यानने चाप्यलम्बुषा ।।२९।।

dakṣiṇe hastijihvā ca pūṣā karṇe ca dakṣiṇe /

yaśasvinī vāmakarṇe hyānane cāpyalambuṣā //29//

Hastijihvā is on the right and *pūṣā* is in the right ear, while *yaśasvinī* is in the left ear and *alambuṣā* is located in the mouth. -1.29

कुहूश्च लिङ्गदेशे तु मूलस्थाने च शङ्खिनी ।

एवं द्वारं समाश्रित्य तिष्ठन्ति दशनाडयः ।।३०।।

kuhūśca liṅgadeśe tu mūlasthāne ca śaṅkhinī /

evaṃ dvāraṃ samāśritya tiṣṭhanti daśanāḍayaḥ //29//

Kuhū is located in the region of the *liṅga* and the *śaṅkhinī* is located in the area of the anus. Thus the ten subtle *prānic* channels are supported by, and situated at, the portals of the body. -1.30

इडापिङ्गलासुषुम्णाः प्राणमार्गे समाश्रिताः ।

सततं प्राणवाहिन्यः सोमसूर्याग्निदेवताः ।।३१।।

iḍāpiṅgalāsuṣumṇāḥ prāṇamārge samāśritāḥ /

satataṃ prāṇavāhinyaḥ somasūryāgnidevatāḥ //31//

Iḍā, *piṅgalā* and *suṣumṇā* are associated with, and depend on, the path of *prāṇa* (i.e. life force). They are constant carriers of *prāṇa*, and their respective *devatās* (deities) are *soma* (the moon), *sūrya* (the sun) and *agni* (fire). -1.31

The Ten Vāyus

प्राणोऽपानः समानश्चोदानोव्यानौ च वायवः ।

नागः कूर्मोथ कृकलो देवदत्तो धनञ्जयः ।। ३२।।

prāṇo'pānaḥ samānaścodānovyānau ca vāyavaḥ /

nāgaḥ kūrmo'tha kṛkalo devadatto dhanañjayaḥ //32//

Prāṇa, *apāna*, *samāna*, *udāna*, *vyāna*, *nāga*, *kūrma*, *kṛkara*, *devadatta* and *dhanañjaya* are the ten *prāṇas* (vital life forces) in the body. 1.32

हृदि प्राणो वसेन्नित्यंअपानो गुदमण्डले ।
समानो नाभिदेशे तु उदानः कण्ठमध्यगः ।।३३।।

hṛdi prāṇo vasennityaṃ apāno gudamaṇḍale /
samāno nābhideśe tu udānaḥ kaṇṭhamadhyagaḥ //33//

Prāṇa always dwells in the heart, *apāna* is in the region of the anus, *samāna* is in the navel region, and *udāna* is in the middle of the throat. -1.33

व्यानो व्यापी शरीरेषु प्रद्धानाः पञ्च वयवः ।
प्राणाद्याः पञ्चविख्याता नागाद्याः पन्च वयवः ।।३४।।

vyāno vyāpī śarīreṣu pradhānāḥ pañca vāyavaḥ /
prāṇādyāḥ pañcavikhyātā nāgādyāḥ pañca vāyavaḥ //34//

Vyāna pervades the whole body. These five *prāṇas* (life forces) are of great renown. Starting with *nāga*, below are the five other (sub) *prāṇas*. -1.34

उद्गारे नाग आख्यातः कूर्म उन्मीलने स्मृतः ।
कृकरः क्षुतकृज् ज्ञेयो देवदत्तो विजृम्भणे ।।३५।।

udgāre nāga ākhyātaḥ kūrma unmīlane smṛtaḥ /
kṛkaraḥ kṣutakṛjjñeyo devadatto vijṛmbhaṇe //35//

It is known that *nāgā* performs belching and *kūrma* blinking of the eyes, *kṛkara* causes hunger and thirst, and *devadatta* yawning and hiccupping. -1.35

न जहाति मृतं चापि सर्वव्यापि धनञ्जयः ।
एते सर्वासु नाडीषु भ्रमन्ते जीवरूपिणः ।।३६।।

na jahāti mṛtaṃ cāpi sarvavyāpi dhanañjayaḥ /
ete sarvāsu nāḍīṣu bhramante jīvarūpiṇaḥ //36//

Dhanañjaya pervades the whole body, and does not depart from it even after death. Therefore, *jīvarūpiṇa* (the embodied Self or Soul in the form of *jīva*) pervades all of these subtle life force channels. -1.36

आक्षिप्तो भुजदण्डेन यथोच्चलति कन्दुकः ।
प्राणापानसमाक्षिप्तस्तथा जीवो न तिष्ठति ।।३७।।

ākṣipto bhujadaṇḍena yathoccalati kandukaḥ /
prāṇāpānasamākṣiptastathā jīvo na tiṣṭhati //37//

As a ball struck with a stick goes up (and comes down), so the *jīva* (the embodied Self), when struck by *prāṇa* and *apāna*, does not remain still. -1.37

Need of Prānāpāna Practice

प्राणापानवशो जीवो ह्य् अधश् चोर्ध्वं च धावति ।
वामदक्षिणमार्गेण चञ्चलत्वान्न दृश्यते ।।३८।।

prāṇāpānavaśo jīvo hyadhaścordhvaṃ ca dhāvati /

vāmadakṣiṇamārgeṇa cañcalatvānna dṛśyate //38//

Being under the control of *prāṇa* and *apāna*, the *jīva* (embodied Self), traverses up and down through the left and right (*prānic*) pathways. Due to its restlessness, it does not perceive its own true form (the nature of the Self). -1.38

रज्जुबद्धो यथा श्येनो गतोऽप्याकृष्यते पुनः ।
गुणबद्धस्तथा जीवः प्राणापानेन कृष्यते ।।३९।।

rajjubaddho yathā śyeno gato'pyākṛṣyate punaḥ /

guṇabaddhastathā jīvaḥ prāṇāpānena kṛṣyate //39//

Like a hawk tied down with a string that can fly away, only to be pulled back again, so the *jīva*, bound by the *guṇas* (i.e. the qualities or modes of nature), is subject to the pull of *prāṇā* and *apāna*. -1.39

अपानः कर्षति प्राणः प्राणोपानं च कर्षति ।
ऊर्ध्वाधः संस्थितावेतौ संयोजयति योगवित् ।।४०।।

apānaḥ karṣati prāṇaṃ prāṇo'pānaṃ ca karṣati /

ūrdhvādhaḥ saṃsthitāvetau saṃyojayati yogavit //40//

The *apāna* draws the *prāṇā*, and the *prāṇā* draws the *apāna*. One who unites these two *prānas*, which are situated above and below (the navel area), is the knower of yoga. -1.40

Haṃsa Mantra and Ajapā Gāyatri

हकारेण बहिर्याति सकारेण विशेत्पुनः ।
हंसहंसेत्यमुं मन्त्रं जीवो जपति सर्वदा ।।४१।।

hakāreṇa bahiryāti sakāreṇa viśetpunaḥ /

haṃsahaṃsetyamuṃ mantraṃ jīvo japati sarvadā //41//

With the sound '*ha*', the *jīva*, in the form of *prāna*, goes out; with the sound '*sa*', it comes back in again. So the *jīva* is always repeating the mantra '*hamsa, haṃsa*'. -1.41

षट्शतानि त्वहोरात्रे सहस्राण्येकविंशतिः ।
एतत्सङ्ख्यान्वितं मन्त्रं जीवो जपति सर्वदा ।।४२।।

ṣaṭśatāni tvahorātre sahasrāṇyekaviṃśatiḥ /

etatsaṅkhyānvitaṃ mantraṃ jīvo japati sarvadā //42//

In fact, the *jīva* continually recites this mantra 21,600 times in each diurnal cycle. -1.42

अजपा नाम गायत्री योगिनां मोक्षदायिनी ।
अस्याः सङ्कल्पमात्रेण सर्वपापैः प्रमुच्यते ।।४३।।

ajapā nāma gāyatrī yogināṃ mokṣadāyinī /

asyāḥ saṅkalpamātreṇa sarvapāpaiḥ pramucyate //43//

The *Gāyatrī* named *Ajapā* bestows liberation upon yogīs, and merely through its power of *saṅkalpa* (resolve or vow), one is released from all sins. -1.43

Note: *Saṅkalpa* means a definite intention, will or vow for doing something. Say a determination/resolution to do something.

अनया सदृशी विद्या अनया सदृशो जपः ।
अनया सदृशं ज्ञानं न भूतं न भविष्यति ।।४४।।

anayā sadṛśī vidyā anayā sadṛśo japaḥ /
anayā sadṛśaṃ jñānaṃ na bhūtaṃ na bhaviṣyati //44//

There is no *vidyā* (wisdom) similar to the *Gāyatrī* named *Ajapā*, there is no *japa* (recitation) similar to it, there is no *jñāna* (knowledge) similar to it, nor was there in the past, nor will there be in the future. -1.44

कुन्दलिन्याः समुद्भूता गायत्री प्राणधारिणी ।
प्राणविद्या महाविद्या यस्तां वेत्ति स योगवित् ।।४५।।

kuṇḍalinyāḥ samudbhūtā gāyatrī prāṇadhāriṇī /
prāṇavidyā mahāvidyā yastāṃ vetti sa yogavit //45//

One who knows this life-supporting *Gāyatrī* (i.e. *Ajapā*), born out of *kuṇḍalinī*, which is *prāṇavidyā* (knowledge) and *mahāvidyā* (supreme wisdom) of *prāṇa* (the life force), is the knower of yoga. -1.45

Awakening of Kuṇḍalī Śakti

कन्दोर्ध्वे कुण्डली शक्तिरष्टधा कुण्डलाकृति ।
ब्रह्मद्वारमुखं नित्यं मुखेनाच्छाद्य तिष्ठति ।। ४६।।

kandordhve kuṇḍalī śaktiraṣṭadhā kuṇḍalākṛti /
brahmadvāramukhaṃ nityaṃ mukhenācchādya tiṣṭhati //46//

The *kuṇḍalī śakti* (power), folded into eight coils, always resides above the *kanda* (bulbous root), closing the opening of the *brahmadvāra* (door of *Brahma*) with its face. -1.46

येन द्वारेण गन्तव्यं ब्रह्मागारमनामयम् ।
मुखेनाच्छाद्य तद्द्वारं प्रसुप्ता परमेश्वरी ।।४७।।

yena dvāreṇa gantavyaṃ brahmāgāramanāmayam /
mukhenācchādya taddvāraṃ prasuptā parameśvarī //47//

The way to *brahmāgāra* (the abode of *Brahma*), which is *anāmaya* (literally, free from any fault and disease), is through this door. But *Parameśvarī* (the Supreme Goddess) is asleep there, covering that door with her face. -1.47

प्रबुद्धा वह्नियोगेन मनसा मारुता सह ।
सूचीव गुणमादाय व्रजत्यूर्ध्वं सुषुम्णया ।।४८।।

prabuddhā buddhiyogena manasā mārutā saha /

sūcīva guṇamādāya vrajatyūrdhvaṃ suṣumṇayā //48//

When *kuṇḍalī* is awakened by intelligence, the mind and *maruta* (*prāṇa*) blend together, and she moves upwards through *suṣumṇā* (the middle pathway) like a needle drawing a thread. -1.48

प्रस्फुरद्भुजगाकारा पद्मतन्तुनिभा शुभा ।
प्रबुद्धा वह्नियोगेन व्रजत्यूर्ध्वं सुषुम्णया ।।४९।।

prasuptabhujagākārā padmatantunibhā śubhā /

prabuddhā vahniyogena vrajatyūrdhvaṃ suṣumṇayā //49//

When awakened by the yogic fire, she raises upwards through the *suṣumṇa* (middle path) in the form of a serpent, bursting up like an auspicious filament of a lotus. -1.49

उद्धटयेत् कपातं तु यथा कुञ्चिकया हठात् ।
कुण्डलिन्या तथा योगी मोक्षद्वारं प्रभेदयेत् ।।५०।।

udghāṭayet kapāṭaṃ tu yathā kuñcikayā haṭhāt /

kuṇḍalinyā tathā yogī mokṣadvāraṃ prabhedayet //50//

Just as one forcibly unlocks a door with a key, so the yogī should break open the door to liberation by means of the *kuṇḍalinī*. -1.50

Śakticālini Mudrā

कृत्वा सम्पुटितौ करौ दृढतरं बद्ध्वा तु पद्मासनं
गाढं वक्षसि सन्निधाय चिबुकं ध्यानं च तच्चेतसि ।
वारम्वारमपानमूर्ध्वमनिलं प्रोच्चारयेत्पूरितं
मुञ्चन्प्राणमुपैति बोधमतुलं शक्तिप्रभावादतः ।।५१।।

kṛtvā sampuṭitau karau dṛḍhataraṃ baddhvā tu padmāsanaṃ

gāḍhaṃ vakṣasi sannidhāya cibukaṃ dhyānaṃ ca taccetasi /

vāramvāramapānamūrdhvamanilaṃ proccārayetpūritaṃ

muñcanprāṇamupaiti bodhamatulaṃ śaktiprabhāvādataḥ //51//

After cupping the hands firmly and assuming the lotus posture while placing the chin tightly against the chest, one should practice meditation focusing his mind on *Tat* (*Brahma* in the Light Form), and after he has filled the chest with *prāna*, should repeatedly expel the *apāna vāyu*. Upon releasing the *prāna*, he acquires *bodhamatula* (incomparable knowledge) through the force of the awakening of *Śakti*. -1.51

Daily Routine of a Yogi

अङ्गानां मर्दनं कृत्व श्रमसञ्जातवारिणा ।
कट्वम्ललवणत्यागी क्षीरभोजनमाचरेत् ।।५२।।

aṅgānāṃ mardanaṃ kṛtva śramasañjātavāriṇā /

kaṭvamlalavaṇatyāgī kṣīrabhojanamācaret //52//

One should rub his limbs with the sweat caused by one's labors. One should consume milk and abstain from bitter, sour, and salty foods. -1.52

ब्रह्मचारी मिताहारी त्यागी योगपरायणः ।
अब्दादूर्ध्वं भवेत्सिद्धो नात्र कार्या विचारणा ।।५३।।

brahmacārī mitāhārī tyāgī yogaparāyaṇaḥ /
abdādūrdhvaṃ bhavetsiddho nātra kāryā vicāraṇā //53//

One who is dedicated to the practice of yoga should be a *brahmacārī* (celibate) and a *tyāgī* (renouncer), and should be a *mitāhārī* (one who takes moderate diet). One will then achieve perfection after one year. There should be no doubt about it. -1.53

सुस्निग्धं मधुराहारं चतुर्थांशविवर्जितम् ।
भुज्यते स्वरसं प्रीत्यै मिताहारी स उच्यते ।।५४।।

susnigdhaṃ madhurāhāraṃ caturthāṃśavivarjitam /
bhujyate svarasaṃ prītyai mitāhārī sa ucyate //54//

One who is called a *mitāhārī* (literally, a moderate eater) eats food that is smooth, oil-rich, sweet and natural in taste after offering it to his God, and leaves one-fourth of his stomach empty. -1.54

कन्दोर्ध्वं कुण्डलीनी शक्ति शुभमोक्षप्रदायिनी ।
बन्धनाय च मूढानां यस्तां वेत्ति स योगवित् ।।५५।।

kandordhvaṃ kuṇḍalīnī śakti śubhamokṣapradāyinī /
bandhanāya ca mūḍhānāṃ yastāṃ vetti sa yogavit //55//

Kuṇḍalīnī śakti, situated above the *kanda* (bulbous root), is the bestower of auspicious liberation for yogīs, but causes bondage for fools. One who realizes this is a knower of yoga. -1.55

Description of Mudrās

महामुद्रां नमोमुद्रां उड्डियानं जलन्धरम् ।
मूलबन्धनं च यो वेत्ति स योगी मुक्तिभाजनः ।।५६।।

mahāmudrāṃ nabhomudrāṃ uḍḍiyānaṃ jalandharam /
mūlabandhanñca yo vetti sa yogī muktibhājanaḥ //56//

A yogī who is familiar with the *mahāmudrā*, *nabhomudrā*, *uḍḍiyāna bandha*, *jalandhara bandha* and *mūlabandha* practices is worthy of liberation. -1.56

Mahāmudrā

वक्षोन्यस्तहनुः प्रपीड्य सुचिरं योनिं च वामाङ्घ्रिणा
हस्ताभ्यामवधारयेत् प्रसरितं पादं तथा दक्षिणम् ।
आपूर्य श्वसनेन कुक्षियुगलं बद्ध्वा शनैरेचयेत्

एषा व्याधिविनाशिनी सुमहती मुद्रा नृणां कत्यते ।।५७।।

vakṣonyastahanuḥ prapīḍya suciraṃ yoniṃ ca vāmāṅghriṇā

hastābhyāmavadhārayet prasaritaṃ pādaṃ tathā dakṣiṇam /

āpūrya śvasanena kukṣiyugalaṃ baddhvā śanaiḥ recayet

eṣā vyādhivināśinī sumahatī mudrā nṛṇāṃ kathyate //57//

Placing the chin on the chest, constantly pressing the left heel against the *yoni* (the perineum), and holding the extended right foot with the hands, the yogī should, after inhaling and holding the air fully inside the chest, exhale it slowly. It is said that this is an extremely great mudra, the destroyer of all human diseases. -1.57

चन्द्राङ्गेन समभ्यस्य सूर्याङ्गेनाभ्यसेत्पुनः ।
यावत्तुल्या भवेत्सङ्ख्या ततो मुद्रां विसर्जयेत् ।।५८।।

candrāṅgena samabhyasya sūryāṅgenābhyasetpunaḥ /

yāvattulyā bhavetsaṅkhyā tato mudrāṃ visarjayet //58//

After practicing the *mahāmudrā* first with *candrāṅga* (the lunar side/part, i.e. the left nostril), one should practice it with *sūryāṅga* (the solar side/part, i.e. the right nostril). One should stop this *mudrā* after practicing an equal number of rounds with both *aṅgas*. -1.58

Results of Mahāmudrā

नहि पथ्यमपथ्यं वा रसाः सर्वेऽपि नीरसाः ।
अपि मुक्तं विषं घोरं पीयूषमिव जीर्यते ।।५९।।

nahi pathyamapathyaṃ vā rasāḥ sarve'pi nīrasāḥ /

api bhuktaṃ viṣaṃ ghoraṃ pīyūṣamiva jīryate //59//

There is no wholesome or unwholesome food (for an expert yogī), and all tastes indeed are tasteless. Even eating a horrible poison is digested like *pīyūṣa* (nectar). -1.59

क्षयकुष्ठगुदावर्तगुल्माजीर्णपुरोगमाः ।
तस्य दोषाः क्षयं यान्ति महामुद्रां तु योभ्यसेत् ।।६०।।

kṣayakuṣṭhagudāvartagulmājīrṇapurogamāḥ /

rogāstasya kṣayaṃ yānti mahāmudrāṃ tu yobhyaset //60//

In addition, for one who practices the *māhamudrā*, diseases like leprosy, constipation, enlargement of the spleen, indigestion, etc. are destroyed. -1.60

कथितेयं महामुद्रा महासिद्धिकरा नृणाम् ।
गोपनीया प्रयत्नेन न देया यस्य कस्यचित् ।।६१।।

kathiteyaṃ mahāmudrā mahāsiddhikari nṛṇām /

gopanīyā prayatnena na deyā yasya kasyacit //61//

It is said that this *mahā mudrā* is the bestower of human perfections. With due effort, one should try to keep it secret. It should not be given to everyone. -1.61

Khecari Mudrā

कपालकुहरे जिह्वा प्रविष्टा विपरीतगा ।
भ्रुवोरन्तर्गता दृष्टिर् मुद्रा भवति खेचरी ।।६२।।

kapālakuhare jihvā praviṣṭā viparītagā /

bhruvorantargatā dṛṣṭirmudrā bhavati khecarī //62//

One should turn the tongue backward into the skull cavity, and fix the gaze between the two eyebrows. This is (the practice of) *khecarī mudrā*. -1.62

Results of Khecari Mudrā

न रोगान्मरणं तस्य न निद्रा न क्षुधा तृषा ।
न मूर्च्छा तु भवेत्तस्य यो मुद्रां वेत्ति खेचरीम् ।।६३।।

na rogānmaraṇaṃ tasya na nidrā na kṣudhā tṛṣā /

na mūrcchā tu bhavettasya yo mudrāṃ vetti khecarīm //63//

For one who knows *khecarī mudrā*, there is no disease, death, tiredness, sleep, hunger, thirst or fainting. - 1.63

पीड्यते न च शिकेन लिप्यते न च कर्मणा ।
बाध्यते न स केनापि यो मुद्रां वेत्ति खेचरीम् ।।६४।।

pīḍyate na ca śokena lipyate na ca karmaṇā /

bādhyate na sa kenāpi yo mudrāṃ vetti khecarīm //64//

One who knows *khecarī mudrā* is not affected by diseases or grief, nor tainted by his karma (actions). One cannot be obstructed by anything. -1.64

चित्तं चलति नो यस्माज्जिह्वा चरति खेचरी ।
तेनेयं खेचरी सिद्धा सर्वसिद्धैर्नमस्कृता ।।६५।।

cittaṃ calati no yasmājjihvā carati khecarī /

teneyaṃ khecarī siddhā sarvasiddhairnamaskṛtā //65//

As the tongue goes into *khecari* (i.e. into the cavity of the skull, or literally, moving in the region of sky), *citta* (the mind) does not move. Consequently, the perfected practice of *khecarī mudrā* is saluted by all the *siddhas*. -1.65

बिन्दुमूल शरीरणां शिरास्तत्र प्रतिष्ठिताः ।
भावयन्ति शरीराणमापादतलमस्तकम् ।।६६।।

bindumūlaṃ śarīraṇāṃ śirāstatra pratiṣṭhitāḥ /

bhāvayanti śarīrāṇamāpādatalamastakam //66//

Bindu (semen) is the foundation of all bodies in which the veins [in the physical body] and the *nādis* (in the *prānic* body) are established.

They compose all bodies from the head to the feet. -1.66

खेचर्या मुद्रितं येन विवरं लम्बिकोर्ध्वतः ।
न तस्य क्षरते बिन्दुः कामिन्यालिङ्गितस्य च ।।६७।।

khecaryā mudritaṃ yena vivaraṃ lambikordhvataḥ /
na tasya kṣarate binduḥ kāminyāliṅgitasya ca //67//

For one who has sealed the cavity of the skull through the *khecarī mudrā*, semen is not ejaculated, even if he is embraced by an amorous woman. -1.67

यावद् बिन्दुः स्थितो देहे तावन्मृतोर्भयं कुतः ।
यावद् बद्धा नभोमुद्रा तावद् बिन्दुर्न गच्छति ।।६८।।

yāvad binduḥ sthito dehe tāvanmṛtorbhayaṃ kutaḥ /
yāvad baddhā nabhomudrā tāvad bindurna gacchati //68//

As long as the *bindu* remains in the body, how can there be fear of death? As long as *nabhomudrā* (meaning *khecarī mudrā*) is maintained, the *bindu* does not go out (of the body). -1.68

Making the Bindu Stable in Its Place

चलितोऽपि यदा बिन्दुः सम्प्राप्तश् च हुताशनम् ।
व्रजत्यूर्ध्वं हृतः शक्त्या निरुद्धो योनिमुद्रया ।।६९।।

calito'pi yadā binduḥ samprāptaśca hutāśanam /
vrajatyūrdhvaṃ hṛtaḥ śaktyā niruddho yonimudrayā //69//

Even if the semen has fallen into the *hutāśana* (literally, it means sacrifice eater or fire, i.e. located in the navel region), it should be taken upward again and controlled by the *Śakti* (power) of the yoni *mudrā*. -1.69

स पुनर्द्विविधो बिन्दुः पण्डुरो लोहितस्तथा ।
पाण्डुरः शुक्रमित्याहुर्लोहिताख्यो महारजः ।।७०।।

sa punardvividho binduḥ panḍuro lohitastathā /
pānḍuraḥ śukramityāhurlohitākhyo mahārajaḥ //70//

In addition, *bindu* is of two kinds: yellowish white and red. It is said that the color of *śukra* (the semen) is yellowish white, and the great *raja* (ovarian fluid) is red. -1.70

सिन्दूरद्रवसङ्काशं नाभिस्थाने स्थितं रजः ।
शशिस्थाने स्थितो बिन्दुस्तयोरैक्यं सुदुर्लभम् ।।७१।।

sindūradravasaṅkāśaṃ nābhisthāne sthitaṃ rajaḥ /
śaśisthāne sthito bindustayoraikyaṃ sudurlabham //71//

The *raja* is located in the navel area and resembles oil mixed with the color vermilion. The *bindu* is located at the place of the moon (i.e. at the palate). It is quite rare to unite them. -1.71

Supreme State: Unity of Bindu and Raja

बिन्दुः शिवो रजः शक्तिर्बिन्दुम् इन्दू रजो रविः ।
अनयोः सङ्गमादेव प्राप्यते परमं पदम् ।।७२।।

binduḥ śivo rajaḥ śaktiscandro bindū rajo raviḥ /
anayoḥ saṅgamādeva prāpyate paramaṃ padam //72//

Bindu is *Śiva* and *raja* is *Śakti*. *Bindu* is the moon and *raja* is the sun. One can accomplish *parama pada* (the Supreme State) through the union of these two. -1.72

वायुना शक्तिचारेण प्रेरितं तु यदा रजः ।
याति बिन्दोः सहैकत्वं भवेद्दिव्यं वपुस्ततः ।।७३।।

vāyunā śakticāreṇa preritaṃ tu yadā rajaḥ /
yāti bindoḥ sahaikatvaṃ bhaveddivyaṃ vapustataḥ //73//

When the activating power of *vāyu* (*prāna*) stimulates *raja*, it unites with the *bindu*. Then, the body becomes divine. -1.73

Harmony of the Sun and the Moon

शुक्रं चन्द्रेण संयुक्तं रजः सूर्येण संयुतम् ।
तयोः समरसैकत्वं यो जानाति स योगवित् ।।७४।।

śukraṃ candreṇa saṃyuktaṃ rajaḥ sūryeṇa saṃyutam /
tayoḥ samarasaikatvaṃ yo jānāti sa yogavit //74//

Śukra is joined with the moon. *Raja* is joined with the sun. Those who know their harmonious unity are knowers of yoga. -1.74

शोधनं नाडिजालस्य चालनं चन्द्रसूर्ययोः ।
रसानां शोषणं चैव महामुद्राभिधीयते ।।७५।।

śodhanaṃ nāḍijālasya cālanaṃ candrasūryayoḥ /
rasānāṃ śoṣaṇaṃ caiva mahāmudrābhidhīyate //75//

The purification of *nāḍijāla* (the *prānic* channels), the activation of *candrasūrya* (the moon and the sun), and the drying up of liquids (from the body) is called *mahāmudrā*. -1.75

Descriptions of Bandhas

उड्डीनं कुरुते यस्मादविश्रान्तं महाखगः ।
उड्डीयानं तदेव स्यान्मृत्युमातङ्गकेशरी ।।७६।।

uḍḍīnaṃ kurute yasmādaviśrāntaṃ mahākhagaḥ /
uḍḍīyānaṃ tadeva syānmṛtyumātaṅgakeśarī //76//

Just like a great bird that flies upward tirelessly, one's practice of *uḍḍīyāna* bandha becomes a lion of immortality over the elephant of death. -1.76

Uḍḍīyāna Bandha

उदरात्पश्चिमे भागे अधो नाभेर्निगद्यते ।

उड्डीयानो ह्यं बन्धस्तत्र बन्धो निगद्यते ।।७७।।

udarātpaścime bhāge adho nābhernigadyate /

uḍḍīyāno hyaṃ bandhastatra bandho nigadyate //77//

It is said that this *bandha* (lock) practice engages the area below the navel, and the back part of the abdomen. This is where it is said that the *bandha uḍḍīyāna* should be performed. -1.77

Jālandhara Bandha

बध्नाति हि सिरोजालं नाधो याति नभोजलम् ।
ततो जालन्धरो बन्धो कण्ठदुःखौघनाशनः ।।७८।।

badhnāti hi sirojālaṃ nādho yāti nabhojalam /

tato jālandharo bandho kaṇṭhaduḥkhaughanāśanaḥ //78//

Jālandhara bandha (the throat lock) certainly blocks *sirājāla* (the network of *prānic* channels in the throat) so that *jala* (the water, meaning nectar) from *nabha* (the sky, i.e. moon) does not trickle down (into the sun). Therefore, it removes a multitude of diseases of the throat. -1.78

जालन्धरे कृते बन्धे कण्ठसंकोचलक्षणे ।
पीयूषं न पतत्यग्नौ न च वायुः प्रकुप्यति ।।७९।।

jālandhare kṛte bandhe kaṇṭhasaṅkocalakṣaṇe /

pīyūṣaṃ na patatyagnau na ca vāyuḥ prakupyati //79//

When *jālandhara bandha* is performed, as characterized (practiced) by the contraction of the throat, the nectar neither falls into the fire, nor is *vāyu* (the air, i.e. '*prāna*') disturbed. -1.79

Mūlabandha

पार्ष्णिभागेनसंपीड्य योनिमाकुञ्चयेद्गुदम् ।
अपानमूर्ध्वमाकृष्य मूलबन्धो विधीयते ।।८०।।

pārṣṇibhāgenasaṃpīḍya yonimākuñcayedgudam /

apānamūrdhvamākṛṣya mūlabandho vidhīyate //80//

One should press the left heel against the perineum and contract the anus while pulling the *apāna* (*vāyu*) upward. This is called *mūla-bandha* (the perineum lock). -1.80

अपानप्राणयोरैक्यात् क्षयोमूत्रपुरीषयोः ।
युवा भवति वृद्धोऽपि सततं मूलबन्धनात् ।।८१।।

apānaprāṇayoraikyāt kṣayo mūtrapurīṣayoḥ /

yuvā bhavati vṛddho'pi satataṃ mūlabandhanāt //81//

Through the union of the *apāna* and *prāṇa*, urine and excrement are decreased. Even the elderly become young by continuously practicing *mūla bandha*. -1.81

Practice of Praṇava

पद्मासनं समारुह्य समकायशिरोधरः ।
नासाग्रदृष्टिरेकान्ते जपेदोङ्कारमव्ययम् ।।८२।।

padmāsanaṃ samāruhya samakāyaśirodharaḥ /
nāsāgradṛṣṭirekānte japedoṅkāramavyayam //82//

After assuming the lotus posture and maintaining *samakāyaśira* (the body and head straight) with *nāsāagradṛṣṭi* (*nāsā agra dṛṣṭi* literally, nostrils, frontal, sight - the sight fixed on the tip of the nose), one should repeat the eternal sound *Om* in *ekānta* (a secluded place). -1.82

भूर्भुवः स्वरिमे लोकाः सोमसूर्याग्निदेवताः ।
यस्या मात्रासु तिष्ठन्ति तत्परं ज्योतिरोमिति ।।८३।।

bhūrbhuvaḥ svarime lokāḥ somasūryāgnidevatāḥ /
yasyā mātrāsu tiṣṭhanti tatparaṃ jyotiromiti //83//

Om is the Supreme Light. In its *mātrā* (metre) abides the three deities of the moon, the sun, and the fire, and the three worlds indicated by the words *bhūḥ*, *bhuvaḥ* and *svaḥ*. -1.83

त्रयः कालास्त्रयो वेदास्त्रयो लोकास्त्रयः स्वराः ।
त्रयो देवाः स्थिता यत्र तत्परं ज्योतिरोमिति ।।८४।।

trayaḥ kālāstrayo vedāstrayo lokāstrayaḥ svarāḥ /
trayo devāḥ sthitā yatra tatparaṃ jyotiromiti //84//

That Supreme Light is *Om*. Therein abide the three times (past, present and future), the three *Vedas* (*Rigveda*, *Yajurveda* and *Sāmaveda*), the three worlds (*bhūḥ*, *bhuvaḥ* and *svaḥ*), the three syllables (*A*, *U* and *M*) and the three deities (*Brahmā*, *Viśnu* and *Maheśvara*. -1.84

क्रिया इच्छा तथा ज्ञानां ब्राह्मी रौद्री च वैष्णवी ।
त्रिधा शक्तिः स्थिता यत्र तत्परं ज्योतिरोमिति ।।८५।।

kriyā icchā tathā jñānāṃ brāhmī raudrī ca vaiṣṇavī /
tridhā śaktiḥ sthitā yatra tatparaṃ jyotiromiti //85//

That Supreme Light is *Om*, wherein abides the threefold *śaktis* (the creative powers) which are *kriyā*, *icchā* and *jñāna* (action, will and knowledge) and *Brāhmī*, *Raudrī* and *Vaiṣṇavī*. -1.85

आकाराश्च उकारश्च मकारो बिन्दुसंज्ञकः ।
त्रिधा मात्राः स्थिता यत्र तत् परं ज्योतिरोमिति ।।८६।।

ākārāśca ukāraśca makāro bindusañjñakaḥ /
tridhā mātrāḥ sthitā yatra tatparaṃ jyotiromiti //86//

The Supreme Light is *Om*, where the three types of letters are situated–the syllable *A*, the syllable *U*, and the syllable *M*–which is known as *bindu*. -1.86

वचसा तज्जयेद् बीजं वपुषा तत् समभ्यसेत् ।
मनसा तत्स्मरेन्नित्यं तत्परं ज्योतिरोमिति ।।८७।।

vacasā tajjaped bījaṃ vapuṣā tat samabhyaset /
manasā tatsmarennityaṃ tatparaṃ jyotiromiti //87//

That Supreme Light is *Om*. One should always recite its *bīja* (the seed syllable) orally, practice it properly with the body, and remember it in the mind. -1.87

शुचिर्वाप्यशुचिर्वापि योजपेत् प्रणवं सदा ।
न स लिप्यति पापेन पद्मपत्रमिवाम्भसा ।।८८।।

śucirvāpyaśucirvāpi yojapet praṇavaṃ sadā /
na sa lipyati pāpena padmapatramivāmbhasā //88//

One who constantly recites *praṇava* (i.e. *Om*), whether one is in a pure or impure state, is not besmeared by sins, just like a lotus leaf which is not tainted by (unclean) water. -1.88

Practice of Breath Control

चले वाते चलो बिन्दुर्निश्चले निश्चलो भवेत् ।
योगी स्थाणुत्वमाप्नोति ततो वायुं निरोधयेत् ।।८९।।

cale vāte calo bindurniścale niścalo bhavet /
yogī sthāṇutvamāpnoti tato vāyuṃ nirodhayet //89//

When *vāta* (the life force) is active, the *bindu* (semen) also becomes active, and when it (the *vāta*) is stable, the *bindu* also becomes still. Therefore, a yogī wishing to obtain pillar-like steadiness should restrain the *vāyu* (the life force). -1.89

यावद् वायुः स्थितो देहे तावज्जीवं न मुञ्चति ।
मरणं तस्य निष्क्रान्तिस्ततो वायुं निरोधयेत् ।।९०।।

yāvadvāyuḥ sthito dehe tāvajjīvaṃ na muñcati /
maraṇaṃ tasya niṣkrāntistato vāyuṃ nirodhayet //90//

As long as *vāyu* (the *prāna*) remains in the body, it is called life. Its departure from the body is death. Therefore, one should restrain the *vāyu* (the life force). -1.90

यावद् बद्धो मरुद् देहे यावच्चित्तं निरामयम् ।
यावद् दृष्टिर्भ्रुवोर्मध्ये तावत्कालभयं कुतः ।।९१।।

yāvadbaddho maruddehe yāvaccittaṃ nirāmayam /
yāvaddṛṣṭirbhruvormadhye tāvatkālabhayaṃ kutaḥ //91//

So long as *maruta* (the life force) is restrained in the body, the mind becomes *nirāmaya* (pure, free from diseases). So long as the gaze is fixed between the two eyebrows, how can there be fear of death? -1.91

अतः कालभयाद् ब्रह्मा प्राणायामपरायणः ।

योगिनो मुनयश्चैव ततो वायुं निरोधयेत् ।।९२।।

ataḥ kālabhayād brahmā prāṇāyāmaparāyaṇaḥ /

yogino munayaścaiva tato vāyuṃ nirodhayet //92//

This is why, due to the fear of death, even *Brahmā* (the Creator) is devoted to the practice of *prāṇāyāma* (the restraint of the life force). The yogīs and sages also do so. Therefore, one should restrain the *vāyu*. -1.92

Haṃsa Form of Prānāpāna Vāyu

षट्त्रिंशदङ्गुलो हंसः प्रयाणं कुरुते बहिः ।
वामदक्षिणमार्गेण ततः प्राणोऽभिधीयते ।।९३।।

ṣaṭtriṃśadaṅgulo haṃsaḥ prayāṇaṃ kurute bahiḥ /

vāmadakṣiṇamārgeṇa tataḥ prāṇo'bhidhīyate //93//

The *prayāṇa* (departure) of the *haṃsa* is of thirty-six fingers distance through the left and right pathways. Therefore, it is called *prāṇa* (the life force). -1.93

शुद्धिमेति यदा सर्वं नाडीचक्रं मलाकुलम् ।
तदैव जायते योगी प्राणसंग्रहणे क्षमः ।।९४।।

śuddhimeti yadā sarvaṃ nāḍīcakraṃ malākulam /

tadaiva jāyate yogī prāṇasaṅgrahaṇe kṣamaḥ //94//

When the *prānic* pathways and *cakras*, which are filled with impurities, are purified, then the yogī acquires the ability of *prāṇa saṅgrahaṇa* (accumulation of the life force). -1.94

Nādi Śodhana Prānāyāma

बद्धपद्मासनो योगी प्राणं चन्द्रेण पूरयेत् ।
धारयित्वा यथाशक्तिभूयः सूर्येण रेचयेत् ।।९५।।

baddhapadmāsano yogī prāṇaṃ candreṇa pūrayet /

dhārayitvā yathāśakti bhūyaḥ sūryeṇa recayet //95//

A yogī in his *baddha padma āsana* (bound lotus posture) should fill in the *prāṇa* (life force) through *candra* (the moon, meaning the left nostril). Then holding it according to his capacity, he should expel it again through *sūrya* (the sun, meaning the right nostril). -1.95

अमृतंदधिसङ्काशं गोक्षीरधवलोपमम् ।
ध्यात्वा चन्द्रमसो बिम्बं प्राणायामी सुखी भवेत् ।।९६।।

amṛtadadhisaṅkāśaṃ gokṣīradhavalopamam /

dhyātvā candramaso bimbaṃ prāṇāyāmī sukhī bhavet //96//

A yogī who, after meditating on the disk of moon--the nectar of immortality which has the appearance (color) of curd or cow's milk or silver--practices *prāṇāyāma* (restraint of the life force/breath) will become happy. -1.96

Iḍa and Piṅgalā Prānāyāma

दक्षिणे श्वासमाकृष्य पूरयेदुत्तरं शनैः ।
कुम्भयित्वा विधानेन पुनश्चन्द्रेण रेचयेत् ।।९७।।

dakṣiṇeśvāsamākṛṣya pūrayeduttaraṃ śanaiḥ /
kumbhayitvā vidhānena punaścandreṇa recayet //97//

Having drawn *śvāsa* (the breath) in through *dakṣiṇa* (the right nostril), one should slowly fill up *udara* (the abdomen). Having retained the breath using the proper method, one should expel it again through the left nostril. -1.97

प्रज्वलज्ज्वलनज्वालापुञ्जमादित्यमण्डलम् ।
ध्यात्वा नाभिस्थितं योगी प्राणायामे सुखी भवेत् ।।९८।।

prajvalajjvalanajvālāpuñjamādityamaṇḍalam /
dhyatva nabhisthitaṃ yogı praṇayami sukhı bhavet //98//

The yogī who, after meditating on the solar disk which is a mass of brightly burning flames located at the navel, practices *prāṇāyāma* (restraint of life force/breath), will become happy. -1.98

प्राणंश्चेदिडया पिबेत्परिमितं भूयोऽन्यया रेचयेत्
पीत्वा पिङ्गलया समीरणमथो बद्ध्वा त्यजेद् वामया ।
सूर्यचन्द्रमसोरनेन विधिना बिम्बद्वयं ध्यायतां
शुद्धा नाडिगणा भवन्ति यमिनां मासत्रयादूर्ध्वतः ।।९९।।

prāṇaścediḍayā pibetparimitaṃ bhūyo'nyayā recayet
pītvā piṅgalayā samīraṇamatho baddhvā tyajed vāmayā /
sūryacandramasoranena vidhinā bimbadvayaṃ dhyāyatāṃ
śuddhā nāḍigaṇā bhavanti yamināṃ māsatrayādūrdhvataḥ //99//

When the breath is drawn in through *iḍa* (the left nostril), one should expel it again through the other (right/opposite nostril). After drawing in the air through *piṅgalā* (the right nostril), one should, after retaining it (inside), release it again through the left nostril. By meditating on the two disks of the sun and the moon according to the prescribed rules, the multitudes of *prānic* pathways become pure after three months. -1.99

The Results of Nādi Śodhana

यथेष्टं धारणं वायोरनलस्य प्रदीपनम् ।
नादाभिव्यक्तिरारोग्यं जायते नाडिशोधने ।।१००।।

yatheṣṭaṃ dhāraṇaṃ vāyoranalasya pradīpanam /
nādābhivyaktirārogyaṃ jāyate nāḍiśodhane //100//

By retaining *vāyu* (the life force) in a comfortable way, the digestive fire is ignited and *nāda* (the subtle mystical sound) becomes manifest through the purification of *nāḍis* (the subtle channels) and one attains *ārogya* (good health, a disease free state). -1.100

इति गोरक्षयोगशास्त्रे पूर्व शतकम् ।।

iti gorakṣayogaśastre pūrva śatakam //

Thus ends the First Part of *Gorakṣa Yogaśāstra.*

UTTARA ŚATAKAM

Part Two

Description of Prāṇāyāma

प्राणो देहे स्थितो वायुरपानस्य निरोधनात् ।
एकश्वसनमात्रेणोद्धाटयेत् गगने गतिम् ।।१।।

prāṇo dehe sthito vāyurapānasya nirodhanāt /
ekaśvasanamātreṇodghāṭayet gagane gatim //1//

A yogī should open his way to *gagana* (space or the sky) with a single breath, through the restraint of the *prāna vāyu* and *apāna vāyu* that remain in the body. -2.1

रेचकः पूरकश्चैव कुम्भकः प्रणवात्मकः ।
प्राणायामो भवेत् त्रेधा मत्रद्वादशसंयुतः ।।२।।

recakaḥ pūrakaścaiva kumbhakaḥ praṇavātmakaḥ /
prāṇāyāmo bhavet tredhā mātrādvādaśasaṃyutaḥ //2//

Prāṇāyāma has three parts. They are *recaka, pūraka and kumbhaka* (exhalation, inhalation and retention) in combination with *praṇava* (*Om*) with twelve *mātrās* (measures). -2.2

मात्राद्वादशसंयुक्तौ दिवाकरनिशाकरौ ।
दोषजालमपध्नन्तौ ज्ञातव्यौ योगिभिः सदा ।।३।।

mātrādvādaśasaṃyuktau divākaraniśākarau /
doṣajālamapaghnantau jñātavyau yogibhiḥ sadā //3//

The sun and moon (i.e. the *prāna* and *apāna*) should be combined with the twelve *mātrās* (measures, i.e. 12 OMs). Through this practice, all *doṣas* (physical disorders, diseases) are destroyed. The yogīs should always know these two (facts). -2.3

Three Types of Prāṇāyāma

पूरके द्वादशीकुर्यात्कुम्भके षोडशी भवेत् ।
रेचके दश ॐकराः प्राणायामः स उच्यते ।।४।।

pūrake dvādaśīkuryātkumbhake ṣoḍaśī bhavet /
recake daśa oṃkārāḥ prāṇāyāmaḥ sa ucyate //4//

One should inhale the breath for twelve *mātrās* (i.e. a count of twelve *Oms*), then retain it for sixteen *mātrās*, and then exhale for ten *mātrās*. This is called *prāṇāyāma* (the restraint of life force). -2.4

प्रथमे द्वादशी मात्रा मध्यमेद्विगुणा मता ।
उत्तमे त्रिगुणा प्राणायामस्य निर्णयः ।।५।।

prathame dvādaśī mātrā madhyame dviguṇā matā /
uttame triguṇā proktā prāṇāyāmasya nirṇayaḥ //5//

In the beginning one should practice using twelve *mātrās*; in the middle stage the *mātrās* should be doubled (i.e. twenty-four); in the highest stage it should be tripled (i.e. thirty-six *mātrās*) as decided for (the practice of) *prāṇāyāma*. -2.5

अधमे चोद्यते घर्मः कम्पो भवति मध्यमे ।
उत्तिष्ठत्युत्तमे योगि ततो वायुं निरोधयेत् ।।६।।

adhame codyate gharmaḥ kampo bhavati madhyame /
uttiṣṭhatyuttame yogī tato vāyuṃ nirodhayet //6//

In the lower stage of *prāṇāyāma*, there is sweating; in the middle stage there is trembling; in the highest stage the yogī rises from the ground. Therefore, he should restrain *vāyu* (the life force). -2.6

Methods of Prānāyāma

बद्ध पद्मासनो योगी नमस्कृत्य गुरुं शिवम् ।
भ्रूमध्ये दृष्टिरेकाकी प्राणायामं समभ्यसेत् ।।७।।

baddhapadmāsano yogī namaskṛtya guruṃ śivam /
bhrūmadhye dṛṣṭirekākī prāṇāyāmaṃ samabhyset //7//

A yogī, bound in *padmāsana*, after saluting his *Guru* and *Śiva*, should practice *prāṇāyāma* with his gaze fixed on the middle of the eyebrows. -2.7

ऊर्ध्वमाकृष्य चापानवायुं प्राणे नियोजयेत् ।
उर्ध्वमानीयते शक्त्या सर्वपापैः प्रमुच्यते ।।८।।

ūrdhvamākṛṣya cāpānavāyuṃ prāṇe niyojayet /
urdhvamānīyate śaktyā sarvapāpaiḥ pramucyate //8//

Raising the *apāna vāyu* upward, he should unite it with the *prāṇa*. When it (*apāna vāyu*) is taken upward along with *Śakti*, he is freed from all sins. -2.8

Kumbhaka Prānāyāma

द्वाराणां नवकं निरुद्ध्य मरुत पीत्वा दृढं धारितं
नीत्वाकाशमपानवह्निसहितं शक्त्या समुच्चालितम् ।
आत्मस्थानयुतस्त्वनेन विधिवद् विन्यस्यमूर्ध्नि ध्रुवं
यावत्तिष्ठति तावदेव महतां संघेन संस्तूयते ।।९।।

dvārāṇāṃ navakaṃ niruddhya maruta pītvā dṛḍhaṃ dhāritaṃ
nītvākāśamapānavahnisahitaṃ śaktyā samuccālitam /
ātmasthānayutastvanena vidhivad vinyasyamūrghniṃ dhruvaṃ
yāvattiṣṭhati tāvadeva mahatāṃ saṃghena saṃstūyate //9//

After closing the nine outlets of the body, one should drink *maruta* (i.e. air) and hold it firmly. Using the *apāna vāyu* and the fire, one should correctly awaken the *Śakti*, and then unite it at the heart space. One should then certainly raise it to the head (i.e. at the *ājñā cakra*) as per the prescribed rule. The yogī who meditates on the *Ātmā* in this way, as long as one remains alive in this world, will be highly praised by the association of the great yogīs. -2.9

Results of Prāṇāyāma

प्राणायामो भवत्येवं पातकेन्धनपावकः ।
भवोदधिमहासेतुः प्रोच्यते योगिभिः सदा ।। १०।।

prāṇāyāmo bhavatyevaṃ pātakendhanapāvakaḥ /
bhavodadhimahāsetuḥ procyate yogibhiḥ sadā //10//

Hence, yogīs always say that *prāṇāyāma* is the fire that burns down the fuel of offences, and is a *mahāsetu* (the great bridge) which helps one get across *bhava udadhi* (the ocean of worldly existence). -2.10

आसनेन रुजो हन्ति प्राणायामेन पातकम् ।
विकारं मानसं योगी प्रत्याहारेण मुण्चति ।।११।।

āsanena rujo hanti prāṇāyāmena pātakam /
vikāraṃ mānasaṃ yogī pratyāhāreṇa muṇcati //11//

By practicing postures, diseases (of the body) are removed; through *prāṇāyāma* (restraint of the life force), offences are destroyed. Through *pratyāhāra* (withdrawal of the senses from external stimuli) the yogī releases his *mānasa vikāra* (mental modifications). -2.11

धारणाभिमतो धैर्यं ध्यानाच्चैतन्यमद्भुतम् ।
समाधौ मोक्षमानोति त्यक्त्व कर्म शुभाशुभम् ।।१२।।

dhāraṇābhimato dhairyaṃ dhyanaccaitanyamadbhutam /
samādhau mokṣamāpnoti tyaktvā karma śubhāśubham //12//

The practice of concentration as desired increases *dhairya* (patience) and through practice of *dhyāna* (meditation) a wonderful state of consciousness is attained. In *samādhi* (the superconscious state of mind), having renounced all auspicious and inauspicious karmas (actions), one attains liberation. -2.12

प्राणायामद्विषटकेन प्रत्याहारः प्रकीर्तितः ।
प्रत्याहारद्विषट्केन ज्ञायते धारणा शुभा ।। १३।।

prāṇāyāmadviṣaṭakena pratyāhāraḥ prakīrtitaḥ /
pratyāhāradviṣaṭkena jñāyate dhāraṇā śubhā //13//

Pratyāhāra (withdrawal of the senses from external stimuli) is said to occur with twice six (twelve) *prāṇāyāmas*. *Śubha dhāraṇā* (auspicious concentration) occurs with twice six (twelve) *pratyāhāras* (one hundred forty-four *prāṇāyāmas*). -2.13

धारणा द्वादश प्रोक्ता ध्यानाद् धानविशारदैः ।
ध्यानद्वादशकेनैव समाधिरभिधीयते ।।१४।।

dhāraṇā dvādaśa proktā dhyānād dhyānaviśāradaiḥ /
dhyānadvādaśakenaiva samādhirabhidhīyate //14//

The state of *dhyāna* is attained with twelve *dhāraṇās* (one thousand seven hundred twenty-eight *prāṇāyāmas*) according to the experts in *dhyāna* (meditation). It is said that the state of *samādhi* is achieved with twelve *dhyānas* (twenty thousand seven hundred thirty-six *prāṇāyāmas*) -2.14

The Nature of Samādhi

यत्समाधौ परं ज्योतिरनन्तं विश्वमोमुखम् ।
तस्मिन् दृष्टे क्रिया कर्म यातायातं न विद्यते ।।१५।।

yatsamādhau paraṃ jyotiranantaṃ viśvatomukham /
tasmin dṛṣṭe kriyā karma yātāyātaṃ na vidyate //15//

One who sees in *samādhi* (the superconscious state of mind) *Parama Jyoti Ananta* (the Supreme Light Infinite) having faces all around, there does not exist any activities, any effects of past karmas, and going and coming (rounds of deaths and births) for him. -2.15

सम्बद्धासनमेढ्रमंध्रियुगलं कर्णाक्षिनासापुटाद्
द्वाराण्यगुलिभिर्नियम्य पवनं वक्त्रेण सम्पूरितम् ।
ध्यात्वा वक्षसि वह्न्यपानसहितं मूर्ध्नि स्थितं धारये
देवं याति विशेषतत्त्वसमतां योगीश्वरस्तन्मयः ।।१६।।

sambaddhāsanameḍhramaṃdhriyugalaṃ karṇākṣināsāpuṭād
dvārāṇyagulibhirniyamya pavanaṃ vaktreṇa sampūritam /
dhyātvā vakṣasi vahnyapānasahitaṃ mūrdhni sthitaṃ dhāraye
devaṃ yāti viśeṣatattvasamatāṃ yogīśvarastanmayaḥ //16//

After performing the posture (preferably, *siddhāsana*) one should close the openings of the ears (with the thumbs), eyes (with the index fingers), the nasal passages (with middle fingers) and mouth (with ring and little fingers) and should inhale the air through the mouth. After concentrating the *prāna* in the chest along with *agni* (the fire in the abdomen) and the *apāna* (in the *mūladhāra*), he should hold them firmly in the crown of the head (*sahasrāra cakra*). In this way, the *Yogīśvara* (lord of the yogīs) absorbed in *samādhi* comes to attain *samatā* (equality or equanimity) with *Viśeṣa Tattva* (the Ultimate Reality). -2.16

The Signs of Yogasiddhi

गगनं पवने प्राप्त ध्वनिरुत्पद्यते महान् ।
घण्टादीनां प्रवाद्यानां तदा सिद्धिरदूरतः ।।१७।।

gaganaṃ pavane prāpte dhvanirutpadyate mahān /
ghaṇṭādīnāṃ pravādyānāṃ tadā siddhiradūrataḥ //17//

When the air reaches *gagana* (the sky or space, meaning *sahasrāra*), a great sound is produced similar to musical instruments such as a bell. Then (it should be known that) *siddhi* (perfection) is not far away. -2.17

प्राणायामेन युक्तेन सर्वरोक्षयो भवेत् ।
आयुक्ताभ्यासयोगेन सर्वरोगस्य संभवः ।।१८ ।।

prāṇāyāmena yuktena sarvarokṣayo bhavet /
ayuktābhyāsaṃyogena sarvarogasya saṃbhavaḥ //18//

Through the proper practice of *prāṇāyāma* all kinds of diseases are destroyed. Through the improper practice of yoga all types of diseases are generated. -2.18

Destruction of Diseases by Prāṇāyāma

हिक्का कासस्तथा श्वासः शिरः कर्णाक्षिवेदनाः ।
भवन्ति विविधा रोगा पवनस्य व्यतिक्रमात् ।।१९।।

hikkā kāsastathā śvāsaḥ śiraḥ karṇākṣivedanāḥ /
bhavanti vividha roga pavanasya vyatikramat //19//

Various disorders like hiccups, cough, asthma, and aching of the head, ears, and eyes are caused through *vyatikrama* (the malpractice) of *pavana* (the air or life force). -2.19

यथा सिंहो गजो व्याघ्रो भवेद्वश्यः शनैः शनैः ।
अन्यथा हन्ति योक्तारं तथा वायुरसेवितः ।।२०।।

yathā siṃho gajo vyāghro bhavedvaśyaḥ śanaiḥ śanaiḥ /
anyathā hanti yoktāraṃ tathā vāyurasevitaḥ //20//

The lion, the elephant, and the tiger are brought under control slowly and slowly; otherwise, they may kill the trainer. Similarly, the improper use and practice of *pavana* (the air or life force) is detrimental. -2.20

युक्तं युक्तं त्यजेद्वायुं युक्तं युक्तं च पूरयेत् ।
युक्तं युक्तं च बध्नीयादेवं सिद्धिरदूरतः ।।२१।।

yuktaṃ yuktaṃ tyajedvāyuṃ yuktaṃ yuktaṃ ca pūrayet /
yuktaṃ yuktaṃ ca badhnīyādevaṃ siddhiradūrataḥ //21//

One should exhale the air slowly and gently, and should also inhale slowly and gently. Also, one should hold the breath slowly and gently. Thus, through such practice *siddhi* (the perfection) is near. -2.21

Description of Pratyāhāra

चरतां चक्षुरादीनां विषयेषु यथाक्रमम् ।
यत्प्रत्याहरणं तेषां प्रत्याहारः स उच्यते ।।२२।।

caratāṃ cakṣurādīnāṃ viṣayeṣu yathākramam /
yatpratyāharaṇaṃ teṣāṃ pratyāhāraḥ sa ucyate //22//

The eyes and other senses wander towards their respective sense-objects. Their withdrawal from such (sense-objects) is called *pratyāhāra* (the withdrawal of senses). -2.22

Three Divisions of the Day

यथा तृतीयकालस्थो रविः प्रत्याहरेत्प्रभाम् ।
तृतौयाङ्गस्थितो योगी विकारं मानसं तथा ।।२३।।

yathā tṛtīyakālastho raviḥ pratyāharetprabhām /
tṛtauyāṅgasthito yogī vikāraṃ mānasaṃ tathā //23//

Just like the sun reaching the third quarter of the day withdraws its luster, so the yogī established in the third limb of yoga should withdraw his mind from its *vikāras* (mental modifications). -2.23

अङ्गमध्ये यथाङ्गन् कूर्मः संकोचयेद् ध्रुवम् ।
योगी प्रत्याहरेदेवमिन्द्रियाणि तथात्मनि ।।२४।।

aṅgamadhye yathāṅgān kūrmaḥ saṅkocayed dhruvam /
yogī pratyāharedevamindriyāṇi tathātmani //24//

Like a tortoise contracts its limbs into the middle of its shell, so the yogī should withdraw his senses from their respective sense-objects within himself. -2.24

Pratyāhāra of Likes and Dislikes

यं यं शृणोति कर्णाभ्यामप्रियं प्रियमेव वा ।
तं तमात्मेति विज्ञाय प्रत्याहरति योगवित् ।।२५।।

yaṃ yaṃ śṛṇoti karṇābhyāmapriyaṃ priyameva vā /
taṃ tamātmeti vijñāya pratyāharati yogavit //25//

Whatever he hears with his ears, whether it is pleasant or unpleasant, knowing that it is *Ātmā* (the Self), the expert in yoga withdraws himself from hearing. -2.25

अगन्धमथवा गन्धं यं यं जिघ्रति नासिका ।
तं तमात्मेति विज्ञाय प्रत्याहरति योगवित् ।।२६।।

agandhamathavā gandhaṃ yaṃ yaṃ jighrati nāsikā /
taṃ tamātmeti vijñāya pratyāharati yogavit //26//

Whatever he smells with his nose, whether fragrant or stinking, knowing that it is *Ātmā* (the Self), the expert in yoga withdraws himself from smelling. -2.26

अमेध्यमथवा मेध्यं यं यं पश्यति चक्षुषा ।
तं तमात्मेति विज्ञाय प्रत्याहरति योगवित ।।२७।।

amedhyamathavā medhyaṃ yaṃ yaṃ paśyati cakṣuṣā /
taṃ tamātmeti vijñāya pratyāharati yogavita //27//

Whatever he sees with his eyes, whether pure or impure, knowing that it is *Ātmā* (the Self), the expert in yoga withdraws himself from seeing or sight -2.27

अस्प्रिश्यमथवा स्प्रिश्यं यं यं स्प्रिशति चर्मणा ।।
तं तमात्मेति विज्ञाय प्रत्याहरति योगवित् ।।२८।।

aspṛśyamathavā spṛśyaṃ yaṃ yaṃ spṛśati carmaṇā /
taṃ tamātmeti vijñāya pratyāharati yogavit //28//

Whatever he senses with his skin, whether perceptible or not perceptible, knowing that it is *Ātmā* (the Self), the expert in yoga withdraws himself from his sense of touch. -2.28

लावण्यमलावण्यं वा यं यं रसति जिह्वया ।
तं तमात्मेति विज्ञाय प्रत्याहरति योगवित् ।।२९।।

lāvaṇyamalāvaṇyaṃ vā yaṃ yaṃ rasati jihvayā /
taṃ tamātmeti vijñāya pratyāharati yogavit //29//

Whatever he tastes with his tongue, whether salty or not salty, knowing that it is *Ātmā* (the Self), the expert in yoga withdraws himself from his sense of taste. -2.29

Pratyāhāra of the Nectar

चन्द्रामृत्मयीं धारां पत्याहरति भास्करः ।
यत्प्रत्यहरणं तस्याः प्रत्याहारः स उच्यते ।।३०।।

candrāmṛtmayīṃ dhārāṃ pratyāharati bhāskaraḥ /
yatpratyāharaṇaṃ tasyāḥ pratyāhāraḥ sa ucyate //30//

The sun devours (withdraws) *dhārā* (the fountain) full of *amṛta* (the nectar) from the moon. One should drink that shower of the nectar, withdrawing it back from the sun. That is called *pratyāhāra* (in the sense of taking the shower of *amṛta* back). -2.30

एकस्त्री भुज्यते द्वाभ्यामागता चन्द्रमण्डलात् ।
तृतीयो यः पुनस्ताभ्यां स भवेदजरामरः ।।३१।।

ekastrī bhujyate dvābhyāmāgatā candramaṇḍalāt /

tṛtīyo yaḥ punastābhyāṃ sa bhavedajarāmaraḥ //31//

There is one female (meaning the fountain of *amṛta*) that comes from the lunar region to be enjoyed by two (the sun and the moon). If the third one enjoys her, he becomes free from old age and death. -2.31

Viparītakaraṇi Mudrā

नाभिदेशे वसत्येको भास्करो दहनात्मनः ।
अमृतात्मा स्थितो नित्यं तालुमूले च चन्द्रमाः ।।३२।।

nābhideśe vasatyeko bhāskaro dahanātmanaḥ /
amṛtātmā sthito nityaṃ tālumūle ca candramāḥ //32//

The one sun dwells in the region of the navel in the form or spirit of fire. The moon in the form or spirit of nectar is always located at *tālumūla* (at the root of the palate). -2.32

वर्षत्यधोमुखश्चन्द्रो ग्रस्त्यूर्ध्वमुखो रविः ।
ज्ञातव्या करणी तत्र यथा पीयूषमाप्यते ।।३३।।

varṣatyadhomukhaścandro grastyūrdhvamukho raviḥ /
jñātavyā karaṇī tatra yathā pīyūṣamāpyate //33//

The downward facing moon drops down the nectar. The upward facing sun devours that nectar (that drops down from the moon). So, one should know *karaṇi* (meaning the inverted pose) in order to get *pīyūṣa* (the nectar). -2.33

ऊर्ध्व नाभिरधस्तालुरुर्ध्वं भानुरधः शशी ।
करणि विपरीताख्या गुरुवाक्येन लभ्यते ।।३४।।

ūrdhva nābhiradhastālurūrdhvaṃ bhānuradhaḥ śaśī /
karaṇi viparītākhyā guruvākyena labhyate //34//

While the navel is above and the palate is below, in other words, while the sun is above and the moon is below, then that is known as *viparīta karaṇi āsana* (the inverted pose). One should receive it through the instructions of a guru (teacher). -2.34

Anāhata Cakra

त्रिधा बद्धो वृषो यत्र रोरवीति महास्वनः ।
अनाहतं च तच्चक्रं हृदये योगिनो विदुः ।।३५।।

tridhā baddho vṛṣo yatra roravīti mahāsvanaḥ /
anāhataṃ ca taccakraṃ hṛdaye yogino viduḥ //35//

Whereas a bull tied up three rounds with a rope bellows in a horrific way, similarly, yogīs should know that it is in the *anāhata cakra* located at the heart where the *jīva* (the embodied Self) yells, being tied up by the snares of this illusory world. -2.35

अनाहतमतिक्रम्य चाक्रम्य मणिपूरकम् ।

प्राप्ते प्राणे महापद्मं योगी स्वयमृतायते ।।३६।।

anāhatamatikramya cākramya maṇipūrakam /

prāpte prāṇe mahāpadmaṃ yogī svayamṛtāyate //36//

When the *prāṇa* (life force) reaches the *mahāpadma* (great lotus i.e. *sahasrāra cakra* - the thousand-petalled lotus at the crown of the head), after having gone beyond the *maṇipūra cakra* and *anāhata cakra*, the yogī by himself attains the state of *amṛtā* (immortality). -2.36

ऊर्धवं षोडशपत्रपद्मगलितं प्राणाद्वाप्तं हठा-
दूर्ध्वस्यो रसनां निधाय विधिवच्छक्तिं परां चिन्तयेत् ।
तत्कल्लोलकलाजलं सुविमलं जिह्वाकुलम् यः पिबे-
न्निर्दोषः समृणालकोपुर्योगी चिरं जीवति ।।३७।।

ūrdhavaṃ ṣoḍaśapatrapadmagalitaṃ prāṇādvāptaṃ haṭhād-

urdhvasyo rasanaṃ nidhaya vidhivacchaktiṃ paraṃ cintayet /

tatkallolakalājalaṃ suvimalaṃ jihvākulam yaḥ pibe-

nnirdoṣaḥ samṛṇālakomalavapuryogī ciraṃ jīvati //37//

After turning his tongue upward into the cavity (of the skull) according to approved method, one should obtain the nectar forcibly by fixing it (the tongue) to the palate so that (the nectar) drops down from the sixteen-petalled lotus above, and then he should contemplate *Parāma Śakti* (the Supreme Power). That flawless yogī, who drinks the extremely pure water flowing from that lotus (mentioned above), from *kula* (the home) of his tongue, lives a long life with a body as soft as a lotus stalk. -2.37

Kāki Mudrā

काकचञ्चुवदास्येन शीतलं सलिलं पिबेत् ।
प्राणापानविधानेन योगी भवति निर्जरः ।।३८।।

kākacañcuvadāsyena śītalaṃ salilaṃ pibet /

praṇapanavidhanena yogı bhavati nirjaraḥ //38//

The yogī should drink the cool flow of air with the mouth formed like the beak of a crow. One does not become old by following the practice of *prāṇa* and *apāna* according to prescribed method. -2.38

रसनातालुमूलेन यः प्राणमनिलं पिबेत् ।
अब्दार्द्धेन भवेतस्य सर्वरोगस्य संक्षयः ।।३९।।

rasanatalumulena yaḥ praṇamanilaṃ pibet /

abdārddhena bhavetasya sarvarogasya saṃkṣayaḥ //39//

One who drinks *prāṇa anila* (meaning *vāyu*) with the tongue located at the root of the palate, their multifarious diseases are totally destroyed after half a year. -2.39

Vishuddha Cakra

विशुद्धे पञ्चमे चक्रे ध्यात्वासौ सकलामृतम् ।
उन्मार्गेण हृतं याति वञ्चयित्वा मुखं रवेः ।।४०।।

viśuddhe pañcame cakre dhyātvāsau sakalāmṛtam /
unmārgeṇa hṛtaṃ yāti vañcayitvā mukhaṃ raveḥ //40//

One who, having contemplated the nectar fully in the fifth *cakra viśuddhi* (also called *viśuddha*), and having the mouth of the sun (located at the navel region) deprived of the nectar, goes to confiscate it (the nectar) through the opposite route. -2.40

विशब्देन स्मृतो हंसः नैर्मल्यं शुद्धिरुच्यते ।
अतः कण्ठे विशुद्धाख्यं चक्रं चक्रविदो विदुः ।।४१।।

viśabdena smṛto haṃsaḥ nairmalyaṃ śuddhirucyate /
ataḥ kaṇṭhe viśuddhākhyaṃ cakraṃ cakravido viduḥ //41//

It is understood that the sound/word '*vi*' means *haṃsa* (literally, a swan that constantly goes out and comes in (here the meaning is: the breath) and it is understood that the word '*śuddhi*' means purity. Therefore, the *cakra* named '*viśuddha*' located at the throat is known well by the expert of the *cakras* in yoga. -2.41

Depriving the Mouth of the Sun

अमृतं कन्दरे कृत्वा नासान्तसुषिरे क्रमात् ।
स्वयमुच्चालितं याति वर्जयित्वा मुखं रवेः ।।४२।।

amṛtaṃ kandare kṛtvā nāsāntasuṣire kramāt /
svayamuccālitaṃ yāti varjayitvā mukhaṃ raveḥ //42//

After one has gradually placed the nectar into the cave at the end of the nose, the *prāna*, after abandoning the mouth of the sun, goes up by itself (in its own way) into the cavity. -2.42

Drinking of the Lunar Nectar

बद्धं सोमकलाजलं सुविमलं कण्ठस्थलादूर्ध्वतो
नासान्ते सुषिरे नयेच्च गगनद्वारान्ततः सर्वतः ।
ऊर्ध्वास्यो भुवि सन्निपत्य निरामुत्तानपादः पिबे
देवं यः कुरुते जितेन्द्रियगणो नैवास्ति तस्य क्षयः ।। ४३।।

baddhaṃ somakalājalaṃ suvimalaṃ kaṇṭhasthalādūrdhvato
nāsānte suṣire nayecca gaganadvārāntataḥ sarvataḥ /
ūrdhvāsyo bhuvi sannipatya nirāmuttānapādaḥ pibed
evaṃ yaḥ kurute jitendriyagaṇo naivāsti tasya kṣayaḥ //43//

Having stopped the extremely pure water (nectar) of the crescent moon located at the upper region of the throat, one should fill it into the cavity at the end of the nostrils. Then, closing all the gates of the *prāna*, one should inhale with *prāna* and *apāna* at the *gagana* (the crown of the head). Then, he should lie flat with extended legs on the ground and drink the nectar (mentioned above). The yogī who regularly does so in this way, and has subdued their senses, there is no destruction for them. -2.43

उर्ध्वं जिह्वां स्थिरीकृत्य सोमपनां करोति यः ।
मासार्द्धेन न सन्देहो मृत्युं जयति योगवित् ।।४४।।

urdhvaṃ jihvāṃ sthirīkṛtya somapānaṃ karoti yaḥ /
māsārddhena na sandeho mṛtyuṃ jayati yogavit //44//

One who is expert in yoga, and drinks *soma* (the nectar from the moon) by establishing his tongue upward in the cavity behind the palate, conquers death within half a month. There is no doubt about it. -2.44

बद्धम् मूलबिल येन तेन विघ्नो विदारितः ।
अजरामरमाप्नोति यथा पञ्चमुखो हरः ।।४५।।

baddhaṃ mūlabila yena tena vighno vidāritaḥ /
ajarāmaramāpnoti yathā pañcamukho haraḥ //45//

The yogī who is successful in locking the main door overcomes all obstacles and attains *ajara* and *amara* (changeless and immortal) states like *Pañcamukha* (five-faced) *Śiva*. -2.45

संपीड्य रसनाग्रेण राजदन्तबिलं महत् ।
ध्यात्वामृतमयीं देवीं षण्मासेन कविर्भवेत् ।।४६।।

sampīdya rasanāgreṇa rājadantabilaṃ mahat /
dhyatvāmṛtamayīṃ devīṃ ṣaṇmāsena kavirbhavet //46//

The yogī who presses the tip of his tongue against the great cavity behind *rājadanta* (the incisor teeth) and contemplates *Amṛtamayī Devī* (the Goddess of Nectar), becomes a *kavi* (poet) within six months. -2.46

सर्वद्वाराणि बध्नाति तदूर्ध्वं धारितं महत् ।
न मुञ्चत्यमृतंकोऽपि स पन्थाः पञ्चधारणाः ।।४७।।

sarvadvārāṇi badhnāti tadūrdhvaṃ dhāritaṃ mahat /
na muñcatyamṛtaṅko'pi sa panthāḥ pañcadhāraṇāḥ //47//

When the great flow of the nectar from above is blocked with the tip of the tongue, the gates of all the *nādis* are closed. Due to the block of the above route, the nectar does not fall anywhere. This way of *dhāraṇā* (concentration on the nectar) is like *pañca dhāraṇā* (the five types of concentration on the five elements). 2.47

Experience of the Nectar Juice

चुम्बन्ती यदि लम्बिकाग्रमनिशं जिह्वा रसस्यन्दिनी
सक्षारं कटुकाम्लदुग्धसदृशं मध्वाज्यतुल्यं तथा ।
व्याधीनां हरणं जरान्तकरणं शास्त्राङ्गमोदगीरणं
तस्य स्यादमरत्वमष्टगुणितं सिद्धाङ्गनाकर्षणम् ।।४८।।

cumbantī yadi lambikāgramaniśaṃ jihvā rasasyandinī
sakṣāraṃ kaṭukāmladugdhasadṛśaṃ madhvājyatulyaṃ tathā /
vyādhīnāṃ haraṇaṃ jarāntakaraṇaṃ śāstrāṅgamodgīraṇaṃ
tasya syādamaratvamaṣṭaguṇitaṃ siddhāṅganākarṣaṇam //48//

The yogi, who regularly kisses the *rasa* (the nectar) donor with the tip of his tongue, experiences its tastes as salty, pungent, sour or like milk, honey, and ghee. All diseases and old age are ended (through this practice) and that yogī comprehends and explains *śāstras* (the scriptures) and their *aṅgas* (the branches) without studying them, and achieves *amaratva* (immortality) and *aṣṭaguṇas* or *aṣṭasiddhis* (the eight supernatural powers) and attracts *siddhas* (adepts) and *aṅganā* (beautiful women). -2.48

अमृतापूर्णदेहस्य योगिनो द्वित्रिवत्सरात् ।
ऊर्ध्वं प्रवर्तते रेतोऽप्यणिमादिगुणोदयः ।।४९।।

amṛtāpūrṇadehasya yogino dvitrivatsarāt /
ūrdhvaṃ pravartate reto'pyaṇimādiguṇodayaḥ //49//

The yogī's body becomes full of the nectar after two or three years and his *reta* (semen) rises upward. Through this he attains *aṇimādiguṇas* (the *aṇimā*, etc. qualities, meaning the supernatural powers). -2.49

ईन्धनानि यथा वह्निस्तैलवर्तिं च दीपकः ।
तथा सोमकलापूर्णं देहं देही न मुञ्चति ।।५०।।

īndhanāni yathā vahnistailavartiṃ ca dīpakaḥ /
tathā somakalāpūrṇaṃ dehaṃ dehī na muñcati //50//

When there is fuel, there is fire, and when there is oil and wick, there is light. Similarly, *Dehī* (the indweller of the body, the Self) does not depart *deha* (the body) of the yogī when it is *somakalāpūrṇa* (full of lunar nectar). -2.50

नित्यसोमकलपूर्णशरीरं यस्य योगिनः ।
तक्षकेणापि दष्टस्य विषं तस्य न सर्पति ।।५१।।

nityaṃ somakalāpūrṇa śarīraṃ yasya yoginaḥ /
takṣakeṇāpi daṣṭasya viṣaṃ tasya na sarpati //51//

A yogī whose body is always full of the lunar nectar, poison does not spread in his body, though a *Takṣaka* (king of serpents) itself bites him.

-2.51

Description of Dhāranā

आसनेन समायुक्तः प्राणायामेन संयुतः ।
प्रत्याहारेण सम्पन्नो धारणां च समभ्यसेत् ।।५२।।

āsanena samāyuktaḥ prāṇāyāmena saṃyutaḥ /
pratyāhāreṇa sampanno dhāraṇāṃ ca samabhyaset //52//

The yogi, who is equipped with posture and breath control, and also rich in (the practice of) *pratyāhāra* (withdrawal of senses), should properly practice *dhāraṇā* (concentration). -2.52

हृदये पञ्चभूतानां धारणा च पृथक् पृथक् ।
मनसो निश्चलत्वेन धारणा साभिधीयते ।।५३।।

hṛdaye pañcabhūtānāṃ dhāraṇā ca pṛthak pṛthak /
manaso niścalatvena dhāraṇā sābhidhīyate //53//

Concentration on each *pañcabhūtā* (the five elements) in the heart with a steady mind is called *dhāraṇā* (concentration). -2.53

Dhāranā on Earth Element

य पृथ्वी हरितालहेमरुचिरा पीता लकारान्विता
संयुक्ता कमलासनेन हि चतुष्कोणाहृदि स्थायिनी ।
प्राणांस्तत्र विलीय पञ्चघटिकं चित्तान्वितान्धारये
देषा स्तम्भकरी सदाक्षितिजयं कुर्यद् भुवो धारणा ।।५४।।

yā pṛthvī haritālahemarucirā pītā lakārānvitā
saṃyuktā kamalāsanena hi catuṣkoṇāhṛdisthāyinī /
prāṇāṃstatra vilīya pañcaghaṭikaṃ cittānvitāndhārayed-
eṣāstambhakarī sadā kṣitijayaṃ kuryadbhuvo dhāraṇā //54//

The earth element has a bright yellow gold or radiant orpiment color, with a *bīja* (the seed) '*lam*' in the middle of a yellowish square altar in the heart, where the God *Brahmā* is seated in lotus pose. One should concentrate on the '*lam*' *bīja* (seed) and dissolve the *prāna* together with the mind there (in the heart) for five *ghaṭikā* (two hours). In this way, this *dhāranā* practice is the bestower of steadying effect (on the *prāna* and mind). One should always practice this concentration to conquer the earth. -2.54

Dhāranā on Water Element

आर्द्धेन्दुप्रतिमं च कुन्दधवलं कण्ठेऽम्बुतत्त्वं स्थितं
यत्पीयूषवकारबीजसहितं युक्तं सदा विष्णुना ।
प्राण तत्रविलीय पञ्चघटिका चित्तानिवितं धारये-
देषा दुःसहकालकूटदहनी स्याद्वारुणी धारणा ।।५५।।

ārddhendupratimaṃ ca kundadhavalaṃ

kaṇṭhe'mbutattvaṃ sthitaṃ
yatpīyūṣavakārabījasahitaṃ yuktaṃ sadā vikṣṇunā /
prāṇaṃ tatravilīya pañcaghaṭikā cittānivitaṃ dhāraye-
deṣā duḥsahakālakūṭadahanī syādvāruṇī dhāraṇā //55//

Ambutattva (the water element) has the color of the crescent moon or white jasmine. Its nectar is bestowed with the *bīja* (seed) '*vam*' located at the throat, and it is always related to Lord *Viṣṇu*. One should concentrate on the '*vam*' *bīja* (seed) and dissolve the prāna together with the mind there (in the heart) for five *ghaṭikā* (two hours). In this way, this *dhāranā* practice is the bestower of steadying effect (on the *prāna* and mind). This is certainly *vāruṇī dhāraṇā* (concentration on water element) which even burns down *duḥsaha kālakūṭa* (the deadliest poison most difficult to digest or eliminate from the body). -2.55

Dhāranā on Fire Element

यत्तालुस्थितमिन्द्रगोपसदृशं तत्त्वं त्रिकोणानलं
तेजो रेफ़युतं प्रवालरुचिरं सत्सङ्गतम् ।
प्राणं तत्र विलीय पञ्चघटिकं चित्तान्वितं धारये
देषा वह्निजयं सदा वितनुते वैश्वानरी धारणा ।।५६।।

yattālusthitamindragopasadṛśaṃ tattvaṃ trikoṇānalaṃ
tejo rephayutaṃ pravālaruciraṃ rudreṇa satsaṅgatam /
prāṇaṃ tatra vilīya pañcaghaṭikaṃ cittānvitaṃ dhārayed
eṣā vahnijayaṃ sadā vitanute vaiśvānarī dhāraṇā //56//

The fire element is red, similar to the cochineal insect, triangular in shape, bright like coral and magnificent with the *bīja* (seed) '*ram*' and is associated with God *Rudra*. One should concentrate on the '*ram*' *bīja* (seed) and dissolve the *prāna* together with the mind there in the fire element for five *ghaṭikā* (two hours). In this way, this *vaiśvānarī dhāranā* (concentration on the fire element) is perfected. This practice always brings *vahnijaya* (victory over the fire element). -2.56

Dhāranā on Air Element

यद्भिन्नाञ्जनपुञ्जसन्निभमिदं स्यूतं भ्रुवोरन्तरे
तत्त्वं वायुमयं यकारसहितं तत्रेश्वरो देवता ।
प्राणं तत्रविलीय पञ्चघटिकं चित्तान्वितं धारये
देषा खेगमनं करोति यमिनः स्याद्वायवीधारणा ।।५७।।

yadbhinnāñjanapuñjasannibhamidaṃ syūtaṃ bhruvorantare
tattvaṃ vāyumayaṃ yakārasahitaṃ tatreśvaro devatā /
prāṇaṃ tatra vilīya pañcaghaṭikaṃ cittānvitaṃ dhārayed-
eṣā khegamanaṃ karoti yaminaḥ syādvāyavīdhāraṇā //57//

The air element is located between the eyebrows. It looks like the black collyrium and is associated with the *bīja* (seed) '*yam*'. Its *devatā* (deity) is *Īśvara*. One should concentrate on the '*yam*' *bīja* (seed) and dissolve the *prāna* together with the mind there in the air element for five *ghaṭikā* (two hours). In this way, through the practice of *vāyavī dhāranā* (concentration on the air element) the practitioner travels in space. -2.57

Dhāranā on Ether Element

आकाशं सुविशुद्धवारिसदृशं यद् ब्रह्मरन्ध्रस्थितं
तन्नादेन सदाशिवेन सहितं तत्वं हकारान्वितम् ।
प्राणं तत्र विलीया पञ्चघटीकं चित्तन्वितं धारये
देषा मोक्षकपाटपाटनपतुः प्रोक्ता नभोधारणा ।।५८।।

ākāśaṃ suviśuddhavārisadṛśaṃ yad brahmarandhrasthitaṃ
tannādena sadāśivena sahitaṃ tatvaṃ hakārānvitam /
prāṇaṃ tatra vilīyā pañcaghaṭīkaṃ cittanvitaṃ dhārayed-
eṣā mokṣakapāṭapāṭanapatuḥ proktā nabhodhāraṇā //58//

The ether element is located at the *brahma randhra* (the hole of *Brahma*) at the crown of the head, which is like perfectly pure water. It is associated with the *devatā Sada Śiva*, *nāda* (the inner mystical sound), and the *bīja* (seed) '*ham*'. One should concentrate on the '*ham*' *bīja* (seed) and dissolve the *prāna* together with the mind there in the ether element for five *ghaṭikā* (two hours). In this way, through the practice of *nabhodhāranā* (concentration on the ether element) the practitioner breaks open the door to liberation. -2.58

स्तम्भिनी द्राविणी चैव दाहिनी भ्रामिणी तथा ।
शोषिणी च भवात्येषा भूतानां पञ्चधारणाः ।।५९।।

stambhinī drāviṇī caiva dāhinī bhrāmiṇī tathā /
śoṣiṇī ca bhavātyeṣā bhūtānāṃ pañcadhāraṇāḥ //59//

Concentration on the earth element is stabilizing, on the water element dissolving, on the fire element burning, on the air element mobile, and on the ether element desiccative, respectively. These are the *pañcadhāraṇā* (the five types of concentration) on the *bhūtās* (the five elements, i.e. earth, water, fire, air, ether). -2.59

कर्मणा मनसा वाचा धारणाः पञ्चदुर्लभाः ।
विज्ञान सततं योगी सर्वदुःखैः प्रमुच्यते ।।६०।।

karmaṇā manasā vācā dhāraṇāḥ pañcadurlabhāḥ /
vijñāna satataṃ yogī sarvaduḥkhaiḥ pramucyate //60//

The practice of *pañcadhāraṇā* (the five types of concentration) by action, mind and speech is rare. The yogī who acquires perpetual knowledge of *pañcadhāraṇā* (through his practice) becomes free from all types of sufferings. -2.60

Description of Dhyāna

स्मृत्येव सर्वचिन्तायां धातुरेकः प्रपद्यते ।
यच्चित्ते निर्मला चिन्ता तद्धि ध्यानं प्रचक्षते ।।६१।।

smṛtyeva sarvacintāyāṃ dhāturekaḥ prapadyate /
yaccitte nirmalā cintā taddhi dhyānaṃ pracakṣate //61//

Smṛti (memory) means constant recollection of the one *Ātmatattva* (the Self Reality) in the mind from among all thoughts. It is called meditation when there are pure thoughts in the mind. 2.61

द्विविधं भवति ध्यानं सकलं निष्कलं तथा ।
चर्याभेदेन सकलं निष्कलं निर्गुणं भवेत् ।। ६२।।

dvividhaṃ bhavati dhyānaṃ sakalaṃ niṣkalaṃ tathā /
caryābhedena sakalaṃ niṣkalaṃ nirguṇaṃ bhavet //62//

Dhyāna (meditation) is of two types: *sakala* (having attributes or qualities) and *niṣkala* (without attributes or qualities). It becomes *sakala dhyāna* while one meditates on God with attributes, and it becomes *niṣkala*, or *nirguṇa dhyāna*, while one meditates on God without attributes. This difference is according to the prescribed routine/activity of meditation practice. -2.62

Elimination of Sins Through Dhyāna

अन्तश्चेतो बहिश्चक्षुरधः स्थाप्य सुखासनः ।
कुण्डलिन्या समायुक्तं ध्यात्वा मुच्येत किल्विषात् ।।६३।।

antaśceto bahiścakṣuradhaḥ sthāpya sukhāsanaḥ /
kuṇḍalinyā samāyuktaṃ dhyātvā mucyeta kilviṣāt //63//

One should perform *sukhāsana* (literally, happy or comfortable pose) with the mind internally focused and eyes externally gazing downward. Contemplating with due attention on *Kuṇḍalini*, one is freed from sins. -2.63

आधारं प्रथमं चक्रं स्वर्णाभं च चतुर्दलम् ।
कुण्डलिन्या समायुक्तं ध्यात्वा मुच्येत किल्विषैः ।।६४।।

ādhāraṃ prathamaṃ cakraṃ svarṇābhaṃ ca caturdalam /
kuṇḍalinyā samāyuktaṃ dhyātvā mucyeta kilviṣaiḥ //64//

Ādhāra is the first *cakra*, with four petals and a color similar to bright gold. Contemplating with due attention on this spot along with *Kuṇḍalini*, one is freed from all sins. -2.64

स्वाधिष्ठाने च षट्पत्रे सन्माणिक्यसमप्रभे ।
नासाग्रदृष्टिरात्मानं ध्यात्वा योगी सुखी भवेत् ।।६५।।

svādhiṣṭhāne ca ṣaṭpatre sanmāṇikyasamaprabhe /

nāsāgradṛṣṭirātmānaṃ dhyātvā yogī sukhī bhavet //65//

Svādhiṣṭhāna (literally, establishment of the Self) *cakra* has six petals and its bright color is similar to a ruby. A yogī who contemplates *Ātmā* (the Self), gazing at the tip of the nose, becomes happy. -2.65

Achievement of Strength Through Dhyāna

तरुणादित्यसंकाशे चक्रे च मणिपूरते ।
नासाग्रदृष्टिरात्मानं ध्यात्वा संक्षोभयेज्जगत् ।।६६।।

taruṇādityasaṅkāśe cakre ca maṇipūrate /

nāsāgradṛṣṭirātmānaṃ dhyātvā saṅkṣobhayejjagat //66//

Maṇipūra cakra is similar to *taruṇa āditya* (literally, the adult sun or rising sun) in the sky. A yogī who contemplates on the Self at this luminous city center, gazing at the tip of the nose, shakes the whole world. -2.66

हृदाकाशे स्थितं शम्भु प्रचण्डरवितेजसम् ।
नासाग्रे दृष्टिमाधाय ध्यात्वा ब्राह्ममयो भवेत् ।।६७।।

hṛdākāśe sthitaṃ śambhu pracaṇḍaravitejasam /

nāsāgre dṛṣṭimādhāya dhyātvā brāhmamayo bhavet //67//

A yogī who contemplates on *Śambhu* (another name of *Śiva*), situated in the space of the heart, fixing the gaze at the tip of the nose, becomes assimilated into *Brahma* (the Absolute Reality). -2.67

विद्युत्प्रभे च हृदत्पद्मे प्राणायामविभेदतः ।
नासाग्रदृष्टिरात्मानं ध्यात्वा ब्रह्ममयो ।।६८।।

vidyutprabhe ca hṛdatpadme praṇayāmavibhedataḥ /

nāsāgradṛṣṭirātmānaṃ dhyātvā brahmamayo bhavet //68//

The *anāhata cakra* in the space of the heart is radiant like lightning. A yogī who contemplates on the space of the heart, fixing the gaze at the tip of the nose, and at the same time practicing various types of *prāṇāyāma*, becomes identical to *Brahma* (the Absolute Reality). -2.68

Immortality Through Ātmā Dhyāna

सततं घण्टिकामध्ये विशुद्धे दीपकप्रभे ।
नासाग्रदृष्टिरात्मानं ध्यात्वानन्दमयो भवेत् ।।६९।।

satataṃ ghaṇṭikāmadhye viśuddhe dīpakaprabhe /

nāsāgradṛṣṭirātmānaṃ dhyatvānandamayo bhavet //69//

One who constantly contemplates on the Self shining like a lamp in the middle of the throat at the *viśuddha cakra*, while fixing the gaze at the tip of the nose, becomes *ānandamaya* (blissful). -2.69

भ्रुवोरन्तर्गतं देवं सन्माणिक्यशिखोपमम् ।
नासाग्रदृष्टिरात्मानं ध्यात्वानन्दमयो भवेत् ।।७०।।

bhruvorantargataṃ devaṃ sanmāṇikyaśikhopamam /
nāsāgradṛṣṭirātmānaṃ dhyātvānandamayo bhavet //70//

The God who is located between the eyebrows looks like a true jewel on the crown. Contemplating on the Self while gazing at the tip of the nose, one becomes blissful. -2.70

ध्यायन्नीलनिभं नित्यं भ्रूमध्ये परमेश्वरम् ।
आत्मानं विजितप्राणो योगी मोक्षमवाप्नुयात् ।।७१।।

dhyāyannīlanibhaṃ nityaṃ bhrūmadhye parameśvaram /
ātmānaṃ vijitaprāṇo yogī mokṣamavāpnuyāt //71//

The yogī who always contemplates on *Nīlanibha* or *Nīlābha* (here it means one having blue color) *Parameśvara* (the Supreme Lord, i.e. *Śiva*) at the spot between the two eyebrows conquers *prāṇa* and attains *mokṣa* (liberation). -2.71

निर्गुणं च शिवं शान्तं गगने विश्वतोमुखम् ।
नासाग्रदृष्टिरेकाकी ध्यात्वा ब्रह्ममयो भवेत् ।।७२।।

nirguṇaṃ ca śivaṃ śāntaṃ gagane viśvatomukham /
nāsāgradṛṣṭirekākī dhvātvā brahmamayo bhavet //72//

While gazing at the tip of the nose, one who contemplates on the absolute, *Śiva* (benevolent), tranquil, having faces on all directions in the sky, assumes the form of the *Brahma* or becomes identical to *Brahma*. -2.72

Attainment of Liberation through Dhyāna

आकाशे यत्र शब्दः स्यात्तदाज्ञाचक्रमुच्यते ।
तत्रात्मानं शिवं ध्यात्वा योगी मुक्तिमवाप्नुयात् ।।७३।।

ākāśe yatra śabdaḥ syāttadājñācakramucyate /
tatrātmānaṃ śivaṃ dhyātvā yogī muktimavāpnuyāt //73//

Space is the place of the mind from where the mystical sound is heard. That space is called *ājñācakra* (the center of command). There in the Self, the yogī contemplating on *Śiva* obtains *mukti* (liberation). -2.73

निर्मलं गगनाकारं मरीचिजलसन्निभम् ।
आत्मानं सर्वगं ध्यात्वा योगीमुक्तिमवाप्नुयात् ।।७४।।

nirmalaṃ gaganākāraṃ marīcijalasannibham /
ātmānaṃ sarvagaṃ dhyātvā yogīmuktimavāpnuyāt //74//

The yogī, after contemplating on the Self Omnipresent, which is pure, has the shape of the sky, and glitters like mirage water, attains *mukti* (liberation). -2.74

Attainment of Siddhis Through Dhyāna

गुदं मेढ्रं च नाभिश्च हृत्पद्मं च तदूर्ध्वतः ।
घण्टिका लंबिकास्थान भ्रूमध्ये च नभोबिलम् ।।७५।।
कथितानि नवैतानि ध्यानस्थानानि योगिभिः ।
उपाधितत्वमुक्तानि कुर्वन्त्यष्टगुणोदयम् ।।७६।।

gudaṃ meḍhraṃ ca nābhiśca hṛtpadmaṃ ca tadūrdhvataḥ /
ghaṇṭikā laṃbikāsthāna bhrūmadhye ca nabhobilam //75//
kathitāni navaitāni dhyānasthānāni yogibhiḥ /
upādhitatvamuktāni kurvantyaṣṭaguṇodayam //76//

Guda (anus), *meḍhra* (penis), *nābhi* (navel), *hṛtpadma* (heart lotus), and above that (i.e. *viśuddha*, the neck center), *ghaṇṭikā* (Adam's apple), *laṃbikā* (uvula in the throat), *bhrūmadhya* (spot between the eyebrows) and *nabhobila* (literally, hole of the sky or cavity at the crown of the head) are nine places of meditation which are told by yogīs. They liberate one from the attributes of the senses, and emanate the eight supernatural powers/qualities. -2.75-76

एषु ब्रह्मात्मकं तेजः शिवज्योतिरनुत्तमम् ।।
ध्यात्वा ज्ञात्वा विमुक्तः स्यादिति गोरक्षभाषित् ।।७७।।

eṣu brahmātmakaṃ tejaḥ śivajyotiraṇuttamam /
dhvātvā jñātvā vimuktaḥ syāditi gorakṣabhāṣitam //77//

The yogī, who after contemplating on those places (mentioned above) and knowing the extremely brilliant light of *Śiva*, which is illuminating and identical to *Brahma* (the Absolute), is liberated. Thus, these words are rarely spoken by *Gorakṣa*. -2.77

Kuṇḍalinī: Union with Shiva

नाभौ संयम्य पवनगतिमधो रोधयंसंप्रयत्नाद्-
आकुण्च्यापानमूलं हुतबहसदृश तंतुवत्सूक्ष्मरूपम् ।
तद्बद्ध्वा हृत्सरोजे तदनु दलणके तालु के ब्रह्मरंध्रे
भित्वाते याति शून्य प्रविशति गगने यत्र देवो महेशः ।।७८।।

nābhau saṃyamya pavanagatimadho rodhayaṃsaṃprayatnād-
ākuṇcyāpānamūlaṃ hutabahasadṛśa tantuvatsūkṣmarūpam /
tadbaddhvā hṛtsaroje tadanu dalaṇake tāluke brahmaraṃdhre
bhitvāte yānti śūnyaṃ praviśati gagane yatra devo maheśaḥ //78//

A yogī should concentrate on the navel (i.e. *maṇipura cakra*) and powerfully contract the root of the *apāna* below and force it to move upward and unite it with the mind and *prāṇa*. Again, in that union he should concentrate on the subtle form of light similar to flaming fire.

By doing that, the light reaches *anāhata cakra* after penetrating the *maṇipura cakra*, and when the practice is perfected, the light reaches *brahmarandhra* (the opening at the crown of the head) after penetrating the *anāhata cakra*. Again, at the time of giving up the body (of the yogī) it abandons *brahmarandhra* and enters into the space of void, and there it dissolves into *Deva Maheśa* (literally, the Great God, i.e. *Śiva*). -2.78

नाभौ शुभ्रारविंद तदुपरि विमलं मंडलं चण्डरश्मेः
संसारस्यैकरूपां त्रिभुवनजननीं धर्मदात्रीं नराणाम् ।
तस्मिनमध्ये त्रिमार्गे त्रितयतनुधरां छिन्नमस्तां प्रशस्तां
तां वंदे ज्ञानरूपां मरणभयहरां योगिनीज्ञानमुद्राम् ।।७९।।

nābhau śubhrāravindaṃ tadupari
vimalaṃ maṇḍalaṃ caṇḍaraśmeḥ
saṃsārasyaikarūpāṃ tribhuvanajananīṃ
dharmadātrīṃ narāṇām /
tasminamadhye trimārge tritayatanudharāṃ
chinnamastāṃ praśastāṃ
tāṃ vande jñānarūpāṃ maraṇabhayaharāṃ
yoginījñānamudrām //79//

The pure rays from the disk of sun are above the bright lotus at the navel where I revere the Goddess (*Kuṇḍalinī*) who is in one universal form, is the mother of the three worlds, the bestower of the truth to human beings, and has three qualities; who branches into three paths and three bodily forms, and is praised as *Chinnamastā* (the beheaded form of the Goddess) who is in the form of wisdom, the destroyer of the fear of death, and is the Supreme *Yoginī* in the form of wisdom. -2.79

Supremacy of Dhyāna Yoga

अश्वमेध्सहस्राणि वाजपेयशतानि च ।
एकस्य ध्यानयोगस्य तुलां नार्हन्ति षोडशीम् ।।८०।।

aśvamedhasahasrāṇi vājapeyaśatāni ca /
ekasya dhyānayogasya tulāṃ nārhanti ṣoḍaśīm //80//

A thousand *Aśvamedha Yajñas* (literally, a horse sacrifice which required one full year to complete, performed to fulfill one's wishes) and a hundred *Vājapeya Yajñas* (a special sacrifice which used to be performed by the kings to gain sovereign power) are not equivalent to one sixteenth of *dhyānayoga* (the yoga of meditation, literally, union through meditation). -2.80

Description of Samādhi

उपाधिश्च तथा तत्त्वं द्वयमेतदुदाहृतम् ।
उपाधिः प्रोच्यते वर्णस्तत्वमात्माभिधीयते ।।८१।।

upādhiśca tathā tattvaṃ dvayametadudāhṛtam /
upādhiḥ procyate varṇastatvamātmābhidhīyate //81//

Upādhi (superimposition) and *Tattva* (literally, essence, real nature, the Truth, i.e. Supreme Spirit) are the two topics described here. *Upādhi* (superimposition) is said to be *varṇa* (literally, coloring, i.e. covering) and *Tattva* (the reality) is called *Ātmā* (the Self). -2.81

उपाधेरन्यथा ज्ञानतत्वसंस्थितिरन्यथा ।
समस्तोपाधिविध्वंसी सदाभ्यासेन जायते ।।८२।।

upādheranyathā jñānatatvasaṃsthitiranyathā /
samastopādhividhvaṃsī sadābhyāsena jāyate //82//

Upādhi (superimposition) creates misunderstanding. In contrast, when wisdom is acquired, then the reality (the Self) is known. Through constant practice and right understanding, all types of superimpositions are destroyed. -2.82

Distinction between Dhyāna and Samādhi

शब्दादीनां च तंमात्रं यावत्कर्णादिषु स्थितम् ।
तावदेवं स्मृतं ध्यानं समाधिः स्यादतः परम् ।।८३।।

śabdādīnāṃ ca tanmātraṃ yāvatkarṇādiṣu sthitam /
tāvadevaṃ smṛtaṃ dhyānaṃ samādhiḥ syādataḥ param //83//

So long as the subject matters of the senses and their objects present in the mind through their respective senses (i.e. the sounds in ears, etc.) it is considered *smṛti dhyāna* (recollective state of meditation). Ultimately, one attains the supreme state of *samadhi* (superconscious state) when the mind and its waves generated through the senses are totally dissolved into *Ātmā* (the Self). -2.83

धारण पञ्चनाडीभिर्ध्यानं च षष्टिनाडीभिः ।
दिनद्वादशकेन स्यात्समाधिः प्राणसंयमात् ।।८४।।

dhāraṇā pañcanāḍībhirdhyānaṃ ca ṣaṣṭināḍībhiḥ /
dinadvādaśakena syātsamādhiḥ prāṇasaṃyamāt //84//

Dhāraṇā (concentration) is achieved in *pañcanāḍī* (two hours), *dhyāna* (meditation) is attained in *ṣaṣṭināḍī* (twenty-four hours) and *samādhi* (superconscious state of mind) is accomplished in *dinadvadaśa* (twelve days) through the control of the *prana* (life force). -2.84

Instances Relating to Samādhi

यत्सर्वं द्वंद्वयोरैक्यं जीवात्मपरमात्मनोः ।
समस्तनष्टसंकल्पः समाधि साभिधीयते ।।८५।।

yatsarvaṃ dvandvayoraikyaṃ jīvātmaparamātmanoḥ /
samastanaṣṭasaṃkalpaḥ samādhi so'bhidhīyate //85//

When all *dvandas* (pairs of opposites i.e. heat and cold, gain and loss, etc.) become alike, and *Jīvātma* and *Paramātmā* become united together and all types of *saṅkalpa* (ideations) are totally eliminated, it is known as *samādhi* (superconscious state of mind). -2.85

अंबुसैंधवयोरैक्यं यथा भवति योगतः ।
तथात्ममनसोरैक्यं समाधिः सोऽभिधीयते ।।८६।।

aṃbusaiṃdhavayoraikyaṃ yathā bhavati yogataḥ /
tathātmamanasoraikyaṃ samādhiḥ so'bhidhīyate //86//

It is just like when salt is added to water, and they become one. Similarly, the union of the mind with the Self is described as *samādhi* (superconscious state). -2.86

यदा संक्षीयते प्राणो मानसं च प्रलीयते ।
यदा समरसत्वं च समाधि सोऽभिधीयते ।।८७।।

yadā saṅkṣīyate prāṇo mānasaṃ ca pralīyate /
yadā samarasatvaṃ ca samādhi so'bhidhīyate //87//

It is described as *samādhi* (superconscious state) when *prāna* is diminished totally, mind is absorbed completely, and *samarasatva* (a harmonious state) is established between the *Jīvātmā* (the Embodied Self) and *Paramātmā* (the Supreme Self). -2.87

Absence of Objective World in Samādhi

न गंधं न रसं रूपं न च स्पर्शं न निःस्वनम् ।
नात्मानं न परस्वं च योगी युक्तः समधिना ।।८८।।

na gaṃdhaṃ na rasaṃ rūpaṃ na ca sparśaṃ na niḥsvanam /
nātmānaṃ na parasvaṃ ca yogī yuktaḥ samadhinā //88//

The yogī who is dissolved in *samādhi* (superconscious state) does not have knowledge of sense-objects i.e. smell, taste, form, touch and sound, or of himself or another. -2.88

अभेद्यः सर्वशस्त्राणाग्वध्यः सर्वदेहिनाम् ।
अग्राह्यो मंत्रयंत्राणां योगी युक्तः समाधिना ।।८९।।

abhedyaḥ sarvaśastrāṇāmavadhyaḥ sarvadehinām /
agrāhyo mantrayantrāṇāṃ yogī yuktaḥ samādhinā //89//

The yogī, who is dissolved in *samādhi* (superconscious state), cannot be penetrated by any type of weapon, harmed by any being or affected by the spell of any mantra and use of any *yantra*. -2.89

बाध्यते न स कालेन लिप्यते न स कर्मणा ।
साध्यते न च केनापि योगीः युक्तः समाधिना ।।९०।।

bādhyate na sa kālena lipyate na sa karmaṇā /

sādhyate na ca kenāpi yogīḥ yuktaḥ samādhinā //90//

The yogī, who is dissolved in *samādhi* (superconscious state), cannot be bound by time, stained by action or controlled by anyone. -2.90

युक्ताहारविहारस्य युक्तचेष्टस्य कर्मसु ।
युक्तस्वप्नावबोधस्य योगो भवति दुखहा ।।९१।।

yuktāhāravihārasya yuktaceṣṭasya karmasu /

yuktasvapnāvabodhasya yogo bhavati dukhahā //91//

Yoga becomes the destroyer of suffering to him who is moderate in eating and recreation, in his effort for work, and in sleep and wakefullness. -2.91

निराद्यन्तं निरालम्बं निष्प्रपञ्चं निरामयम् ।
निराश्रयं निराकारं तत्वं जानति योगवित् ।।९२।।

nirādyantaṃ nirālambaṃ niṣprapañcaṃ nirāmayam /

nirāśrayaṃ nirākāraṃ tatvaṃ janati yogavit //92//

The expert yogī knows that the Reality is without beginning and end, without support, free from illusion and fault, without (need of any) shelter or protection and formless. -2.92

निर्मलं निश्चलं नित्यं निष्क्रियं निर्गुणं महत् ।
व्योमाविज्ञानमानन्दं ब्रह्मं ब्रह्मविदो विदुः ।।९३।।

nirmalaṃ niścalaṃ nityaṃ niṣkriyaṃ nirguṇaṃ mahat /

vyomāvijñānamānandaṃ brahmaṃ brahmavido viduḥ //93//

The *Brahma* (i.e. the Absolute) is known as pure, immovable, inactive, attributeless, ultimate, space, beyond the knowledge (of the mind and intellect) and blissful according to the experts of the Absolute. -2.93

हेतुदृष्टान्तनिर्मुक्तं मनोबुद्ध्योरगोचरम् ।
व्योम विज्ञानमानन्दं तत्वं तत्वविदो विदुः ।।९४।।

hetudṛṣṭāntanirmuktaṃ manobuddhyoragocaram /

vyoma vijñānamānandaṃ tatvaṃ tatvavido viduḥ //94//

The Reality is outside of *hetu* and *dṛṣṭānta* (logical reason and evidence), not perceptible by *mana* and *buddhi* (the mind and intellect). It is space, consciousness and bliss according to the experts of *Tattva* (Reality). -2.94

Attainment of Beatific State by Yoga

निरातङ्के निरालम्बे निराधारे निरामये ।
योगी योगविधानेन परे ब्रह्मणि लीयते ।।९५।।

nirātaṅke nirālambe nirādhāre nirāmaye /

yogī yogavidhānena pare brahmaṇi līyate //95//

The yogī, through the prescribed methods of yoga, is dissolved into the *Brahman* (Supreme Absolute), which is free from fear, without support, without foundation and faultless. -2.95

यथा घृते घृतं क्षिप्तं घृतमेव हि जायते ।
क्षीरं क्षीरे तथा योगी तत्त्वमेव हि जायते ।।९६।।

yathā ghṛte ghṛtaṃ kṣiptaṃ ghṛtameva hi jāyate /
kṣīraṃ kṣīre tathā yogī tattvameva hi jayate //96//

Just like ghee poured into ghee disappears and only ghee remains, milk poured into milk disappears and only milk remains, so the yogī becomes one with the Reality. -2.96

दुग्धे क्षीरं धृते सर्पिरग्नौ वह्निरिवार्पितः ।
तन्मयत्वं व्रजत्येवं योगी लीनः परे पदे ।।९७।।

dugdhe kṣīraṃ dhṛte sarpiragnau vahnirivārpitaḥ /
tanmayatvaṃ vrajatyevaṃ yogī līnaḥ pare pade //97//

The form of a yogī, dissolved into *Parama Pada* (the Highest State), becomes identical to *Parabrahma* (the Supreme Reality) just like the milk in milk, the ghee in ghee and the fire into fire. -2.97

भवभयहरं नृणां मुक्तिसोपानसंज्ञकम् ।
गुह्याद् गुह्यतर गुह्यं गोरक्षेण प्रकाशितम् ।।९८।।

bhavabhayaharaṃ nṛṇāṃ muktisopānasaṃjñakam /
guhyād guhyatara guhyaṃ gorakṣeṇa prakāśitam //98//

The mystery (*guhya*) disclosed by *Gorakṣa*, is the highest mystery which is known as the ladder to liberation for men that destroys the fear of the rounds of death and birth). -2.98

गोरक्षसंहितामेतां योगभूतां जनः पठेत् ।
सर्वपापविनिर्मुक्तो योगसिद्धिं लभेद् ध्रुवम् ।।९९।।

gorakṣasaṃhitāmetāṃ yogabhūtāṃ janaḥ paṭhet /
sarvapāpavinirmukto yogasiddhiṃ labhed dhruvam //99//

One devoted to yoga should study this *Gorakṣa Saṃhitā* (the Compilation of *Gorakṣa*) made with the essence of yoga. They will certainly attain freedom from all sins and achieve *yogasiddhi* (perfection in yoga). -2.99

योगशास्त्रं पठेन्नित्यं किमान्यैः शास्त्रविस्तरैः ।
यत्स्वयं आदिनाथस्य निर्गतं वदनाम्बुजात् ।।१००।।

yogaśāstraṃ paṭhennityaṃ kimāanyaiḥ śāstravistaraiḥ /
yatsvayaṃ ādināthasya nirgataṃ vadanāmbujāt //100//

One should regularly study this *Yogaśāstra* (the sacred Yoga Scripture), which has come out of the lotus mouth of *Ādinātha* (i.e. Lord *Śiva*) himself. There is no need/use for extensive studies of other scriptures. -2.100

Fulfillment of Ultimate Goal by Yoga Śāstra

स्नातं तेन समस्ततीर्थसलिलं दत्ता द्विजेभ्यो धरा
यज्ञानां च हुतं सहस्रमयुतं दे वाश्च सम्पूजिताः ।
स्वाद्वन्नेन सुतर्पिताश्च पितरः स्वर्गं च नीताः पुन
यस्य ब्रह्मविचारणे क्षणमपि प्राप्नोति धैर्यं मनः ।।१०१।।

snātaṃ tena samastatīrthasalilaṃ dattā dvijebhyo dharā
yajñānāṃ ca hutaṃ sahasramayutaṃ devāśca sampūjitāḥ /
svādvannena sutarpitāśca pitaraḥ svarga ca nītāḥ puna
yasya brahmavicaraṇe kṣaṇamapi prāpnoti dhairyaṃ manaḥ //101//

Suppose one who studied this *Yogaśāstra* completed the holy baths of all the religious places, donated the earth to priests, offered oblations to thousands of sacrifices, worshiped all the Gods and deities, and helped his ancestors attain heavenly abode again having offered libations of water to them. This is because all the above-mentioned results are instantly attained through the study of it (the *Yogaśāstra*) with a calm mind. -2.101

इति श्रीगोरक्षयोगशास्त्रे उत्तरशतकम् ।।

iti śrīgorakṣayogaśāstre uttaraśatakam //

Thus ends the Second Part of *Gorakṣa Yogaśāstra*.

A KEY TO TRANSLITERATION

Vowels

अ आ इ ई उ ऊ ऋ ॠ

a ā i ī u ū ṛ ṝ

ऌ ॡ ए ऐ ओ औ अं अः

lṛ lṝ e ai o au aṃ aḥ

Consonants

क ख ग घ ङ - Gutturals:

ka kha ga gha ṅa

च छ ज झ ञ - Palatals:

ca cha ja jha ña

ट ठ ड ढ ण - Cerebrals:

ṭa ṭha ḍa ḍha ṇa

त थ द ध न - Dentals:

ta tha da dha na

प फ ब भ म - Labials:

pa pha ba bha ma

य र ल व - Semivowels:

ya ra la va

श ष स ह - Sibilants:

śa ṣa sa ha

क्ष त्र ज्ञ - Compound Letters:

kṣa tra jña

Aspirate: ह - ha, Anusvara: अं - aṃ

Visharga - aḥ - अः

Unpronounced अ - a - ऽ - ’, आ - ā - ऽऽ - ”

ALSO BY THIS AUTHOR

Three Classical Yogic Texts (in English)
Yoga Kundalini Upanishad (in English)
Yoga Darshana Upanishad (in English)
Minor Yoga Upanishads (in English)
Dattatreya Yogashastra (in English)
Hatha Yoga Pradipika (in English)
Yogatattva Upanishad (in English)
Triyoga Upanishad (in English)
Shiva Samhita (in English)
Shiva Samhita (in Nepali)
Durga Strotram (in Nepali)
Surya Namskara (in Nepali)
Vagalamukhi Stotram (in Nepali)
Amogha Śivakavacham (in Nepali)

ABOUT THE AUTHOR

Swami Vishnuswaroop (Thakur Krishna Uprety), B. A. (Majored in English & Economics), received his Diploma in Yogic Studies (First Class) from Bihar Yoga Bharati, Munger, Bihar, India. He was formally trained under the direct guidance and supervision of Swami Niranjanananda Saraswati in the Guru Kula tradition of the Bihar School of Yoga. He was initiated into the lineage of Swami Satyananda Saraswati, the founder of Bihar School of Yoga and the direct disciple of Swami Sivananda Saraswati of Rishikesh. His guru gave his spiritual name 'Vishnuswaroop' while he was initiated into the sannyasa tradition.

Divine Yoga Institute has published his nine books on classical yoga, meditation and tantra. He is one of the few yoga practitioners registered with Nepal Health Professional Council established by The Government of Nepal. He has been teaching on the theory and practice of traditional yoga and the yogic way of life to Nepalese and foreign nationals for more than twenty-five years.

Swami Vishnuswaroop has designed a comprehensive yoga program called 'Yoga Passport' in order to give a broader theoretical and practical knowledge of yoga which includes various aspects of yogic practice in a graded orer from beginner's level one to advanced level ten. Many health professionals, yoga practitioners and people from various backgrounds of more than forty-seven countries from various parts of the world have gone through his yoga courses and programs. He currently works as the President of Divine Yoga Institute, Kathmandu, Nepal and travels abroad to provide yogic teaching and training.

ABOUT THE PUBLISHER

Divine Yoga Institute, which follows Satyananda Yoga tradition, offers a wide variety of group and individual courses in Yogic art and science. Classes at the Institute contribute to the development of a healthy body, a healthy mind, and healthy thought. Institute teachers help students achieve balanced, harmonious and integrated development of all the aspects of their personalities.

The goal of the Divine Yoga Institute is to promote a Yogic system of life with Yoga as a pathway to true, happy, and healthy living. Yogic training eventually prepares one for spiritual awakening, the supreme aim of human life. Keeping in view of this fact Divine Yoga Institute has published nine books on classical yoga, meditation and tantra authored and translated by Swami Vishnuswaroop.

He is one of the few yoga practitioners registered with Nepal Health Professional Council established by The Government of Nepal. He has been teaching on the theory and practice of traditional yoga and the yogic way of life to Nepalese and foreign nationals for more than twenty-five years.

Divine Yoga Institute was established in 1998 by a team of qualified Yoga professionals who received their academic degrees from Bihar Yoga Bharati (BYB) in the *Guru Kula* tradition of Bihar School of Yoga (BSY), Munger, India. BYB is the first Yoga Institute for advanced yogic studies of its kind in the world. Divine Yoga Institute follows the BSY/BYB method of teaching, founded by *Swami Satyananda Saraswati*, a direct disciple of *Swami Shivananda Saraswati* of Rishikesh. *Swami Satyananda* promoted the most profound and holistic aspects of Yoga, covering body, mind, emotions, intellect, spirit and karma. He was the first to widely popularize and spread the therapeutic effects of Yoga.

Printed in Great Britain
by Amazon

66614820R00095